SafeThink™
to prevent illness and injury

The Exemplary Worker Book Series

SafeThink™ ...to prevent illness and injury

SafeThink is a structured critical thinking strategy you can use to identify, predict, and control hazardous situations before, during, and after completing work. This cognitive-based safety strategy can be used on the fly, at work, at home, at play, and while driving. *SafeThink* also provides strategies for you to remain focused on your tasks.

WorkThink™ ...to achieve excellent results

WorkThink is a thinking strategy you can use to achieve quality results with the least amount of effort. It usually takes little extra effort to do quality work instead of inferior work. *WorkThink* also emphasizes understanding the expectations of your supervisor, team leader, and customers so that you can achieve the excellent results they expect.

EquipThink™ ...to achieve optimal results

EquipThink is a thinking strategy for you to use tools, mobile equipment, and stationary equipment effectively and efficiently. The goals are for you to achieve the desired results with minimal stress on equipment, to conserve energy, and to extend equipment life. The input–process–output thinking strategy, in conjunction with identifying critical variables, is used to achieve optimal results.

MatThink™ ...to optimize materials

MatThink is a thinking strategy you can use to make the most effective use of materials. The thinking strategy applies to recovering, processing, modifying, applying, transporting, and storing materials. Because equipment and materials are usually closely related, the input–process–output thinking strategy, in conjunction with identifying critical variables, is used to optimize material recovery and use.

EnviroThink™ ...to protect the environment

Both industry and individuals have a responsibility to protect the environment. *EnviroThink* is a critical thinking strategy you can use to identify and respond to environmental issues for any job position that you might hold. *EnviroThink* helps you think through your work by asking yourself specific questions relating to environmental issues important to organizations.

JobThink™ ...to contribute to job and corporate performance

Exemplary workers understand what is important to their organizations. They know the issues critical to business success and where to focus their efforts. *JobThink* addresses the critical thinking strategies you can use to identify what is important for job and corporate performance.

MetaThink™ ...for exemplary performance

MetaThink applies some of the thinking strategies addressed in previous books in different ways and also addresses new thinking strategies useful for the workplace. You can use these thinking strategies, along with the detailed thinking strategies addressed in other books of this series, to achieve exemplary performance.

The Exemplary Worker Book Series

" Rarely can workers from any sector access self-paced instructional materials that are easy-to-use, step-by-step guides to workplace learning. *The Exemplary Worker* book set is an exception. These books offer a good breadth of learning for workers in contexts ranging from: exemplary performance; job and corporate performance; results optimization; and work excellence. With meticulous organization, these essential training references are helpful guides for workers seeking to improve their performance. With prefaces designed to help trainers/instructors assist workplace learners, these books use critical thinking strategies that identify what matters to workers and supervisors considering people, equipment, materials, environments, and organization in concert."

—**Eugene G. Kowch, Ph.D.**, Leading Complex and Adaptive Learning Systems/Organizations, University of Calgary, Canada

" The power of thinking in determining our safety, health, and welfare is obvious, but how to manage such cognition or self-talk for injury prevention, self-motivation, and self-improvement is not so obvious. Answers are provided in this action-focused series of self-help books on *The Exemplary Worker* by Gordon D. Shand. He offers much practical information for leadership, safety, and well-being. Each of these books provides critical and structured thinking strategies for optimizing performance on several fronts, from improving safety and productivity in the workplace to actively caring as a teacher, parent, or friend."

—**E. Scott Geller, Ph.D.**, author of The Psychology of Safety Handbook; Alumni Distinguished Professor, Virginia Tech; Senior Partner, Safety Performance Solutions

" These are very practical books. I, myself, have been interested in the fundamental processes of human thinking. For creativity there is Lateral Thinking. For exploration there is the parallel thinking of the Six Thinking Hats. For perception there is the CoRT school programme. *The Exemplary Worker* series of books provide frameworks for focused thinking about specific situations. The frameworks guide the thinker to deal with the situation instead of messing about. That is why the books are so practical."

—**Dr. Edward de Bono**, Author of Lateral Thinking and Six Thinking Hats and creator of CoRT

The Exemplary Worker Book Series

Gordon D. Shand

HDC Human Development Consultants Ltd.
PO Box 4710, Edmonton, AB, Canada T6E 5G5
www.hdc.ca
www.safethink.ca

© 2014 by HDC Human Development Consultants Ltd.

All rights reserved. No part of this publication may be reproduced, stored in a retrieval system, or transmitted in any form or by any means, electronic, mechanical, photocopying, recording, or otherwise, without the prior written permission of HDC Human Development Consultants Ltd. (HDC).

This publication is designed to provide general information regarding the subject matter covered. Care has been taken to ensure the accuracy of the information and that the instructions contained in this publication are clear and reflect sound practice. The user understands that HDC is not providing engineering services. The user understands that any procedures (task steps) that are published or referenced may have to be modified to comply with specific equipment, work conditions, company standards, company policies and practices, legislation, and user qualifications. HDC does not make any representations, guarantees, or warranties of any kind whatsoever with respect to the content hereof and the results to be achieved by implementing the procedures (task steps) herein. To the maximum extent permitted by applicable law, in no event shall HDC be liable for any damages whatsoever (including without limitation, direct or indirect damages for personal injury, damages to the environment, damages to business property, loss of business profit, or any other pecuniary loss). The use of the information and procedures (task steps) herein is undertaken at the sole risk of the user.

SafeThink™ is a registered trademark of HDC Human Development Consultants Ltd.

Library and Archives Canada Cataloguing in Publication
Shand, Gordon D.
    SafeThink to prevent illness and injury / Gordon D. Shand.
(The exemplary worker book series)
ISBN 978-1-55338-041-2
    1. Safety measures. 2. Critical thinking. 3. Employees--
Training of. 4. Accidents--Prevention. I. HDC Human
Development Consultants II. Title. III. Series: Exemplary worker
T55.S52 2014   363.11'7   C2014-902761-8

Published by HDC Human Development Consultants Ltd.

Published in Canada

Website: www.hdc.ca
E-mail: hdc@hdc.ca
Phone: (780) 463-3909

> ### Notice to Reader
>
> While *SafeThink* is one of the series of self-taught books, *SafeThink* training is normally delivered as a series of workshops. The advantages of delivering the training in a workshop setting is that participants dialogue with each other, learn from each other, motivate each other, and receive feedback in applying the *SafeThink* strategy to their jobs and workplaces. More information about *SafeThink* workshops can be found at www.safethink.ca.
>
> HDC Human Development Consultants Ltd. (HDC) has proprietary rights to the SafeThink course. Anyone wishing to provide *SafeThink* training must be certified by HDC.

The *SafeThink* program is well developed. Over 6500 hours were dedicated to the research and development. Industry volunteered an additional 1600+ hours. However, there are always opportunities to improve.

As part of the commitment to continuous improvement, any suggestions to make the *SafeThink* strategy and book more effective are appreciated.
info@safethink.ca
www.safethink.ca

Acknowledgements

Developing *The Exemplary Worker* book series has been challenging and rewarding. I am certainly grateful for all the help I have received to produce quality products. Over one hundred people have contributed to the quality of the content and presentation.

Generally, I developed the first draft of the books working on evenings and weekends. I would blitz the first draft for a book—I produced the draft in a month to three months. During those times, my family's gracious support allowed me to concentrate on the task and to dialogue with them about the concepts. Once a first draft was produced, consultants in my firm carried out several edits as time allowed. HDC's Production Department developed illustrations and formats to produce a book ready for validation by industry. Because the people from industry volunteered their time and some validations were conducted in sequence, the validation process for each book took up to six months or more.

Many staff contributed to the development process. I would like to acknowledge those consultants who struggled to gather relevant content when working with customers—they gave cause to identify the thinking strategies used by exemplary workers and to develop the training for HDC consultants. Many thanks to the consultants who worked so diligently with me to produce the books. They were adamant in adhering to our standards for quality, even when I was burned out and wanted to put closure to a topic. Thanks to Janelle Beblow, Art Deane, Alice Graham, Jean MacGregor, and Bruno Schoenfelder for the wonderful edits and feedback. Thanks to Phil Jenkins, Kris Vasey, and Denise Hodgins for developing the illustrations, formatting the documents, and creating the book covers. Thanks to Maria Peck for coordinating the validations and field tests and proofing text. Their personal support, commitment to quality, and attention to detail are greatly appreciated.

I have been exceptionally fortunate to work with so many wonderful people from industry. They have been great mentors—they have made many contributions to my personal growth. A special thanks to nearly a hundred people who have volunteered their time to validate and field test the strategies.

Who is *The Exemplary Worker* series for?

The Exemplary Worker series benefits:

- **Individuals** who want to have outstanding performance
- **Apprentices and students** who want to work safely and effectively
- **Supervisors** who want staff to be more effective
- **Trainers** who want to contribute to improved corporate, job, and employee performance
- **Trades and technology instructors** who want their apprentices and students to work safely and effectively
- **Instructional designers** who want to ensure that training is relevant, useful, and practical
- **HR managers** who want to improve the development and retention of exemplary workers
- **Operations staff** who want to optimize production and minimize losses

Contents

Preface	xv
Job Aid	xxxii
The Objective: Preventing illness and injury	xxxiv
Part 1 Prevention: a Better Way	1
1 Prevention: a Better Way	2
1.1 Prevention: Zero Illness and Injury	4
1.2 Occupational Injuries and Fatalities	5
1.3 Effective Safety Programs	8
Learning Activity 1—Thinking about safety	11
Food for Thought	13
Part 2 Overview of the SafeThink Strategy	17
2 Overview of the SafeThink Strategy	18
2.1 Use the SafeThink Strategy	22
2.2 Learn the SafeThink Strategy	24
2.3 Benefits of SafeThink	29
2.4 Introduction to the Learning Activities—	31
Learning Activity 2—What categories of hazard are present in my workplace? What conditions, actions, and events could expose me to the hazards?	31
Food for Thought	37

Table of Contents (continued)

Part 3	**Hazardous Materials**	39
3	Hazardous Materials	42
3.1	Compressed Gases	45
3.2	Flammable and Combustible Materials	47
3.3	Oxidizing Materials	51
3.4	Poisonous and Infectious Materials	53
3.5	Corrosive Materials	61
3.6	Dangerously Reactive Materials	62
3.7	Waste Materials	64
3.8	What Can Go Wrong?	68
	Learning Activity 3—Does the work involve hazardous materials? What conditions, actions, and events could expose me to the hazardous materials?	72
	Food for Thought	79
Part 4	**Objects, Motion, Force**	83
4	Objects, Motion, Force	86
4.1	Stationary Objects	86
4.2	Motion (Moving Objects)	93
4.3	Force	103
4.4	What Can Go Wrong?	110
	Learning Activity 4—Does the work involve objects, motion, or force that could cause harm? What conditions, actions, and events could cause the objects, motion, or force to harm me?	112
	Food for Thought	122
Part 5	**Non-Ambient Conditions**	127
5	Non-Ambient Conditions	130
5.1	Pressure	130
5.2	Temperature	133
5.3	Light	135

Table of Contents (continued)

5.4	Noise	136
5.5	Hazardous Emissions	137
5.6	Oxygen-Deficient Atmospheres	140
5.7	What Can Go Wrong?	142

Learning Activity 5—Does the work involve non-ambient conditions that could cause harm? What conditions, actions, and events could expose me to non-ambient conditions?   145

Food for Thought   149

Part 6 Electricity   151

6	Electricity	153
6.1	Current Electricity	153
6.2	Static Electricity	159
6.3	What Can Go Wrong?	160

Learning Activity 6—Is current or static electricity a factor in doing the work? What conditions, actions, and events could cause current or static electricity to harm me?   163

Food for Thought   168

Part 7 Radiation   173

7	Radiation	175
7.1	Ionizing Radiation	175
7.2	Non-Ionizing Radiation	180
7.3	Ultrasound	185
7.4	What Can Go Wrong?	187

Learning Activity 7—Is radiation present when doing the work? What conditions, actions, and events could expose me to excessive radiation?   189

Food for Thought   196

Part 8 Changes   199

8	Changes	201
8.1	Worker-Initiated Changes	202

Table of Contents (continued)

8.2	Technology-Initiated Changes	209
8.3	Externally-Initiated Changes	211
8.4	Predicting Changes, Determining Consequences, and Using Controls	213
8.5	What Can Go Wrong?	214
	Learning Activity 8—Could changes lead to or create a hazardous situation?	218
	Food for Thought	227

Part 9 Apply Your Safethink Strategy — 237

9	Apply Your SafeThink Strategy	239
9.1	Controls Used to Protect People	239
9.2	Lockout and Tagout	241
9.3	Thinking and Planning Ahead	245
9.4	SafeThink Thinking Processes	247
9.5	Strategies for Working Safely, Effectively, and Efficiently	248
9.6	Reporting	249
9.7	Continuous Improvement	250
9.8	What Can Go Wrong?	251
	Learning Activity 9—Apply your SafeThink strategy and select controls to eliminate or reduce the hazard.	252
	Food for Thought	258

Appendices — 269

Appendix 1—Learning Concepts and Generalizations	270
Appendix 2—Safety Models	273
Appendix 3—SafeThink: Philosophy and Concepts	277
Appendix 4—Hazard and Control Tables	281

Preface

In addition to being skilled, exemplary workers use a broad range of *critical thinking strategies* to maintain outstanding performance. Exemplary workers know what is important to their jobs and organizations—they put their efforts in the right places by doing the most important things, doing them effectively, and doing them efficiently. Because they know what is important to the job and the organization, they effectively coordinate their actions with others and make decisions in the best interest of their organizations. Knowledge and thinking skills empower workers to achieve exemplary performance, be flexible as workplaces continue to evolve, and provide leadership within the workplace.

Exemplary performance can have many benefits for you, the line worker, lead operator, foreman, or supervisor, including:
- increased job satisfaction
- being recognized by your peers and supervisors as an effective employee
- increased potential for keeping your job during slow economic times
- increased potential for receiving salary/wage increases or bonuses
- increased opportunity for new or different work assignments
- increased potential for promotion

Each of the seven books in *The Exemplary Worker* series focuses on one of five domains (**PEMEO**):
- **P**eople
- **E**quipment
- **M**aterials
- **E**nvironment
- **O**rganization

Loss and/or optimization (LO) are the main themes for the domains, creating the word **LO-PEMEO™**. LO-PEMEO stands for Loss and Optimization of People, Equipment, Materials, Environment, and Organization. As an example: **L**oss to **P**eople is illness and injury; **O**ptimizing **P**eoples' performance is working effectively and efficiently; **L**oss to **E**quipment is damage and shortened operating life; and **O**ptimizing **E**quipment is using equipment effectively and efficiently. The books place a strong emphasis on using **thinking strategies** and **asking quality questions**—the goals are to minimize losses and optimize performance of PEMEO.

The series of books addresses both loss and optimization of each domain. We recommend that you complete each of the first six books in the sequence. However, the books can be studied in any order without difficulty. The last book in the sequence, *MetaThink*, should be read last. *MetaThink* applies some of the thinking strategies addressed in previous books but in different ways and also addresses new thinking strategies useful for the workplace.

Introduction to *The Exemplary Worker* Series

Over the last twenty-five years, the process of discovering *what's important* for exemplary worker performance has gone full circle. The process began for me when I interviewed exemplary workers to identify relevant training content. My premise was that exemplary workers know what is important for people to do their jobs effectively. Over time, it became apparent to me that one of the reasons exemplary workers perform so well is that they use a set of generic thinking strategies. After starting a consulting firm to design and develop training, I developed a comprehensive internal training program for our consultants and technical writers who develop training programs. The training focused on using generic thinking strategies and critical questions to identify training content that helps workers perform effectively. With a lot of support, I have revised our consultant training program and made it available to the public for people to learn and refine their personal thinking strategies to be exemplary workers.

The Exemplary Worker books are presented as a series. The same concepts underlie all seven books. For example, a safety incident may cause harm to a person and result in other losses—work may be suspended, equipment and materials damaged, the environment harmed. The organization could also experience unpredicted costs and have its reputation harmed. This introduction provides a framework and the key concepts that apply to the series. The discovery process and happenstances that led to the development of *The Exemplary Worker* series are explained to provide a setting and context to give meaning to the underlying concepts.

The Discovery Process

For me, the real discovery process began in 1985 when I founded the consulting firm HDC Human Development Consultants Ltd. (HDC) to design and develop customized technical training programs. I believed that it was possible to develop quality training for any industry without having an in-depth understanding of the organization, its technology, or the tasks that its people perform. The premise was that a well-thought-out instructional design and development process combined with effective consulting skills would be sufficient.

As founder of the company, I felt that I was successful in providing leadership to identify training content important to my customers—customers often asked me to do additional work. If I could do the work well, then certainly others in the firm could as well and, for some deliverables, do better.

The Plan

The plan was that I would work with customers to develop the outline of the training program (curriculum) and identify critical content for the program. The training program would be documented in one of three ways:
- a list of specific courses
- a list of general training objectives
- a competency-based training profile

Competency-Based Training Profile

The following illustration is a *partial* example of a competency-based training profile. The profile is a visual presentation of the competencies (tasks and support knowledge) that specific work groups require to do their work safely and effectively.

ORIENTATION	Complete Company Orientation	Describe Roles and Responsibilities	Identify Local Structures and Facilities	Describe and Use Communication Systems	Identify Customers and their Expectations
SAFETY	Describe and Use Personal Safety Equipment	Review Safety Handbook	Complete First Aid Training	Decribe and Operate Personal Gas Monitors	Describe Codes of Practice
ENVIRONMENT	Describe Environmental Responsibilities	Describe and Store Hazardous Wastes	Describe and Monitor Gas Emissions	Take Waste Water Samples	Describe and Participate in Spill Response Exercises
GENERAL KNOWLEDGE AND SKILLS	Describe Flammable Gas Measurements	Use Portable Multi-Gas Monitor	Describe Reciprocating Compressors	Prepare Maintenance Requests	
ROUTINE TASKS	Carry out Routine Equipment Checks	Change Process Filters	Describe and Change Corrosion Coupons	Monitor and Adjust Inhibitor Injection	Perform Housekeeping
SITE-SPECIFIC KNOWLEDGE AND TASKS	Describe Remore Process	Start and Adjust Remore Process	Describe and Change Remore Output Parameters	Perform Emergency Shutdown of Remore Process	Shut down Remore Process for Maintenance

Critical content for each competency is a list of the key issues a buddy or supervisor would emphasize when coaching the trainee. The end product is a *scope document* listing the key issues and ensuring continuity between competencies—no overlaps or gaps in content. As an example of a scope document, here is a partial list of key issues for the competency *Purge Piping and Station Systems:*

- replacing one medium with another to prevent combustible or toxic condition
- important to prevent:
  – people being exposed to toxic gases
  – possibility of a fire
- piping should only be purged after system has been opened and exposed to a foreign substance
- stations purged in preparation for startup
- some stations have automatic purging for specific piping and equipment
- automatic purging sequence must be checked
- always purge in direction gas migrates (up or down)
- criteria for length of time to purge include volume, pressure, and amount of connected equipment

Preface

In a profiling workshop, I used a brainstorming technique with four to sixteen of the customer's employees to identify competencies and critical content. The workshops were mentally demanding. On the one hand, I was concerned that the scope of training and performance requirements be limited and only address competencies and content that were considered important to the workers, their supervisors, and the organization. On the other hand, I was concerned that critical issues affecting people and the business were not overlooked. During these workshop sessions, I was constantly searching for relevant, useful, and practical content. What do the workers do? Is there a special way of doing the task? How do they know they are doing a good job? What can go wrong? How can the equipment be damaged or its life shortened? What do you mean by product quality? What about safety and the environment? Does the organization have special policies and ways of doing business? What is important and to whom or what? What questions should I be asking the group? I did not have a clear set of criteria or a structured thinking process that I could use to provide leadership in identifying training content that was important to the worker and the supervisor.

Working with Subject Matter Experts (SMEs)

I certainly believed that asking quality questions was more important than providing content. Answers to the questions could be provided by the customer's experienced employees. The term *subject matter experts* (*SMEs*) is often used to refer to the organization's staff who provide content to training consultants and technical writers. Unfortunately, some SMEs, having in-depth knowledge of the tasks, technology, and the organization, had difficulties identifying content important for training. These SMEs expected consultants to provide leadership to identify relevant content. I soon discovered that my consultants often had difficulties in providing leadership to SMEs trying to identify content that was relevant, practical, and useful. When reviewing the first draft of training modules, information that would help trainees do their jobs more effectively, efficiently, and safely would often be missing. Nor would the supervisor's concerns always be addressed. Sometimes, information would be included that was of little value in helping workers do their jobs well and making decisions in the best interest of their organizations. When consultants asked me for direction as to the types of content that were relevant for training, I could not provide a comprehensive explanation. If the company was going to be successful in the future, I needed to find ways to define content that was relevant, practical, and useful—content that contributed to employee, job, and corporate performance.

Customer feedback gave me reason to believe that I was providing adequate leadership to identify relevant content; that I was asking quality questions. The truth of the matter was I did not have a formal list of types of question I should ask. In many ways, I was relying on intuition to ask the right questions. I needed to find a way to articulate a content gathering strategy that consultants could use with a variety of customers in different lines of business, different technologies, different hiring practices and performance expectations, and different ways of conducting business. I needed to find a way to identify the specific types of question consultants could ask SMEs to identify important training content—content that would help workers perform their jobs safely and effectively and contribute to meeting corporate objectives.

To help our training consultants and technical writers gain a better understanding of our customers, their businesses, goals, and concerns, I took consultants along to the competency-based profiling sessions. Listening to the group discussions and individual insights about the work and the business always provided learning beyond the information recorded in the program outline and scope document. This learning should be valuable when working with SMEs to identify detailed content for the training resources. Having this preliminary knowledge about the customer seemed to help some consultants be better at identifying relevant training content, but other consultants continued to struggle. I concluded that knowledge about the customer was valuable but didn't give consultants the strategies they needed to provide leadership when working with SMEs.

The Importance of Training Content Being Relevant to the Organization, Job, and Employees

Project reviews with customers were very useful for gaining ideas on how to improve services and products. Feedback from SMEs was that HDC consultants asked more questions than anyone they had ever worked with before. On the other hand, our consultants felt that they didn't ask enough questions because relevant information had been missed. The real issue was to ask fewer questions but more *quality* questions—questions that addressed issues that were important to employees, the job, and the organization. Certainly, customers strongly indicated that identifying relevant, useful, and practical content was the most important quality concern they had regarding the development of training resources. Customers also were adamant that consultants provide direction and leadership when working with SMEs to identify relevant content.

At the close of each project, I would ask the customer what additional training might be useful for consultants to help them be more effective at identifying relevant content. Suggestions included that consultants could increase their technical knowledge, or have a better understanding about safety management systems, environment management systems, or management styles. In response to suggestions, we began providing additional internal training using off-the-shelf technical training materials when possible. The additional training helped consultants to better understand what SMEs were telling them but only resulted in marginal improvements in consultants being able to provide leadership to identify relevant content. I concluded that the knowledge is useful but not sufficient in helping consultants (and workers) to identify issues important to employee, job, and corporate performance.

To compound the problem of identifying relevant content, expectations in industry were changing from developing entry level training (do as I tell and show you and don't ask why) to exemplary level training (maximizing productivity and making quality decisions) and every level between those two extremes. These changing expectations created difficulties in determining the content and amount of detail to include in training and keeping within training development budgets. Customers were upset if training materials included content they did not want and were not willing to pay for. Customers could also be disappointed if the training did not include content that they considered important. In many ways, the concerns consultants had in understanding the customer's expectations are the same concerns an employee new to a job would have.

When I had worked with exemplary workers, I discovered that one of their strategies was to confirm expectations. So we used the same strategy and built more confirmation checks into the development process to ensure the content was what customers wanted. Unfortunately, the confirmation checks were good at confirming that the documented content was what customers wanted but did not effectively address concerns about omissions of content important to customers (e.g., safety, equipment life).

Identifying Thinking Strategies Used by Exemplary Workers

Developing internal training for consultants to effectively identify relevant, useful, and practical content proved to be very difficult. Having consultants participate in the profiling sessions to learn about the customer, developing scope documents, providing technical and organization training, and building in confirmation checks had some value but weren't sufficient in helping them to provide leadership to identify relevant training content.

The instructional systems design models I was familiar with generally placed a strong emphasis on instructional development processes and only provided marginal direction and strategies on how to provide leadership to identify content that was important to customers. Certainly, the design of instruction and the nature of the content had an effect on each other. I suspected that there were instructional designs in which generic module structures and generic types of content would work for some types of technology and associated training outcomes. It would be several more years, after we had a large inventory of customized self-instructional modules, before we were able to develop a set of generic boilerplates (list of section and sub-section titles) for specific technologies and training outcomes. These *boilerplates* provided general structures for self-instruction and listed the types of content that *could* be included (but not necessarily included) in each section. No doubt, the SMEs that I worked with had mentally created their own boilerplates to be effective when working with specific types of equipment.

My initial effort to develop training to identify relevant content proved to be fairly impractical. Fortunately, several events provided me with the fundamental concepts needed to develop strategies that consultants could use to identify relevant content.

One of HDC's customers had a very demanding supervisor who was exceptionally analytical. In fact, he was by far the most powerful analytical thinker I have met. He was also driven to prevent anything negative from happening. He would always be analyzing situations and wanted to know all the *hows* and *whys* about every aspect of the instructional design that came to mind. Once a week I would make a personal visit to address his concerns. On one of those visits, he demanded to know what type of content should be addressed in the training. He said he asked our consultant the same question and the consultant's response was that *he would write self-instruction on anything as long as we told him the content*. Obviously, the consultant was not providing leadership when working with the SME to identify training content that would help the operators perform their work safely and effectively. For me, it was confirmation that our internal training was not very effective in helping our consultants to provide leadership.

My immediate response to his demand was to give some general criteria for identifying relevant content. *Well, safety, environment, equipment life, product quality, and customer satisfaction are important. Adhering to legislation and making decisions are important, too.*

There was a long silence—a lot of mental processing was going on in his head. Finally, he nodded and said, *Good. Let's tell the consultant and the senior operator what you just said.* The bottom line for this customer was that the training we were developing would contribute to his staff doing their work effectively and safely and making good decisions.

The interaction I had with that customer was the moment of discovery for me! The three-hour drive back to the office gave me time to reflect on what had just happened. Obviously, until I was asked, I had not been able to see the forest for the trees. Ask any business person what is important to their business success and he or she would give a list of areas of concern similar to the one I gave to my customer. No doubt the business person's list would be more extensive and include additional concerns affecting productivity and controlling losses—all businesses want to get the most out of their assets, including their people. Businesses prefer to have exemplary workers, workers that contribute to business success. Certainly, the training we develop for customers must help workers be effective in doing their jobs.

Creating the LO-PEMEO Model to Identify Relevant Training

I reflected on the thinking process I was using to identify relevant content when developing training profiles and scope documents. The questions that I had been asking myself during the sessions addressed the optimization and prevention of losses primarily to People, Equipment, Materials, Environment, and the Organization as a whole. Surely, the questions would take on meaning when the work environment was considered. And one way of assessing the work environment was to consider the conditions, actions, and events within the workplace that affect PEMEO.

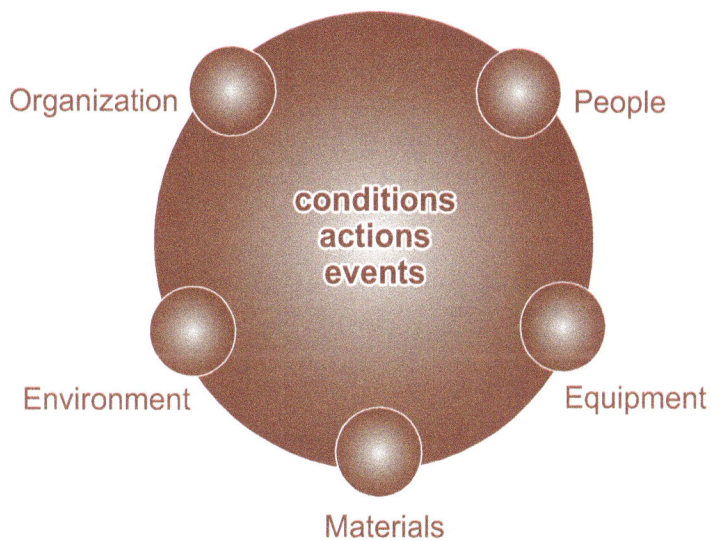

Most exciting for me, I could combine the concepts of optimization and controlling losses of organizational assets such as people and equipment to create a model and strategy for identifying relevant content. The LO-PEMEO model was born. Each of the five domains (people, equipment, materials, etc.) shown in the above illustration had potential for optimization and loss. An example of loss to people is illness and

injury. Loss of materials when processing ore is the inefficient recovery of the desired products. Optimization of materials in construction is to use the right materials and maximize the use of the materials. The following illustration shows the combinations of loss and optimization of PEMEO.

LOSS					OPTIMIZATION	
Loss:	People	LP	P	OP	Optimization:	People
Loss:	Equipment	LE	E	OE	Optimization:	Equipment
Loss:	Materials	LM	M	OM	Optimization:	Materials
Loss:	Environment	LE	E	OE	Optimization:	Environment
Loss:	Organization	LO	O	OO	Optimization:	Organization

Exemplary workers consider the potential for Loss and Optimization of each domain of PEMEO (i.e., LO-PEMEO) while they work. So LO-PEMEO was used as the framework and structure for *The Exemplary Worker* series of books. For example, loss to people (LP) is safety—the book *SafeThink* focuses on using a structured critical thinking strategy to identify and predict hazardous situations to prevent illness and injury.

Interestingly, several years later, I was introduced to a loss control model created by Frank E. Bird that used PEME as an acronym. I have always wondered if it would have saved me a lot of effort if I had known of Bird's loss control model earlier. Or would that knowledge have put in place constraints such that I would never have created the LO-PEMEO model?

While driving back to my office, I thought about how fortunate I had been over the years to work with a lot of exemplary performers, many of them my SMEs. Our customers gave us SMEs who are exemplary workers because the belief is that exemplary workers know what is important for business success and will provide training content that is relevant to corporate, job, and employee performance. When I had asked the SMEs if there were any concerns about issues such as safety, equipment, or materials, they would often look at the ceiling and ponder for a while. If they said yes, they would go on and give me further clarification. If they said no, I would continue to ask different questions. When I thought about it, the questions that I asked SMEs usually focused on concerns about LO-PEMEO. I always wondered what the SMEs were thinking when they were looking at the ceiling and pondering the answers to my questions. Eventually, I asked them. Interestingly, different SMEs from different companies and lines of business had similar concerns. For example, damage to equipment often involved shock from a sudden change in physical forces or temperature. The sources for causing damage could be people, material, or any of the other three domains. In fact, *each domain has the potential to affect the other domains*. Whether the SMEs were aware of it or not, they were mentally searching for specific workplace concerns relating to LO-PEMEO. In many ways, even at the detailed level, *the thinking strategies of exemplary workers were similar and generic.* Certainly, being aware of one's own thinking strategies contributes to planning and working effectively and helps to communicate effectively when collaborating with others and mentoring apprentices.

Linking Corporate, Job, and Employee Performance

When organizations develop standards, procedures, and training, they want to realize an improvement in corporate performance. Improving *corporate performance* is often achieved by either filling a gap in performance or by preparing the organization to move towards new goals. The following illustration lists some criteria that can be used to measure corporate performance.

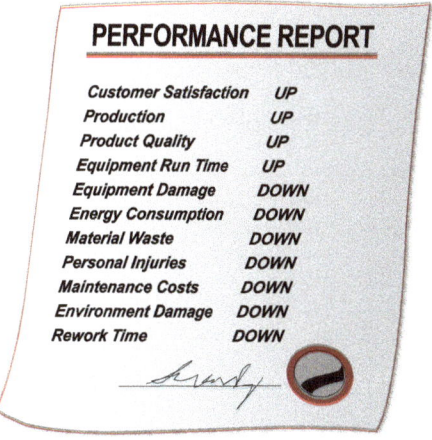

At the operational or job level, the supervisor also has concerns about performance. Within his or her roles, responsibilities, and authority, the supervisor is expected to maximize productivity and minimize losses. Improved *job performance* contributes to improved corporate performance. The supervisor therefore represents the concerns and goals of the organization and must use specific resources and assets (including people) to effectively achieve the goals. The supervisor must also be able to motivate, coordinate, and assign staff to effectively carry out the work. Furthermore, worker performance affects job performance which, in turn, affects corporate performance.

Employee performance affects business results. Employees are expected to work effectively and efficiently and make good use of materials and technology. Expectations of performance are articulated to line employees both orally and in writing. In turn, employees have concerns about understanding the expectations and working safely, effectively, and efficiently to meet the expectations. The following illustration is of a person new to a job asking questions relating to corporate, job, and employee performance issues.

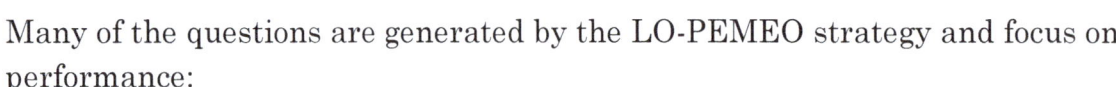

- What's important to the business?
- What does the team leader expect of me?
- What am I supposed to do?
- How am I supposed to do it?
- How do I know I've done well?
- How does my work affect others?
- Is there a better way?
- What tools and equipment are used?

- Could I get hurt?
- Could I injure others?
- Could I damage the equipment?
- Does this product affect the environment?
- How much waste is acceptable?
- How can I prevent…?
- Will the customer be satisfied?
- What should I do if …?

- What would happen if …?
- Do I have the authority to take action?
- What action?
- Whom should I inform?
- What does …?
- How does …?
- What caused …?
- What is the reason?
- What are the consequences for …?

- What questions should I be asking?
- What answers do I need?

Many of the questions are generated by the LO-PEMEO strategy and focus on performance:
- What is important?
- What are the issues?
- What questions should I ask?

The person new to the job needs answers to the questions in the illustration to quickly learn to do that job effectively and efficiently. Interestingly, two employees with similar experiences and skills who are new to a job can perform quite differently. One employee will be uncertain about the work and become stressed if work conditions change. The other employee will initiate actions and make good work-related decisions for the organization within a few weeks. One of the factors that makes the difference in performance between the two employees is the knowledge about what is important to job and corporate performance. Understanding *what is important* provides criteria for focusing one's efforts and for making decisions. LO-PEMEO is a good start in identifying what is important to the organization. Although many of the issues identified by LO-PEMEO are generic, each organization has its own business strategies, resources, and priorities. As such, each organization could place a different emphasis on each issue identified by LO-PEMEO. And that's why asking the *right* questions is so valuable. Questions focus on key issues; the answers to the questions are unique to the organization, workplace, and specific circumstances. *The Exemplary Worker* series provides many of the questions that workers need to ask of themselves and of others to achieve exemplary performance.

Understanding Organizations for Exemplary Worker Performance

Exemplary workers understand what is important to the organization so that they put their efforts in the right places, do the right things, and make good decisions in the best interests of their organizations. For workers to have exemplary performance, they need to have an understanding of organizations in general, and a specific understanding of their own organization. Training and performance consultants also need to have a general understanding of organizations to be effective at developing customized training—training that is relevant, useful, practical, and reflects the organization for what it is. There is a lot of literature on organizations but most of it is more complex than training consultants need. Generally, the literature does not directly address issues important to designing and developing customized training for industry.

So, what issues are important? For consultants at HDC (and exemplary workers in other organizations) to be effective, they must be able to identify and understand organizational issues from different points of view. Imagine a roomful of statues facing in different directions. The room has many doors, each opened by a different work group or discipline. Each doorway has a different view of the statues.

For consultants to get a broader understanding of the organization, they need to view the statues from different doors. Ideally, consultants would walk around the statues to get many different points of view. The consultant must be prepared to consider different points of view within a specific organization to be effective at understanding the organization and identifying issues important to employee, job, and corporate performance.

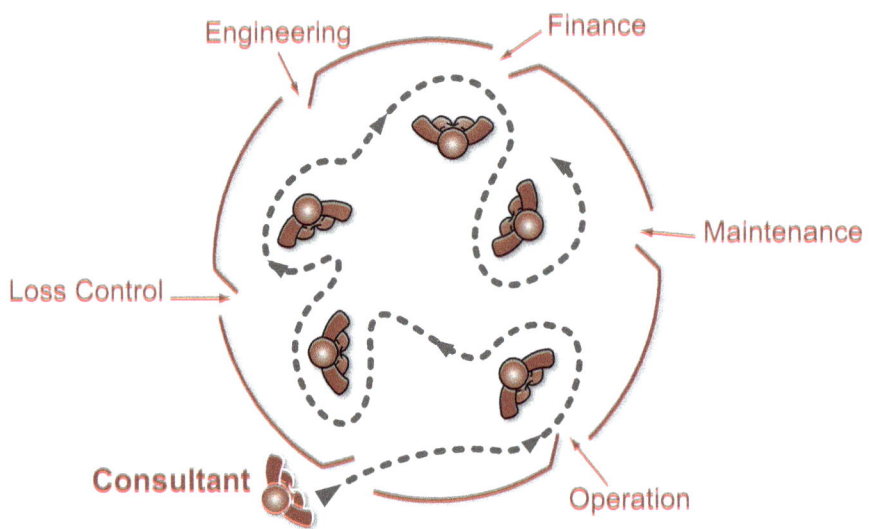

Both exemplary workers and training/performance consultants benefit from an understanding of relationships between business resources, organizational structure, business strategies, corporate objectives, and performance standards. Exemplary workers gain an understanding as to how their line of work fits into the organization as a whole. In doing so, they appreciate how their work affects others and they potentially make better use of organizational resources. This understanding about organizations also helps training consultants and technical writers to be more effective at designing and developing training that is customized, reflects the business, and has excellent value for the customer.

The approach I take with consultants to learn about organizations is to pretend to build a new business. Would the line of business be a service or a product? What is the mission? If the business is a service, then performing tasks is the main way to generate revenue and tools/equipment provide support for carrying out the work. If the line of business is to use technology to make products, then the technology dictates many of the tasks that workers must do. Having resources to achieve specific results is essential but not sufficient for business success. The resources must also be managed effectively. The following illustration identifies some key constituents of a business.

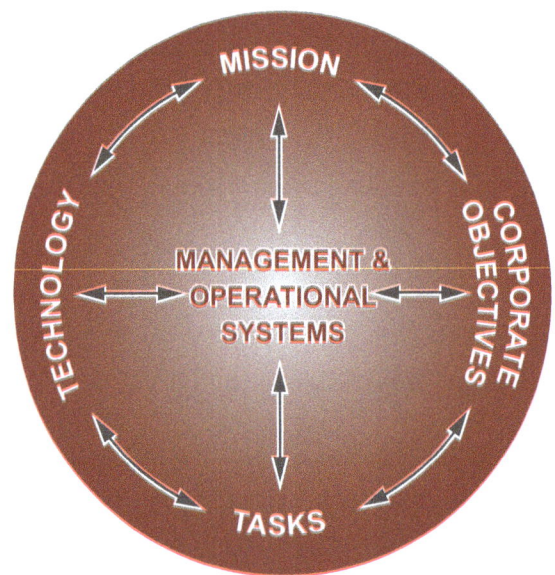

The book *JobThink* uses the previous model to provide a practical way for workers to understand organizations. This understanding helps workers to effectively focus their efforts and make decisions in the best interests of their organizations.

Of particular interest are the *corporate objectives*. Corporate objectives provide direction for using technology, performing tasks, and coordinating work to effectively achieve the corporate mission. The following table lists areas of concern, common to many organizations, for which corporate objectives may be developed.

Areas addressed by Corporate Objectives

- safety
- environment
- legislation
- equipment reliability and life
- equipment optimization
- energy use
- quality
- waste control
- loss control
- cost control
- customer satisfaction
- public image
- public disruption
- reputation
- communication
- teamwork

For a specific organization, a list of corporate objectives can be generated by expanding the organization's strategic business objectives or by using LO-PEMEO. Some companies issue strategic business objectives to provide direction to employees as to where to put their energy and focus for business success. Strategic business objectives identify what the organization must do well to be successful. For example, leaders in an organization may believe that it is essential for business success to have reliable service and satisfied customers. Organizations may identify five to eight strategic objectives. Within a department, the list of objectives (or goals) may be expanded in more detail to address issues specific to the department's mandate.

The expanded list of corporate objectives can also be generated using LO-PEMEO— each of the items in the above table relates to one or more of the LO-PEMEO domains.

Corporate objectives are fundamental to exemplary performance because they define what is *important* to the organization, the job, and workers. Corporate objectives provide a ***formal link*** between organizational goals and worker performance. Workers can use corporate objectives as criteria for working effectively and efficiently and for making decisions in the best interest of their organizations. Training consultants and technical writers can use corporate objectives to identify relevant, useful, and practical training content. Refer to my book, *Interviewing to Gather Relevant Content for Training* for:

- information about applying critical thinking skills to identify relevant content for training
- an interviewing process that consultants and technical writers can use to interview SMEs to gather relevant content

Developing Training to Identify What is Important to Employee, Job, and Corporate Performance

With the LO-PEMEO and business models, I could now develop training for consultants to provide leadership to identify relevant content. The LO-PEMEO model was the most practical approach to use to structure the training because it relates directly to work and job issues. The organizational model can be integrated into the training on loss and optimization of organization, LO-O. For the training on these models to be useful, the training needs to be flexible and apply to a broad range of work, technology, and organizations. The training must also provide strategies for people to think through their work. That is what exemplary workers do—they think through their work. And, the thinking processes are generic so they apply to all types of industries, work environments, and jobs.

All of the training to identify relevant content is founded on using thinking strategies. An emphasis is placed on *concepts* and *generalities* to maintain a broad application of the thinking strategies. Furthermore, the thinking involves asking questions relating to LO-PEMEO. Asking questions is important to maintaining the broad application of the thinking strategies and helping people remain mentally engaged. Asking the *right* questions is often more important than finding the answers, because if the right questions are asked, answers can usually be found—answers that contribute to exemplary employee, job, and corporate performance.

Over several years, I developed training for all the combinations of LO-PEMEO. I also expanded the training to include consulting processes and a performance and training model to design, develop, and implement competency-based training and performance management systems. I was very fortunate to have excellent support from staff to edit and refine the training. HDC staff made important contributions to the training content and presentation. And, after the training resources were in use, we refined them further.

Developing *The Exemplary Worker* Series

After the HDC consultants' training resources had been used for ten years, I decided to go full circle and modify the resources for general use. A major rewrite was required; the new audience was very broad and the lines of work very diverse. The instructional design content had to be deleted. New and different examples of applying the thinking strategies were required for the books. To help the reader, each book required new learning activities. Exemplary workers in industry needed to field test and validate the content. Staff also needed to make major contributions to ensure the quality of each book. It took over six thousand hours to develop *The Exemplary Worker* series. In addition, industry has volunteered more than a thousand hours to field test and validate the content.

The Exemplary Worker series has many suggestions to help you not only be aware of your own thinking strategies but also help you to refine your strategies to achieve exemplary performance. You will also be better at mentoring others to perform better.

Gordon D. Shand
Edmonton, Alberta
Canada

Job Aid

Apply the strategy before working, while working, and after the work has been completed.

Six Critical Thinking Questions (General Questions)

- Does the work involve hazardous materials?
- Does the work involve objects, motion, or force that could cause harm?
- Does the work involve non-ambient conditions that could cause harm?
- Is current or static electricity a factor in doing the work?
- Is radiation present when doing the work?
- Could changes lead to or create a hazardous situation?

For each question, determine if conditions, actions, or events could lead to or create a hazardous situation.

Does the work involve hazardous materials?

Is it a compressed gas?	What type of harm does the material pose?
Is it flammable or combustible?	What recommended first aid should be used if I get exposed?
Is it an oxidizing material?	
Is it poisonous or infectious?	What conditions, actions, and events could expose me to the hazard?
Is it corrosive?	What can I do to prevent exposure?
Is it dangerously reactive?	How can I store the material safely?
	How can I dispose of the material safely?

Does the work involve objects, motion, or force that could cause harm?

- What type of harm does the object, motion, or force pose?
- What conditions, actions, and events could cause the object, motion, or force to harm me?
- What can I do to prevent being harmed by the object, motion, or force?

Does the work involve non-ambient conditions that could cause harm?

- Is pressure involved?
- Is temperature involved?
- Are there unusual light conditions?
- Will noise be excessive?
- Will there be hazardous emissions?
- Will there be an oxygen-deficient (or excessive oxygen) atmosphere?
- What type of harm does the non-ambient condition pose?
- What conditions, actions, and events could expose me to non-ambient conditions?
- What can I do to prevent being harmed by non-ambient conditions?

Is current or static electricity a factor in doing the work?

- What conditions, actions, and events could cause electrically-driven equipment to automatically start and harm me?
- What conditions, actions, or events could cause me to come in contact with current electricity?
- What conditions, actions, or events could create an electrical spark that could cause a fire or explosion?
- What can I do to prevent being harmed by current and static electricity?

Is radiation present when doing the work?

- What type of radiation is involved?
- What type of harm does the radiation pose?
- What conditions, actions, and events could expose me to excessive radiation?
- What can I do to prevent being exposed to excessive radiation?

Could changes lead to or create a hazardous situation?

If a change is identified by questions 1, 2, or 3, go to question 4.

1. What worker-initiated changes will occur?
   - What equipment will be started, operated, adjusted, switched, or stopped?
   - What maintenance activities are or will be taking place?
2. What technology-initiated changes will occur?
   - What equipment will be automatically started, adjusted, switched, or stopped?
   - What could go wrong with the equipment and materials?
3. What externally-initiated changes could occur?
   - Could there be off-site changes that affect the workplace?
   - Will inclement weather create a hazardous situation or power failure?
4. Could these changes lead to or create a hazardous situation?
   - What are the possible consequences of the hazardous situation?
   - What can I do to prevent or minimize the hazardous situation?
   - How can I prevent being harmed?

The Objective: Preventing illness and injury

Upon completion of this book, you will be able to apply a structured critical thinking strategy to identify, predict, and control hazardous situations all day, every day.

Part 1

Prevention: a Better Way

How effective are you at preventing harm to yourself and others?

How committed are you to being safe all day, every day, at work and at home?

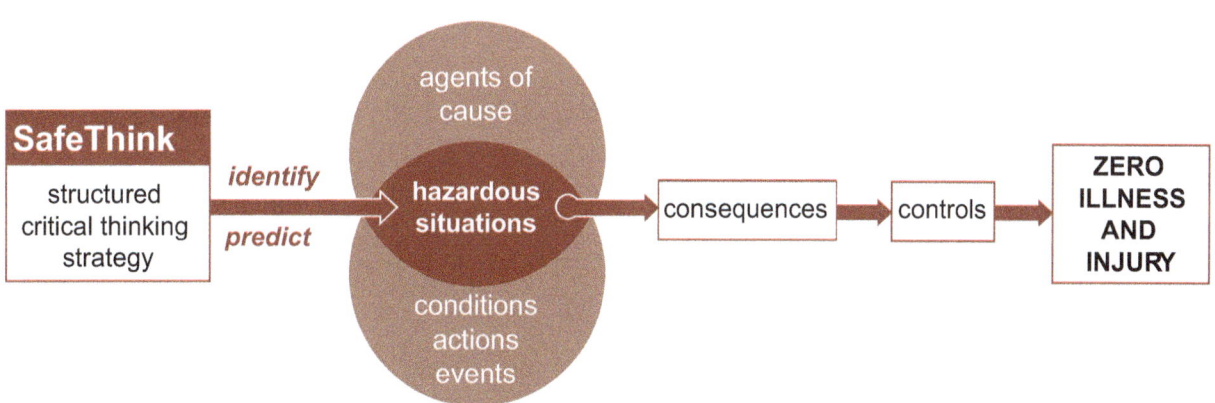

 SafeThink™

> **Training Objectives**
>
> Upon completion of this part, you will be able to describe the focus of the *SafeThink* strategy to prevent illness and injury.
>
> - Explain why all PEMEO (people, equipment, materials, environment, organization) domains must be considered when identifying and predicting hazardous situations.
> - Describe the level of predictable and preventable illnesses and injuries occurring on and off the job.
> - Describe the benefits of the *SafeThink* strategy to prevent illness and injury.
> - Describe the *SafeThink* philosophy and concepts.
> - Consider the quality of your thinking processes and commitment to preventing illness and injury.

1 Prevention: a Better Way

This book is one of *The Exemplary Worker* series of books. Books in the series all focus on using critical thinking strategies to identify **what is important** to employees, the job, and the organization. Each book focuses on one of five domains (**PEMEO**):

P People

E Equipment

M Materials

E Environment

O Organization

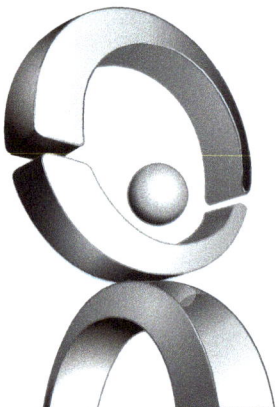

Within each book, loss and/or optimization (LO) are the main themes, hence the word LO-PEMEO™.

Themes	Books
L-P Loss to People (Safety)	*SafeThink* Use a structured thinking strategy to identify and predict hazardous situations.
O-P Optimize People's Performance	*WorkThink* Work effectively and efficiently.
LO-E Loss and Optimization of Equipment	*EquipThink* Use tools and equipment effectively and efficiently.
LO-M Loss and Optimization of Materials	*MatThink* Use materials effectively and efficiently.
LO-E Loss and Optimization of the Environment	*EnviroThink* Protect the environment.
LO-O Loss and Optimization of the Organization	*JobThink* Contribute to job and corporate performance.
LO-PEMEO Use thinking strategies for the workplace	*MetaThink* Integrate thinking strategies for exemplary performance.

The fundamental premise of LO-PEMEO is to ask questions. By asking yourself questions, you remain alert. By seeking answers, you continually learn and become more effective in the workplace and adaptable to changes. The big question is, *What questions should I ask?* The questions identified in LO-PEMEO help you to ask many of the right questions.

This book *SafeThink* focuses on loss to people (i.e., health and safety). Because safety is an integral part of work and the work environment, all PEMEO domains must be considered when identifying hazardous situations. For example, equipment, materials, and the work environment can create hazards. The Job Aid for this book lists the key questions you need to ask yourself to identify and predict hazardous situations to prevent illness or injury.

1.1 Prevention: Zero Illness and Injury

SafeThink is a *thinking strategy*. Everyone can use the *SafeThink* strategy to quickly analyze what could cause harm before, during, and after completion of work. When used with a company's safety initiatives, the *SafeThink* strategy can further reduce workplace illness and injury. The strategy can be adapted for use in all industries, all organizations, and all types of jobs.

The *SafeThink* strategy is useful for workers, supervisors, and team leaders. It is especially useful when they work as a group to develop and practice the strategy and incorporate it into their work routine. Workers can continually apply the strategy before work, during work, and after the work is complete. Supervisors and team leaders can use the strategy during pre-job meetings, safety meetings, and walkabouts.

When you use the *SafeThink* strategy, you ask yourself six questions. These six questions help you to analyze the hazards and the conditions, actions, and events that are common to many workplaces that have the potential to cause harm.

Common sense

"There is nothing more uncommon than common sense."
Frank Lloyd Wright

Some experienced workers may argue that the *SafeThink* strategy is just common sense. Unfortunately, workers are not born with common sense; common sense is learned. Often the learning comes from trial and error and, in some cases, resulting in severe negative consequences.

In specialized work, such as in the trades, issues affecting health and safety are specific to each type of work. Some workers may never have been exposed to the trade-specific conditions, actions, and events that could cause harm. Health and safety issues become common to the work group only after all workers understand the specific hazards and the conditions, actions, and events that create the hazardous situations. Communication about safety-related issues is more effective when the SafeThink strategy is common to all workers. Sense can mean being sensible, that is, thinking about the job and the potential hazards. The willingness and ability to think about health and safety issues, predict consequences, and take action to minimize or prevent illness and injury varies from one worker to the next.

Some workers already have:
- a strong desire for self-preservation
- a low personal risk threshold (they do not take chances)
- the ability to analyze situations and predict consequences
- the patience to take a few moments to think about their work before taking action
- the confidence to take action to minimize the risk of being in harm's way

Other workers need guidance to develop their critical thinking skills about health and safety

1.2 Occupational Injuries and Fatalities

Every industrialized country has a different rate of fatalities and injuries. Below is some information about the fatalities and injuries of one industrialized country, Canada, which has a diverse economy. Read the information and then give your opinion about *acceptable* rates of fatalities and injuries.

Fatalities and Injuries

In Canada (population 34.6 million in 2008[1]), worker compensation boards reported that 3 work-related deaths occur every day of the year.[2] That amounts to nearly 5 work-related deaths occurring each workday.[3] But this number does not represent Canada's total number of work-related deaths—many workers such as farmers and ranchers are not registered with worker compensation boards. In the province of Alberta, in 2008, the Alberta Workers Compensation Board (AWCB) reported 166 fatality claims accepted.[4] Yet, for the same period, the Alberta Centre for Injury Control and Research (ACICR) reported 1777 predictable and preventable deaths. That's ten times more deaths than the AWCB reported. ACICR also reported 52,400 hospital admissions and 436,935 emergency department visits resulting from injury.

Compared with many other nations, Canada does not fare well in *preventing* illness and injury. The International Labor Organization (ILO) workplace fatality database shows that, in 2003, Canada had the fifth *highest* workplace fatality rate out of twenty-nine Organization for Economic and Co-operative Development (OECD) countries. Only Korea, Mexico, Portugal, and Turkey had higher workplace fatality rates.[5]

In Canada, in 2008, there were almost one million occupational claims (loss time injuries).[6] For that year, WCBs across Canada paid $7.67 billion in benefits. An additional $2.03 billion was paid for health care and rehabilitation. The total direct and indirect costs exceeded $19 billion annually.[7] And there is a huge intangible cost to families, friends, and co-workers—loss, grief, and sadness that comes with death and injury cannot be measured in a meaningful way.

Youth

Youth and inexperienced workers are more at risk because of their lack of knowledge about hazards and their inability to manage risk.

Statistically, young people and new hires are more at risk of injury on the job. Among injured workers under the age of 25, more than 50% were hurt in the first six months on the job. Nearly 20% of the injuries and fatalities happened during the first month on the job.[8]

Many youth lack the ability to recognize hazardous situations. When they do recognize hazardous situations, they can make poor judgments about the degree of risk and the need to take preventive measures. Neuroscientists[9] are learning that the part of the brain involved in making sound judgments and controlling emotions is the last part of the brain to mature. Few workplace safety programs address the special learning needs of young workers.

Part 1 Prevention: a better way

> **What do you think?**
>
> 1. Are Canada's rates of fatalities and injuries reasonable for an industrialized country? ☐ yes ☐ no
>
> 2. If no, what percentage decrease in rates do you think would be reasonable? Explain why. _____%
>
>   _____
>   _____
>   _____
>
> 3. Is it possible to achieve zero illnesses and injuries in workplaces? Explain. ☐ yes ☐ no
>
>   _____
>   _____
>   _____
>
> 4. Is it possible to significantly reduce the number of injuries and fatalities on highways of industrial countries? Explain. ☐ yes ☐ no
>
>   _____
>   _____
>   _____

We can do better! It is no longer acceptable for workers to learn by trial and error about hazardous situations and controls. There is a better way and that better way is *SafeThink*. *SafeThink* is a structured critical thinking strategy you and others can continually use to identify, predict, and control hazardous situations. The strategy can be used throughout the day, at work, at home, while driving, and on vacation.

1.3 Effective Safety Programs

Many companies invest large amounts of money and resources to maintain safe, healthy workplaces. Companies develop written policies, practices, and procedures that aim to safeguard worker health and safety; companies also provide safety training and hold regular safety meetings. Yet work-related illnesses and injuries still occur.

Preventing illnesses and injuries becomes more difficult as workplaces become more complex and varied:
- implementation of complex technology and processes to improve productivity and quality
- frequent workplace changes
- multi-disciplinary and cross-functional jobs can potentially place people in work situations where they have little previous experience

Adding more safety rules to deal with workplace complexities may not be an effective solution to reduce illness and injury. Workers become overwhelmed with all the information they have to apply to their varied work situations.

Encouraging workers to think for themselves to identify hazardous situations can help reduce illnesses and injury. Often workers are in the best position to identify hazardous situations associated with moment-to-moment work activities. And, as part of planning work, workers are often in the best position to predict potentially hazardous situations associated with the work assignment because they understand what is involved with the tasks.

The *SafeThink* strategy helps you identify agents of cause and the conditions, actions, and events that create or lead to a hazardous situation. When you apply the strategy, you ask yourself a set of critical thinking questions before, during, and after completing the work. The strategy helps you be more thoughtful and careful and provides you with a means to be better at meeting your responsibility for your own health and safety and for the health and safety of others.

Benefits of the Strategy

When you apply the *SafeThink* strategy, you are better at identifying and predicting hazardous situations on the job. *SafeThink* has value for both inexperienced and experienced workers:

- Inexperienced workers personalize the *SafeThink* strategy for their particular work and learn more about the specific health and safety issues associated with their workplace and jobs.
- Experienced workers sharpen their thinking skills and reinforce their understanding about health and safety issues associated with their workplace and jobs.

The strategy is also useful for experienced workers confronted with new or changing work conditions:

- workers from other specialties performing work in their area
- workers who have new job functions, change jobs, or change the type of work that they do

For an extensive list of benefits, refer to Part 2—*Overview of the SafeThink Strategy*.

SafeThink is a cognitive-based safety model (i.e., it relates to thinking processes). To learn more about safety models, refer to Appendix 2—*Safety Models*. For a summary of *SafeThink* concepts, refer to Appendix 3—*Safethink: Philosophy and Concepts*.

References

[1] Retrieved February 15, 2012 from http://Wikipedia.org/wiki/Poputation_Canada_by_year#since_confederation_1867_.E2.80.94_present

[2] Human Resources and Skills Development Canada. *Occupational Injuries and Diseases in Canada,* 1996-2008: Injury Rates and Cost to the Economy. Retrieved February 15, 2012, from http://www.hrsdc.gc.ca/eng/labour/publications/health_safety/oidc/page02.shtml#highlights

[3] Centre for the Study of Living Standards. Five Deaths a day: *Workplace Fatalities in Canada*, 1993-2005. Ottawa, Ontario. Retrieved February 15, 2012 from http://www.csls.ca/reports/csls2006-04-E.pdf

[4] WCB-Alberta. 2010 *Accountability Framework: supplementary measures* Report. Workers Compensation Board-Alberta. Retrieved February 15, 2012, from http://www.wcb.ab.ca/pdfs/public/accountability_framework.pdf

[5] Centre for the Study of Living Standards. *Five Deaths a day: Workplace Fatalities in Canada*, 1993-2005. Ottawa, Ontario. Retrieved February 15, 2012 from http://www.csls.ca/reports/csls2006-04-E.pdf

[6] Human Resources and Skills Development Canada. Occupational Injuries and Diseases in Canada, 1996-2008: Injury Rates and Cost to the Economy. Retrieved February 15, 2012, from http://www.hrsdc.gc.ca/eng/labour/publications/health_safety/oidc/page02.shtml#highlights

[7] ibid

[8] ENFORM, The Safety association for Canada's upstream oil and gas industry, *Risk Management of Young New and Inexperienced Workers*. Retrieved February 15, 2012 from http://ww2.enform.ca/safety_resources/companies/resourcesandtools/greenhands.aspx

[9] Giedd, J.N.; Blumenthal, J.; Jeffries, N.O.; Catellanos, F.X.; Liu, H.; Zijdenbos, A., *Brain development during childhood and adolescence: a longitudinal MRI study.* Nature Neuroscience, 1999, 2, 861 – 863

Part 1 Prevention: a better way

 **Thinking about safety**

Each of us has a personal strategy to prevent being harmed. This learning activity will help you think about the quality of your own strategy and your commitment to preventing illness and injury.

1. Did you ever experience a near miss (near hit) or injury? Did you beat yourself up for not preventing the incident? Explain.

    _____

    _____

    _____

2. How do you prevent that type of incident now?

    _____

    _____

3. Do you still take shortcuts or fail to follow good safety practices, even when you know there is a safer way?

    ☐ never   ☐ sometimes   ☐ often   ☐ a lot

4. Do you ever consider the potential consequences for yourself, family, friends, and co-workers when you take shortcuts or fail to follow good safety practices?

    ☐ occasionally   ☐ sometimes   ☐ quite often   ☐ a lot

5. People have different thresholds for risk. To what degree do you have a commitment to keeping yourself safe from illness and injury?

    ☐ a little   ☐ somewhat   ☐ quite a bit   ☐ very

6. To what degree do you have a commitment to keeping others (family, friends, co-workers, visitors) safe from illness and injury?

    ☐ a little   ☐ somewhat   ☐ quite a bit   ☐ very

7. Rate your ability to think ahead to identify and predict hazardous situations that exist or could be created as part of an activity (at work and at home)?

☐ poor   ☐ weak   ☐ good   ☐ excellent

8. To what degree is safety part of how you think about work, plan work, do work, and follow up on work?

☐ a little   ☐ somewhat   ☐ quite a bit   ☐ a lot

9. When you are at work, how confident are you that others will not do something that could potentially harm you?

☐ a little   ☐ somewhat   ☐ considerably   ☐ very

10. What do you do at work to prevent other workers' activities from causing you harm?

_____

_____

11. At work, you are required to use specific safety measures (e.g., using personal protective equipment such as eye protection and steel-toe shoes). Do you use similar safety measures at home when performing tasks that could cause you harm (e.g., cutting the lawn)?

☐ yes   ☐ sometimes   ☐ no

Each and every one of us has a personal responsibility to keep ourselves and others from becoming ill or injured. One of our first lines of defense is to *think for ourselves*—to continually identify, predict, and control hazardous situations. To do so, we need to use quality thinking processes.

FOOD for THOUGHT

Being thoughtful

When I make *SafeThink* presentations or facilitate courses, I often ask participants to think of someone they *trust* to be safe to work with. Then I ask them the following question:

What is it about that person—their actions, behaviors, attributes—that makes you feel safe when working with or around him or her?

The participants' responses vary. For example, participants say that he or she:
- is competent to do the work
- communicates concerns about safety
- takes time to think the work through
- stops me if he or she thinks I am about to do something that could harm me

Thoughtful

Across groups, there is a common attribute of a person that can be trusted to be safe: *the person is thoughtful*. Being thoughtful involves two things:
- taking the time to think about health and safety issues.
- using a quality thinking strategy to ensure all safety issues are considered.

Some people take the **time** to be safe. Before working, while working, and after work these people take time to think about safety. These people also continue to think ahead when work stops (e.g., during a natural break between sub-tasks, during coffee or rest periods, while going to the washroom). They think through the work to be done. They think ahead. Issues that are considered include:

What has to be done?

How will it be done?

Who is going to do the work?

How will the work affect other workers and vice versa?

What are the safety concerns?

In addition to taking the time to think ahead about work, being thoughtful also depends on the **quality** of the thinking process. As one worker said to me, *I want to work with someone who is very logical and thorough in thinking.*

Have you ever been in a situation where, after an incident, you thought, *What was that person thinking?* You may never know. That's where *SafeThink* is so useful; it's about the quality of the thinking process. *SafeThink* is a *structured critical thinking strategy* to identify, predict, and control hazardous situations:

- It is structured to provide a framework to deal with the complex health and safety issues.
- It is critical thinking because the focus is on those issues that are critical to a person's health and safety.
- It is thinking critically because workers have to use higher level thinking skills to assess and analyze their work and environment.
- It's a strategy because it provides a process for going about the thinking to identify, predict, and control hazardous situations.

Learn to *SafeThink*—it helps you to be rigorous at identifying, predicting, and controlling hazardous situations *on the fly*. Don't put people in the situation when some day they will have to ask, *What were you thinking?*

The main focus of this book is on helping you learn to continually apply the *SafeThink* strategy at work, at home, at play, while driving, and on vacation. To effectively apply the *SafeThink* strategy (thinking process), you need to learn the *SafeThink* questions (see Job Aid) so well that you can recall them automatically, just like you automatically know the answer to the question, *What is 2 x 2?*

The information on agents of cause, conditions, actions, events, and controls provides support knowledge and is not the main focus of this book. Support knowledge is essential but not sufficient to be able to *SafeThink*. Everyone needs a structured critical thinking strategy to apply their knowledge rigorously to identify and predict hazardous situations.

To learn to *SafeThink*:
- read the self-instruction for a part
- complete the learning activities for that part to help you learn to apply that part of the *SafeThink* strategy to your work and personal life
- learn the questions for that part
- apply the *SafeThink* strategy at work, at home, while driving, and on vacation

When you have learned to *SafeThink*, it's in your head—you can't leave home without it!

Part 2
Overview of the SafeThink Strategy

What categories of hazard are present in my workplace?

What conditions, actions, and events could expose me to the hazards?

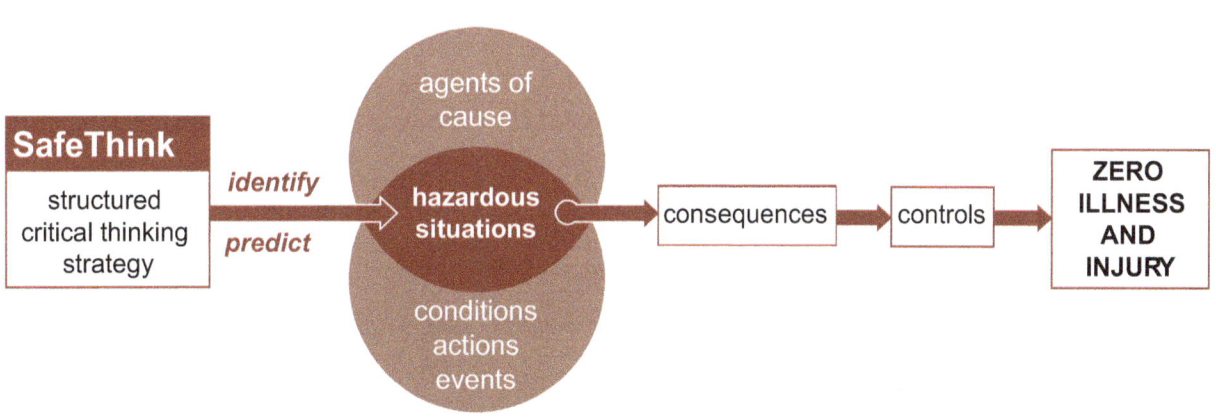

SafeThink™

> **Training Objectives**
>
> Upon completion of this part, you will be able to describe the structure of the SafeThink strategy and how the strategy is applied in the workplace.
>
> - Describe why it is important to personalize the *SafeThink* strategy to your work and work environment, (i.e., develop your own personal protective strategy)
> - Identify the six categories of hazard that may be present on industrial workplaces
> - Provide examples of questions related to the six categories of hazard
> - Identify some conditions, actions, and events that can expose workers to each category of hazard:
>   – before working
>   – while working
>   – after completing the task
>
> A learning activity at the end of Part 2 helps you to apply your learning to identify agents of cause (hazards) and the conditions, actions, and events that create hazardous situations at your workplace.

2 Overview of the SafeThink Strategy

We all have a natural instinct to protect ourselves from harm. Keeping out of harm's way is especially important in the workplace. Your company likely has written policies, practices, and procedures to protect your health and safety. You've probably attended safety meetings and specialized safety courses. Despite your company's best efforts to inform everyone about workplace hazards and how to control them, accidents still occur. Your company may have an excellent health and safety program, but it is impossible for you to predict and protect against potentially hazardous situations associated with every moment-to-moment set of actions that occur on the job.

This training will help you learn and *personalize* the *SafeThink* strategy so that you can apply the strategy to your own particular workplace or to any new work situation that arises. By personalizing *SafeThink*, you are refining

your personal protective strategy. The strategy involves continually asking yourself a set of critical thinking questions to identify agents of cause (hazards) and the conditions, actions, and events that could lead to or create a hazardous situation. The questions relate to six categories of hazards that are common to many workplaces:
- hazardous materials
- objects, motion, and force
- non-ambient conditions
- electricity
- radiation
- changes

Conditions:
the nature of the workplace, including physical surroundings, quality of atmosphere, status of equipment operation, and nature of work being performed

In the workplace, workers are normally protected from exposure to these six categories of hazard. However, workplaces are dynamic. Specific *conditions, actions,* or *events* can make one or more of the categories hazardous to workers. For example, the following situation could occur in the workplace:

- **safe condition:** a hazardous material is stored in approved containers in a fire cabinet
- **action:** a worker carries several containers of the hazardous material at one time to the work area and drops a container
- **hazardous condition:** the container breaks open and releases flammable vapors
- **event:** plumbing in the area is being repaired. A plumber is using a lighted torch.
- **potential consequence:** if flammable vapors travel towards the plumber, the torch will ignite the vapors and cause injury to nearby workers

Actions:
worker's activities required to perform a task

Events:
planned and unplanned happenings such as a temporary shutdown of a mill for repair or a pressurized vessel rupture

Part 2 introduces the six questions and describes the *SafeThink* strategy.

Individual initiative

You can take the initiative to protect yourself and others by:
- having a personal commitment to working safely
- using a personal protective strategy (i.e., thinking for yourself)
- acquiring the knowledge and developing the skills you need to work safely and effectively at all workplaces
- following your company's practices and procedures for hazardous tasks

Continual, Continuous

Continual refers to something that happens frequently or regularly but with interruption (e.g., the phone rang continually). Continuous refers to something that occurs constantly or without interruption (e.g., the air conditioning unit hummed continuously).

Commitment

Wanting to be safe is essential but not sufficient to protect yourself and others. Part of your commitment to safety involves making a continuous effort to be safe throughout the workday.

Before starting a task, **while** doing a task, and **after** completing a task, you must think about what you are doing:
- analyze the workplace and work to identify agents of cause (e.g., hazards) and conditions, actions, and events that could lead to or create hazardous situations
- take action to reduce the likelihood of illness or injury
- learn from illnesses and injuries that have occurred in the workplace

Personal protective strategy

Employees who are doing the work are often in the best position to recognize and predict situations that could cause harm. All employees have a personal thinking strategy for identifying hazardous situations. However, some people are more thorough than others. To be able to rigorously identify and predict potentially hazardous situations before, during, and after completing the work, all employees need a structured critical thinking strategy. This book provides instructions to help you learn the *SafeThink* strategy and personalize it.

SafeThink is a structured critical thinking strategy you can use to identify and predict hazardous situations at work, at home, while driving, at school, and at play. The strategy involves asking yourself a series of questions to determine if agents of cause exist or can be created as a result of doing work (or doing anything else). An agent of cause is anything that, under specific circumstances, can result in a hazardous situation. Agents of cause include hazards such as pinch points, toxic materials, static electricity, and dust as well as items that are usually not considered hazardous such as a desk drawer, a corner of a wall, and legs of furniture. It is the interaction between agents of cause and specific conditions, actions, and events that can lead to or create a hazardous situation.

Part 2 Overview of the SafeThink Strategy

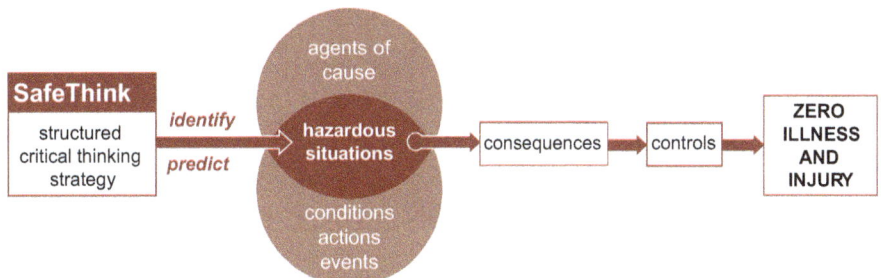

Knowledge and skills

To use the *SafeThink* strategy effectively, you need to know about your workplace and the tasks you perform. You must have basic information about your surroundings, equipment, materials, and processes so that you can identify and predict potentially hazardous situations. For example, when working near a piece of equipment containing a radioactive source, you need to:

- know that radiation can be harmful (agent of cause)
- know that the equipment contains a source of radiation (work environment)
- determine if there is any possibility that conditions, actions, or events could expose you to harmful levels of radiation while performing the task (hazardous situation)
- determine the consequences of exposure
- take action to reduce your risk of exposure to radiation (use controls)

Controls:
methods used to prevent agents of cause and hazardous conditions, actions, and events from causing harm

One way to gain critical safety knowledge for your work is to:
- ask yourself six questions to identify agents of cause
- if an agent of cause exists, determine if conditions, actions, or events can lead to or create a hazardous situation

As part of your learning, you must always keep in mind that the types of task being performed and the different locations for carrying out the tasks can result in:
- different agents of cause being present
- conditions, actions, and events being different

Practices and procedures

For hazardous tasks, you must follow your company's written practices and procedures to minimize the risk of illness or injury. These practices and procedures were rigorously

developed by your company's operators, maintenance personnel, and specialists (e.g., engineers, and health, safety, and environmental specialists). When developing practices and procedures, a formal task analysis strategy is used to identify potential hazards and establish controls to keep people safe.

The *SafeThink* strategy you will learn in this book is an informal task analysis strategy—the goal is for you to be able to recognize and predict potentially hazardous situations. The strategy takes very little time to apply on the job. With practice, you will be applying the strategy continually throughout the workday.

2.1 Use the SafeThink Strategy

To effectively use the *SafeThink* strategy as part of your personal protective strategy, you must:
- identify conditions, actions, and events that can expose you to the agents of cause
- continually think about your work to recognize and predict situations that could cause harm

SafeThink can also be applied to a job new to you. Asking yourself questions about agents of cause and conditions, actions, and events common to many workplaces before taking action helps you to consider some of the possibilities that could cause harm. And, if you are unsure about the answers to your questions, you can ask others or review site documentation.

Using the *SafeThink* strategy, combined with your knowledge about your workplace, your tasks, and your company's health and safety program, will go a long way towards keeping yourself and others out of harm's way.

> **Objectives**
> - Before working, while working, and after work is completed, use *SafeThink*, a structured critical thinking strategy, to identify and predict agents of cause and the conditions, actions, and events that can create or lead to a hazardous situation.
> - Determine possible controls to keep you and others from being harmed.

A safe workplace

When everyone follows safe work practices and procedures and applies the *SafeThink* strategy before, during, and after completing the work, hazardous situations are controlled. There may be times, however, when you feel a condition, action, or event is potentially hazardous and that additional measures should be taken to protect you while performing the work. You are responsible for discussing the situation with your team leader or supervisor. You not only have the right but also the obligation to refuse to do work that puts you and others at risk.

Many different types of controls can be used to control workplace hazards, including:
- elimination (e.g., replacing a flammable solvent with a non-flammable solvent, removing a sharp object protruding from a concrete wall)
- engineering controls (e.g., installing a ventilation system in a welding area)
- administrative controls (e.g., limiting the number of people involved in a hazardous task, providing safe work procedures, providing close supervision, scheduling work to minimize exposure to hazards, providing training)
- personal protective equipment (e.g., using supplied-air respirators, safety lines, and gas detectors in a confined space where hazardous gas may be present)

To minimize the risk associated with the work, a variety of measures (controls) can be taken. For *SafeThink*, the controls of interest are the ones that can be used as part of doing the work; for example:
- putting up temporary barriers around excavations and construction areas

- using personal protective equipment such as safety lines and respirators
- when carrying out the steps of a task, performing specific actions in ways that are safe
- asking for help when lifting something that is awkward or too heavy for one person to lift safely
- putting warning signs on low overhangs
- developing written work processes and procedures

Your company probably has safety rules requiring that you wear personal protective equipment for specific tasks and areas (e.g., wear hard hats in the shop, wear approved safety eyewear when operating grinders). For some tasks you may need highly specialized equipment such as fall arrest equipment, supplied-air respirators, and chemical-resistant gloves.

2.2 Learn the SafeThink Strategy

The SafeThink Strategy

The *SafeThink* strategy involves asking yourself critical thinking questions that are progressively more specific. You ask yourself the questions before doing a task, while doing the task, and after doing the task. First, you ask yourself six critical thinking questions to determine if specific agents of cause exist or can be created while doing the work. The six questions relate to six different categories of hazard that are common to many workplaces. Each category of hazard, under specific conditions, actions, or events, has the potential to cause harm. The table on the following page lists the categories and questions.

	The SafeThink Strategy	
Part	**Category of hazard**	**Six critical thinking questions**
Part 3	Hazardous Materials	Does the work involve hazardous materials?
Part 4	Objects, Motion, Force	Does the work involve objects, motion, or force that could cause harm?
Part 5	Non-Ambient Conditions	Does the work involve non-ambient conditions that could cause harm?
Part 6	Electricity	Is current or static electricity a factor in doing the work?
Part 7	Radiation	Is radiation present when doing the work?
Part 8	Changes	Could changes lead to or create a hazardous situation?

The exact wording of the questions is not critical. You can rephrase each question to better suit your particular work, workplace, and way of thinking.

To use the strategy, you continually ask yourself the six critical thinking questions **before** you start work, **while** you are working, and **after** you have completed the work. You ask yourself each question, one at a time. If there are no workplace hazards in one category, proceed to the next question. If there are workplace hazards, think about the work and look for conditions, actions, and events that can potentially expose you to that hazard. If you do not identify a situation that potentially can cause harm, you go to the next question. However, if you identify a condition, action, or event that could create or lead to a hazardous situation, ask yourself additional questions to:
- identify the health or safety issues
- determine possible controls to keep you and others from being harmed.

The primary focus of *SafeThink* is to identify agents of cause and determine if conditions, actions, and events can create or lead to a hazardous situation. For example:
- the action of a worker putting force on a sharp tool in the direction of his or her body could lead to an injury if the tool slips

- a very dusty atmosphere (condition) could lead to respiratory problems
- opening (action) a container of solvent in a poorly ventilated space (condition) could expose the worker to excessive concentrations of a hazardous material
- the combination of a pipe containing flammable gas rupturing (event) and a worker welding nearby (action) could cause a fire or explosion

 A hazardous situation can be created by one or more conditions, actions, and events. Logically, these terms should be written as condition(s), **and/or** action(s), **and/or** event(s). However, for ease of reading, the terms are written in this book as *conditions, actions, and events*.

To use the strategy, you continually ask yourself six questions to determine which categories of hazard exist in the workplace. If a category of hazard does exist, you ask additional questions to determine if you could be harmed, what would be the consequences, and how to control the hazard to prevent being harmed. Although the specific questions for each category of hazard vary, four types of question that address key concepts are common to all categories of hazard:

- Does the category of hazard exist?
- What conditions, actions, and events could expose me to the hazard? (How could I be harmed?)
- What type of harm does the hazard pose? (consequences)
- What can I do to prevent being harmed? (control)

The following flow diagram shows the basic *SafeThink* process to prevent illness and injury.

The specific critical thinking questions for each category of hazard are provided throughout this book. All questions are also listed in the *Job Aid*. You must learn these questions well enough so that you can instantly recall them when needed, just like you can automatically remember that two plus two equals four.

Apply the SafeThink Strategy

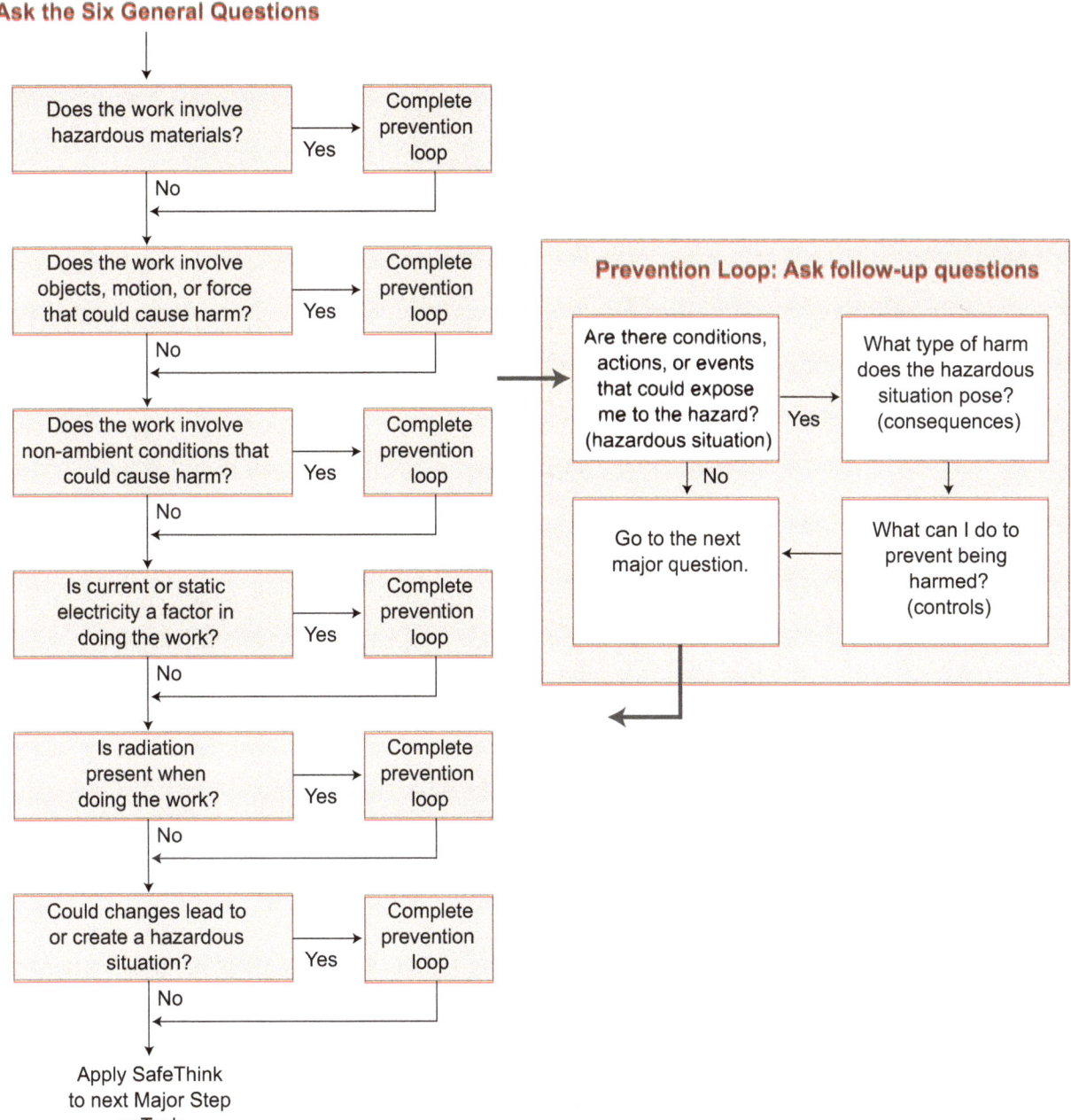

The learning structure of this book

Parts 3 to 8 address the six categories of hazards that are common to many workplaces. Each of these six parts describes one category of hazard and associated agents of cause. Each part is presented as a question that you can ask

yourself; for example, *Is radiation present when doing work?* A learning activity at the end of each part directs you to apply the critical thinking to your work and workplace.

To use the *SafeThink* strategy effectively, you need some basic knowledge about agents of cause. Examples common to many workplaces are provided for each category of hazard. Because every workplace is different, this book cannot provide examples for every possible situation. Some of the examples provided may not apply to your work situation. However, the learning activities help you to learn to use the *SafeThink* strategy and gain knowledge about the specific health and safety issues that apply to your work and workplace.

Important
*The focus of the SafeThink book is on developing your critical thinking skills about health and safety and to practice using your personal protective SafeThink strategy in your workplace. The focus is **not** on memorizing a lot of information.*

Some hazard categories (e.g., radiation) may not apply to your current job or workplace. Nevertheless, you should develop your critical thinking skills for that category because your work may change in the future.

Examples of different types of hazard controls are also identified in each part. You can use the list of controls to help you complete the learning activities. You are also encouraged to identify controls that are not listed but are used in your work and workplace. Appendix 4 provides summary tables listing different types of hazards and hazard controls. Part 9—*Apply Your SafeThink Strategy* combines all six questions as a strategy to identify potentially hazardous situations in the workplace. A learning activity at the end of Part 9 gives you the opportunity to practice using the strategy in your work and workplace.

Learning to use SafeThink

Appendix 1—*Learning Concepts and Generalizations* provides suggestions for learning and for coaching others to use the *SafeThink* strategy.

Learning concepts and generalizations: Traditionally, health and safety courses tended to focus on memorizing information, rules, and regulations. This book, however, focuses on learning concepts and learning how to apply the concepts to the job. Concepts give you the flexibility to identify hazardous situations in many different workplaces. The goal is to have you think for yourself to identify and predict hazardous situations and to predict consequences. Appendix 1 describes a way to learn concepts.

Mentoring Others: Refer to Food for Thought in Part 7—*Radiation* for suggestions on mentoring others about generalities. Of most importance for effective learning is to *practice* applying the concepts in your workplace throughout the day.

2.3 Benefits of SafeThink

There are many benefits of using this structured critical thinking strategy to identify and predict hazardous situations:
- useful for both new and experienced workers
- workers are often in the best position to identify and predict hazardous situations because they know their jobs the best and are part of a dynamic work environment
- the structured thinking strategy can be used "on the fly" throughout the workday
- can be used continually on the job before, while, and after work is complete
- useful for identifying hazardous situations created by change
- can be used in unfamiliar work conditions
- reduces overlooking hazardous situations
- improves monitoring of contractors and third parties
- provides a method for more effective communication
- useful when working alone or with others
- reduces stress with the knowledge that all workers are using a structured critical thinking strategy to identify and predict hazards
- gives workers more control over their own health and safety, and workers have the most to lose
- useful when tired, over-confident, complacent, distracted, emotionally upset, or rushed
- contributes to group collaboration, team work, and cohesion
- fosters a personal commitment to safety

- complements existing health and safety initiatives and programs
- contributes to a safer workplace
- contributes to achieving corporate health and safety goals
- can be used at work, while driving, at home, and at play

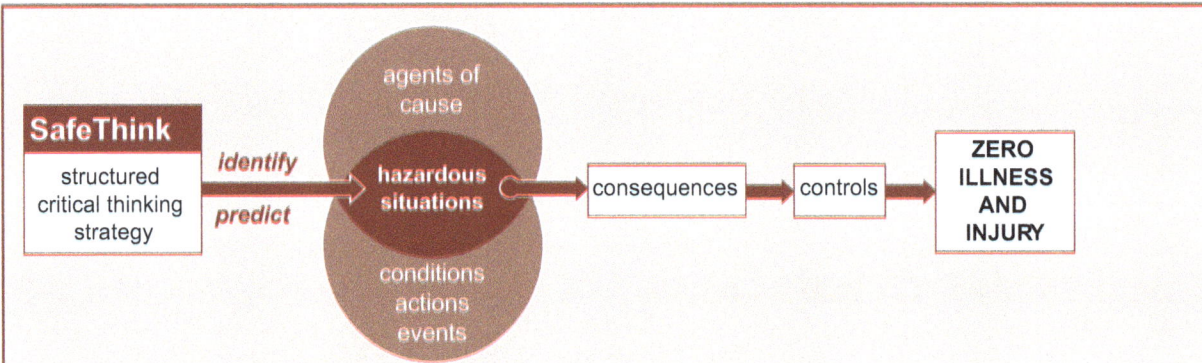

The SafeThink Strategy

A structured critical thinking strategy forms the basis of the *SafeThink* Strategy. The thinking strategy requires you to identify and predict hazardous situations by asking yourself a series of questions. First you ask yourself six critical thinking questions to determine if one or more categories of hazard exist:

- Does the work involve hazardous materials?
- Does the work involve objects, motion, or force that could cause harm?
- Does the work involve non-ambient conditions that could cause harm?
- Is current or static electricity a factor in doing the work?
- Is radiation present when doing the work?
- Could changes lead to or create a hazardous situation?

If you answer *yes* to a question, you must ask yourself more detailed questions. There are three generic detailed questions that apply to each category of hazard:

- What conditions, actions, and events could expose me to the hazard?
- What type of harm does the hazard pose? (consequences)
- What can I do to prevent being harmed? (controls)

Learn the six critical thinking questions and the three generic questions as soon as possible. If you learn these questions, you will find it easier to learn the detailed questions of the *SafeThink* strategy.

2.4 Introduction to the Learning Activities

Your goal is to personalize *SafeThink* and continually apply the strategy in your work and workplace. You will know that you are using the strategy effectively when you are aware that you are continually asking yourself questions to identify and predict hazardous situations.

The learning activities at the end of each part help you to:
- apply the knowledge in the book to your work and workplace
- identify specific health and safety issues that apply to your work and workplace
- apply the specific critical thinking questions for each hazard category

It is recommended that after completing a learning activity you reread the part of the book that you are studying. The information will then have more meaning for you and will reinforce your learning.

To become proficient, you need to continually practice applying the strategy in your workplace. With practice, you will automatically apply the strategy as part of planning and doing work and ensuring that the workplace is safe after the work is complete.

A hazardous situation can be created as a result of one or more conditions, actions, and events. When completing the learning activities to identify conditions, actions, and events, you may not be able to identify all three because some may not exist.

What categories of hazard are present in my workplace? What conditions, actions, and events could expose me to the hazards?

This learning activity will help you learn about the *SafeThink* strategy for identifying and predicting hazardous situations before, during, and after work is completed.

1. Describe three hazardous incidents (accidents or near-misses) that have occurred at your workplace during the past 5 years.

   Incident 1 _____
   _____

   Incident 2 _____
   _____

   Incident 3 _____
   _____

1a. In the table below, identify the three incidents and check off the categories of hazard that were associated with each incident.

Category of Hazard	Incident 1	Incident 2	Incident 3
hazardous materials (Part 3)			
objects, motion, force (Part 4)			
non-ambient conditions (Part 5)			
electricity (Part 6)			
radiation (Part 7)			
changes (Part 8)			

1b. Select one incident from the table in question 1a. What were the conditions, actions, and events that made the categories of hazard you identified hazardous to workers? Incident _____

_____
_____
_____
_____
_____

1c. Using the incident you identified in question 1b, what types of controls were put in place after the incident to prevent the incident from re-occurring?

_____
_____
_____
_____
_____
_____

2. Describe a hazardous task at your workplace.

_____
_____
_____
_____
_____
_____

2a. Before, during, and after performing a task, conditions, actions, and events can lead to or create a hazardous situation. Using the task you identified in question 2,

list in the table below the conditions, actions, and events associated with each hazard category that makes the work potentially hazardous. Not all categories may apply to a specific task. A partial example has been provided.

Name of Task	Install roof decking on a building		
Category of Hazard	Conditions, actions, events before doing the task	Conditions, actions, events while doing the task	Conditions, actions, events after doing the task
Hazardous Material	propane bottles have been placed nearby		propane bottles have been placed nearby
Objects, Motion, Force		a crane is used to lift materials	scrap materials are on floor
Non-Ambient			

Name of Task			
Category of Hazard	Conditions, actions, events before doing the task	Conditions, actions, events while doing the task	Conditions, actions, events after doing the task
Hazardous Material			
Objects, Motion, Force			
Non-Ambient Conditions			
Current and/or Static Electricity			
Changes			

2b. Referring to the table you completed in question 2a, list three controls that could be used to minimize or eliminate some of the hazards you have identified.

_____
_____
_____
_____
_____
_____

The SafeThink Strategy

The structured critical thinking strategy forms the basis of the *SafeThink* Strategy. The thinking strategy requires you to identify and predict hazardous situations by asking yourself a series of questions. First you ask yourself six critical thinking questions to determine if one or more categories of hazard exist:

- **Does the work involve hazardous materials?**
- **Does the work involve objects, motion, or force that could cause harm?**
- **Does the work involve non-ambient conditions that could cause harm?**
- **Is current or static electricity a factor in doing the work?**
- **Is radiation present when doing the work?**
- **Could changes lead to or create a hazardous situation?**

If you answer *yes* to a question, you must ask yourself more detailed questions. There are three generic detailed questions that apply to each category of hazard:

- **What conditions, actions, and events could expose me to the hazard?**
- **What type of harm does the hazard pose? (consequences)**
- **What can I do to prevent being harmed? (controls)**

Learn the six critical thinking questions and the three generic detailed questions as soon as possible. If you learn these questions, you will find it easier to learn the detailed questions of the *SafeThink* strategy.

Option

Many participants have found that writing helps them learn and remember the questions. In the box on the next page, write the six critical thinking questions and the three generic detailed questions that apply to each of the six critical thinking questions. The questions are listed above.

■ FOOD for THOUGHT

■ Hazardous situations

In the workplace or personal environment, a hazardous situation may be created by an agent of cause interacting with the conditions, actions, and events. It is the interaction (i.e., causal relationship) between the agent of cause and the conditions, actions, and events that leads to the hazardous situation. At first, when people are learning the *SafeThink* strategy, they try to identify a condition, an action, and an event (i.e., three separate factors) that lead to a hazardous situation. These efforts produce examples that do not reflect realistic situations. In many cases where a hazardous situation is created, only one or two of the three possible factors exist (i.e., a condition, **and/or** an action, **and/or** an event). When applying the *SafeThink* strategy, think of the conditions and/or actions, and/or events that interact with the agent of cause to create the hazardous situation.

Sometimes when learning to apply the *SafeThink* strategy, people confuse the **action** that created the hazardous situation with the **action** that can be taken to prevent illness or injury (i.e., the controls). You must first identify the potentially hazardous situation before you can take preventive action.

■ When to use the SafeThink strategy

When using the *SafeThink* strategy as part of planning work or personal activities, you may identify a hazardous situation that exists before work starts, while working, and after the work is complete (e.g., the presence of a toxic substance). You can then take precautions that prevent illness or injury throughout the work process before, during, and after the work is complete. You must apply the *SafeThink* strategy continually to identify and predict hazardous situations because work or personal activities (e.g., using power tools) can create additional hazardous situations.

■ The six general questions and the three generic questions

Page 35 lists the six general questions that you must ask yourself to identify agents of cause. These questions are the framework of the *SafeThink* strategy. If you say *yes* to one of the six general questions about agents of cause, you then move on to the first of three generic questions, *What conditions, actions, and events could expose me to the agent of cause?* (i.e., create a hazardous situation). If you identify that a condition and/or action and/or event can interact with the agent of cause to create a hazardous situation, you ask the next two generic questions about *consequences* and *controls* to prevent an incident.

To help you learn to *SafeThink*, learn the six general questions and the three generic questions first because these questions form the framework of the *SafeThink* strategy. For each general question there are specific questions. Each set of specific questions includes the three generic questions. Knowing that the generic questions are repeated in each of the six sets of specific questions makes learning the *SafeThink* questions easier.

All of the *SafeThink* questions are listed in the **Job Aid**. Ideally, you should learn all the *SafeThink* questions in the Job Aid so that you will be more effective at identifying and controlling hazardous situations. The purpose of *SafeThinking* is to prevent you and others from becoming ill or injured.

Part 3
Hazardous Materials

Does the work involve hazardous materials?

What conditions, actions, and events could expose me to the hazardous materials?

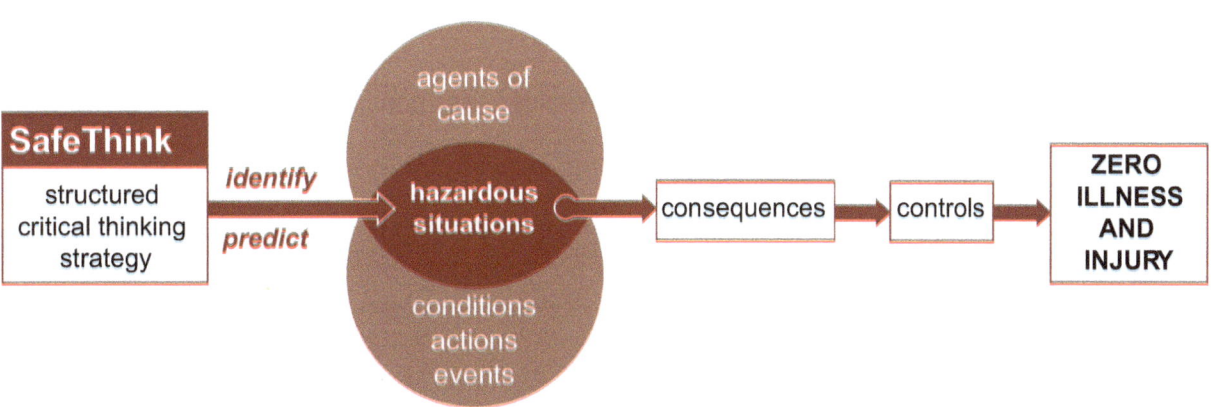

Training Objectives

Upon completion of this part, you will be able to identify and predict conditions, actions, and events that could make hazardous materials hazardous to workers.

- Identify materials in your workplace that are hazardous
- Identify the harm the hazardous materials can cause
- Identify the recommended first aid measures to take if you or a co-worker is exposed to a hazardous material
- Identify conditions, actions, and events that could expose you to the hazardous material
- Identify the correct method(s) for handling and storing hazardous materials
- Identify the correct method(s) for disposing of hazardous materials
- To prevent being harmed by hazardous materials, identify precautions that could be taken:
  - before starting a task
  - during the task
  - after the task is complete

The SafeThink Strategy		
Part	Category of hazard	Critical thinking question
Part 3	*Hazardous Materials*	*Does the work involve hazardous materials?*
Part 4	Objects, Motion, Force	Does the work involve objects, motion, or force that could cause harm?
Part 5	Non-Ambient Conditions	Does the work involve non-ambient conditions that could cause harm?
Part 6	Electricity	Is current or static electricity a factor in doing the work?
Part 7	Radiation	Is radiation present when doing the work?
Part 8	Changes	Could changes lead to or create a hazardous situation?

Part 3 Hazardous Materials

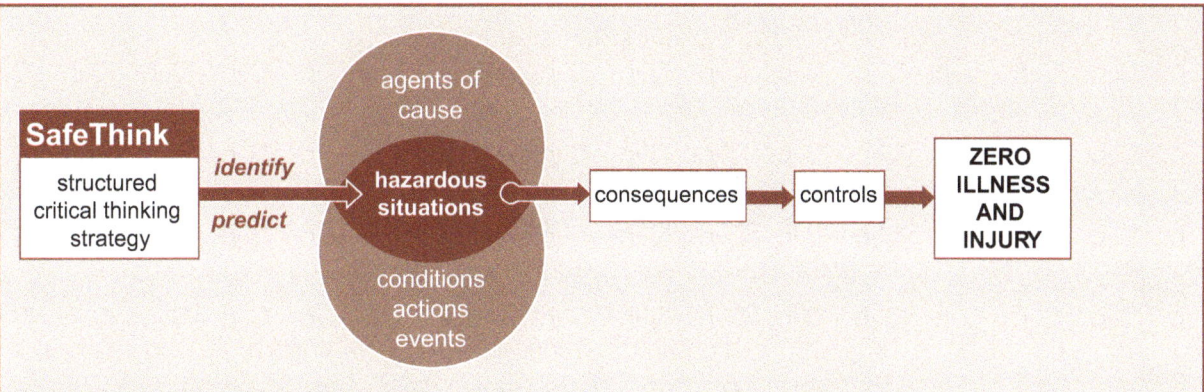

Using the SafeThink strategy

Does the work involve hazardous materials?

1. **To determine if the material is hazardous, ask:**
   - Is it a compressed gas?
   - Is it flammable or combustible?
   - Is it an oxidizing material?
   - Is it poisonous or infectious?
   - Is it corrosive?
   - Is it dangerously reactive?

2. **If the answer to any of the above questions is YES, ask:**
   - What type(s) of harm does the material pose?
   - What recommended first aid should be used if I get exposed?
   - What conditions, actions, and events could expose me to the hazard?
   - What can I do to prevent exposure?
   - How can I store the material safely?
   - How can I dispose of the material safely?

With practice, when you think about the work or see materials that could be hazardous, you will automatically ask these questions.

A learning activity at the end of Part 3 helps you learn to apply the *SafeThink* strategy to your work and workplace. The goal is to identify the conditions, actions, and events which lead to hazardous situations involving hazardous materials.

3 Hazardous Materials

Hazardous materials are substances or products that can cause illness or injuries to people. Some hazardous materials can also damage the environment, workplace equipment, or other materials. Hazardous materials may—or may not—be regulated by governments to prevent illness or injuries. For example, manufactured products (e.g., acids and combustible liquids) are regulated. Other hazardous materials that you could be exposed to are **not** regulated, for example, bird and mouse droppings, and poisonous plants.

Regulatory controls

Industrialized countries provide controls in the form of regulations and guidelines for storing, handling, transporting, and disposing of hazardous materials. All companies and workers who use hazardous materials must comply with the regulations—failure to comply can result in penalties (fines and/or imprisonment) for you and your company.

Regulatory controls for storing and handling hazardous materials include the following:

- Hazardous materials must be labeled correctly. There are specific requirements for labeling different types of hazardous materials.
- Suppliers of hazardous products must provide a Material Safety Data Sheet (MSDS) for each product. The MSDS describes the product's:
  - hazardous ingredients
  - physical properties
  - fire and explosion hazard
  - reactivity data
  - oxidizing data
  - first aid measures in case of exposure
  - exposure prevention measures, including personal protective clothing and equipment, waste disposal, storage, and ventilation
- Suppliers must periodically update MSDSs for their hazardous products. Workers at every workplace where the products are used must have ready access to up-to-date MSDSs.

Hazard:
the property or ability of a machine, equipment, process, material, physical factors, or work activities to cause harm to people

Material Safety Data Sheet (MSDS):
a technical document which provides information about a hazardous material

- Companies must provide general and workplace-specific training to workers who work with or near hazardous materials. Training programs must be reviewed every year and refresher training must be provided regularly.
- Companies must provide workplace controls to prevent workers from being injured or made ill by hazardous materials. The controls may include providing workers with specialized equipment, personal protective equipment, respirators, and instruments to detect the presence of hazardous materials (e.g., gas detector). Workers must use the controls provided.

Regulatory controls for transporting hazardous materials (dangerous goods) include the following:
- All packages must be labeled and vehicles transporting dangerous goods must display warning placards.
- All shipments of dangerous goods must be accompanied by a shipping bill showing the shipper's and receiver's name(s) and address(es) and the classification and quantity of items being shipped.

Regulatory controls for hazardous waste materials govern waste handling, storage, labeling, documentation, transportation, and disposal.

Primary concerns

Your six primary concerns when dealing with **regulated** and **non-regulated** hazardous materials are:
- What kind of hazard does the material pose?
- What recommended first aid should be used if I get exposed?
- What conditions, actions, and events could expose me to the hazard?
- What can I do before, during, and after work to prevent exposure?
- How can I store the material safely?
- How can I dispose of the material safely?

Classification of hazardous materials

Hazardous materials can be classified according to the type(s) of hazard the materials present. One classification system

used by governments divides the materials into six classes; some classes are further divided into subclasses. The six classes are:
- compressed gas
- flammable and combustible materials
- oxidizing materials
- poisonous and infectious materials
- corrosive materials
- dangerously reactive materials

Radioactive hazardous materials are **not** included in this part. Radiation hazards are described in Part 7.

SafeThink uses the six classes of regulated hazards described above to organize content about hazardous materials. Keep in mind that the thinking strategy applies to both **regulated** and **non-regulated** hazardous materials. The goal is to prevent all types of hazardous material from causing illness or injury to you and others.

Your workplace may not have all six classes of hazardous materials and some of the examples provided in this book may not have meaning for you. Nevertheless, it is important that you learn all six classes of hazardous materials: you may change jobs or be required to work near people who are using these hazardous materials. The importance is to learn the critical thinking strategy:
- to identify materials that are hazardous
- to identify the conditions, actions, and events that could cause you to be exposed to the hazardous materials, and
- to determine the appropriate controls.

Many hazardous materials pose more than one type of hazard. For example, a material may be flammable, toxic, and corrosive. When working around or with materials, make sure you know *all* the hazards each material poses.

3.1 Compressed Gases

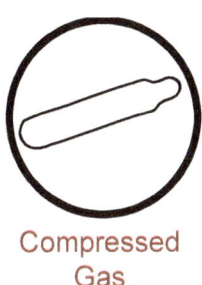

Compressed Gas

Compressed gases such as propane, oxygen, acetylene, argon, helium, and nitrogen are common at industrial workplaces. Compressed gases are kept in containers under pressure, for example, pressurized cylinders and aerosol cans. Often gases stored in cylinders are liquefied due to the high pressure. Spills or leaks of liquefied gases can cause frostbite to exposed skin. Puncturing or damaging a pressurized container or allowing the container to become hot could result in an explosion.

The cap for a compressed gas cylinder protects the valve from mechanical damage. A damaged valve can leak, potentially exposing workers to flammable and/or toxic gas hazards. If the valve breaks off, the rapidly escaping gas will cause the cylinder to rocket (i.e., travel like a rocket).

You must take care when handling and working around compressed gas cylinders to prevent the cylinders from being dented or gouged. The cylinder wall can develop a weak spot which will continue to weaken if corrosion sets in.

Some types of cylinders (e.g., acetylene) must remain upright. Do **not** lay the cylinders down for transportation or storage. All cylinders must be secured during transportation, storage, and use to prevent them from falling over. Do **not** store cylinders of oxygen with other types of gas cylinders.

Compressed gas is produced in large volumes at gas plants, refineries, and chemical plants; the gas is transported by tanker truck, railcar, and pipeline. At these workplaces, gases are contained in pressurized process vessels, storage bullets and spheres, and piping.

To learn about the characteristics of a compressed gas at your workplace, refer to the MSDS for that product.

Hazardous situations

Examples of conditions, actions, and events causing compressed gas to create or lead to hazardous situations are:

condition—a barbecue propane tank could not be properly secured in the trunk of a car

condition—aerosol cans are stored in a furnace room

action—a worker drops a small oxygen cylinder on a concrete floor

action—a worker is drilling post holes for a fence and pierces a natural gas pipeline

event—a train pulling compressed gas cars (tankers) derails

event—a building is on fire. The building contains compressed gas cylinders.

Consequences

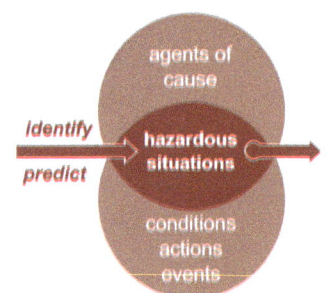

Potential consequences of mishandling compressed gas include:
- If a pressurized container is heated, pressure may build up inside, causing the container to rocket or explode. Flying shrapnel from an exploding container could cause serious injury.
- Some compressed gases are poisonous; a poisonous gas leak could cause illness or death.
- Some compressed gases are flammable; leaking flammable gas could ignite, causing a fire or explosion.

Controls

Many types of control can be used to reduce the risk of harm from compressed gases. In addition to the controls mentioned previously, some other controls that you can use are:
- Check the container label and hazard symbols before using the gas. Follow your site-specific procedures for using that gas to eliminate or reduce the potential for illness or injury.

- Check gauges on compressed gas piping and vessels regularly. Piping and vessels are built to withstand a specified maximum operating pressure and temperature.
- Do not transport small cylinders of compressed gas, for example, propane, in the passenger compartment of a vehicle. If the cylinder leaks, you will be exposed to potentially toxic and/or flammable gas. Usually, cylinders (including aerosol cans) cannot be properly secured in the passenger compartment. In a vehicle accident, the cylinder becomes a projectile, potentially injuring the occupants. The cylinder could also become damaged and leak.

Critical thinking questions

When working with or in an area where there is compressed gas, ask yourself the following questions before, while, and after working:
- What kind of hazard does the material pose?
- What recommended first aid should be used if I get exposed?
- What conditions, actions, and events could expose me to
- the hazard?
- What can I do to prevent exposure?
- How can I store the material safely?
- How can I dispose of the material safely?

These critical thinking questions are an important part of the *SafeThink* strategy. Asking these questions before, while, and after working helps you develop good habits that prevent illness and injury. To help you learn the questions, they are repeated for each of the next five classes of hazardous material. Learning these questions will also help you complete the learning activities for this part.

3.2 Flammable and Combustible Materials

A flammable or combustible material is any solid, liquid, or gas that ignites and burns. Flammable materials (e.g., propane) burn readily at room temperature; combustible materials (e.g., paper) burn when heated.

Almost all industrial workplaces use flammable and combustible materials such as:
- fuels (e.g., propane and gasoline)
- solvents for cleaning and degreasing; paint thinner
- adhesives
- paints, lacquers, and other coatings
- asphalts
- waxes
- wood
- plastic
- paper

 Solid materials that are normally difficult to ignite can be a serious fire and explosion hazard when they are in the form of a powder or dust (e.g., wood, coal, grains, metals).

Products such as fuels and solvents give off flammable vapors. The vapors can accumulate in poorly ventilated areas, increasing the risk of a fire or explosion. The vapors can also drift to other areas that may have sources of ignition. When using flammable products, you must eliminate or control sources of ignition.

Sources of ignition include:
- open flames
- hot fragments created by grinding, cutting, and welding metals
- metal sparks created by metal-to-metal contact (e.g., impact of hand tools on equipment)
- electrical sparks created by motors of power tools
- sparks created by discharging static electricity
- space heaters
- cigarettes

Large volumes of flammable and combustible gases and liquids are produced at gas plants, refineries, and chemical plants. At these workplaces, the products are contained in pressurized process vessels, storage vessels, and piping. Portable and fixed flammable gas detectors are used at these sites to detect leaks and measure the concentration of the gas in the atmosphere. Audible and visible alarms activate if the concentration of flammable gas reaches a specific level.

At facilities such as medium density fiberboard mills that produce large volumes of dust, spark detectors are installed in the dust collectors. Audible and visible alarms activate if the number of sparks per second reaches a specific level.

When working at sites that have systems to detect flammable and combustible materials in the atmosphere, make sure you know:
- the type of material that is being monitored
- the concentrations that trigger alarms
- the meaning of each type of audible and visible alarm
- your response to each type of alarm

To learn about the flammable and combustible characteristics of a manufactured product, refer to the MSDS for that product. For wastes, refer to provincial/state waste regulations.

Hazardous situations

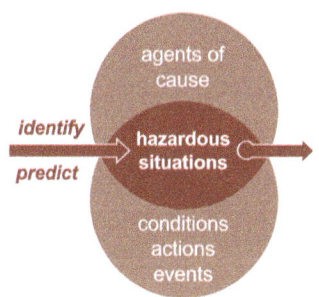

Examples of conditions, actions, and events causing flammable and combustible materials to create or lead to hazardous situations are:

condition—a pipe beside a large propane tank must be welded

condition—solvent-soaked rags are in a pile on the garage floor

action—a person is heating candle wax on the stove. The wax overheats and ignites.

action—a person lights a match to check the operation of the pilot light on a furnace

event—a high pressure gas pipeline is corroded, ruptures, and bursts into flames

event—lightning strikes a home and starts a fire

Consequences

Potential consequences of mishandling flammable and combustible materials include:
- fires and explosions could cause burns, shrapnel injuries, or death
- the burning material (or its byproducts) may be toxic, causing illness or death (e.g., creosote-treated railway ties)

Controls

Many types of control can be used to reduce the risk of harm from flammable and combustible materials. In addition to the controls mentioned previously, some other controls that you can use are:

- Before using flammable or combustible materials, eliminate sources of ignition.
- If you work around flammable and combustible gases and liquids, wear flame-resistant clothing and follow all site safety rules.
- Store flammable and combustible materials away from sources of heat, sparks, or open flames (for example, not in furnace rooms, beside electrical panels, or near grinders or welders).
- For manufactured products, check the container label and hazard symbols before use. Follow your site-specific procedures for using that material.
- When you pour a flammable liquid from one container into another or fuel your equipment and vehicles:
  - follow your site's electrical grounding procedure. The procedure is designed to prevent flammable vapors from being ignited by a spark from static electricity.
  - leave sufficient room in the container for thermal expansion (e.g., do **not** fill the container to more than 90% capacity). Overfilling may cause flammable vapors to leak or the container to rupture if the container is heated.
- When using a solvent to clean components on stationary equipment, use a catch basin to collect runoff.
- Store oily- or solvent-soaked rags in closed metal containers.
- Follow site-specific procedures for disposing of flammable and combustible wastes (e.g., used oil, spent solvents, paint cans).
- Keep work areas clear of combustible materials such as wood chips and dust.
- In areas that are monitored by fixed flammable gas detectors, learn the meaning of the different alarms and how you should respond.
- If you use portable equipment to monitor for flammable gases at your workplace, learn how to use the equipment correctly and how to respond when the equipment alarms.

- Do **not** transport flammable or combustible products, (e.g., paint thinner) in the passenger compartment of a vehicle.
- Before adding fuel to a portable engine or a vehicle, shut off the engine to eliminate the source of ignition. Do not smoke while fuelling.

Critical thinking questions

When working with or in an area where there are flammable or combustible materials, ask yourself the following questions before, while, and after working:
- What type of harm does the material pose?
- What recommended first aid should be used if I get exposed?
- What conditions, actions, and events could expose me to the hazard?
- What can I do to prevent exposure?
- How can I store the material safely?
- How can I dispose of the material safely?

3.3 Oxidizing Materials

Oxidizing materials are liquids or solids that easily give off oxygen or other oxidizing substances. Oxidizers feed a fire; they help the fire to develop quickly and burn vigorously. Some oxidizers explode when they contact contaminants or are exposed to heat, shock, or friction. Common oxidizers are:
- sodium hypochlorite (bleach)
- chlorine gas, chlorine dioxide
- oxygen
- perchloric acid solutions, sodium perchlorate
- potassium dichromate, chromic acid
- silver nitrate, aluminum nitrate
- hydrogen peroxide, zinc peroxide

Hazardous situations

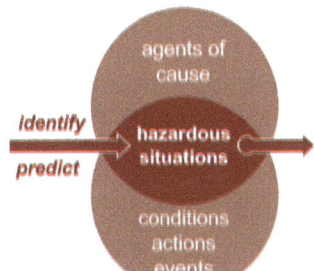

When mixed with water, some oxidizers form corrosive acids. When an oxidizer comes in contact with body moisture, it can cause severe burns to the skin, eyes, nose, throat, and lungs.

Household bleach is often used to clean and disinfect surfaces. Never mix bleach with other cleaners; the bleach

can react violently with other chemicals to produce poisonous byproducts.

To learn about the oxidizing characteristics of a manufactured product, refer to the MSDS for that product.

Consequences

Potential consequences of exposure to oxidizing materials include:
- fires and explosions can cause burns, shrapnel injuries, or death
- contacting body tissue (eyes, skin, throat, lungs) can cause burns and permanent organ damage
- formation of corrosive acids can cause tissue damage
- formation of toxic products or byproducts can cause poisoning and/or asphyxiation

Controls

Controls you can use to reduce the risk of harm from oxidizing materials include:
- Check the label and hazard symbols before using the product. Follow your site-specific procedures for using that material.
- Read and follow the posted hazard warnings before entering storage areas.
- Store oxidizing materials as recommended in the MSDS. For example, most oxidizers must be stored:
    - in a cool dry area
    - away from direct sunlight, heat sources
    - away from incompatible materials
    - away from processing or handling areas
    - away from exit doors. Containers near doors are more likely to be bumped. Burning or exploding containers could block your escape route.
    - away from fuels, grease, lubricants, or solvents
    - away from ignition sources
- Wear the recommended personal protective equipment (e.g., rubber gloves, goggles, face shield, respirator).
- Never use oxygen (e.g., from gas welders) to clean parts. Oxygen can cause oil and grease to ignite spontaneously.
- Follow site-specific procedures to dispose of waste oxidizing materials.

- Do **not** transport oxidizers such as bleach in the passenger compartment of a vehicle.
- Monitor oxygen levels when working in combustible atmospheres. Excessive oxygen concentrations are highly dangerous because they greatly increase the risk of a fire and/or explosion.

Critical thinking questions

When working with or in an area where there are oxidizing materials, ask yourself the following questions:
- What type of harm does the material pose?
- What recommended first aid should be used if I get exposed?
- What conditions, actions, and events could expose me to the hazard?
- What can I do to prevent exposure?
- How can I store the material safely?
- How can I dispose of the material safely?

3.4 Poisonous and Infectious Materials

Material Causing Immediate Toxic Effects

You can be exposed to poisonous and infectious materials at your workplace, at public facilities, in your home, or outdoors. The materials can be manufactured industrial products, naturally-occurring materials in the environment, or disease agents. The materials are sometimes classified as follows:
- **materials causing immediate toxic effects**—This category includes:
  - manufactured gases (e.g., chlorine)
  - naturally-occurring gases (e.g., hydrogen sulfide)
  - poisonous plants and the poisonous venom of insects and snakes
  - insecticides

Material Causing Other Toxic Effects

- **materials causing delayed toxic effects**—Exposure to grain, wood, and sandblasting dusts can create respiratory problems. Repeated exposure to fuel and solvent vapors and pesticides can damage the nervous system. Materials such as asbestos, lead, chromium, and benzene cause diseases, including cancer, which may show up many years after exposure.

Biohazardous Infectious Material

- **infectious materials**—Agents such as bacteria, viruses, fungi, and prions can cause diseases in both humans and animals. Sources of these agents include:
  - humans, animals, and insects
  - untreated water
  - soil
  - meats, vegetables, and other food products
  - surfaces such as keyboards, washroom counters, and telephones
  - damp materials (containing fungi, mildew)

Routes of entry

Hazardous materials (including disease agents) can harm body cells, tissues, and organs. Materials can enter your body by several routes, including:

absorption—through your skin, eyes, or a body opening
inhalation—through your mouth and nose
ingestion—by mouth
injection—when a sharp object or high-pressure gas or liquid stream punctures your skin

NOTE Routes of entry also apply to compressed gases and liquids, and corrosive materials.

Hazardous situations

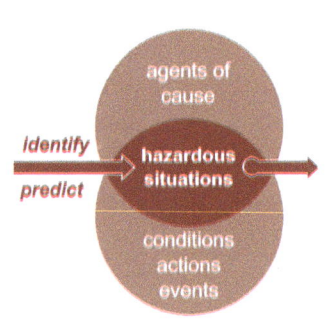

Many activities can expose workers to poisonous and infectious materials:

- handling food products, handling carcasses, handling soil
- sampling water from lagoons and ponds
- cleaning out sludge in sumps and septic tanks
- cleaning up rodent and bird droppings
- emptying waste containers

- renovating buildings
- working outdoors
- being bitten by animals and insects

Examples of conditions, actions, and events causing poisonous and/or infectious materials to create or lead to hazardous situations are:

condition—surveyors must work in an area that has poison ivy

condition—bird and mouse droppings cover the top of air ducts that must be removed for renovation

action—a worker dispenses concentrated hydrofluoric acid (used to etch glass) from a large container to a smaller one, but does not label the small container. The worker places the small container on a workbench shared by several workers, and then leaves for the day.

action—a worker is using an airless sprayer to apply paint in a poorly ventilated area. The atmosphere quickly fills with spray droplets which are toxic and flammable.

event—a supplier puts the wrong label on a container of a highly toxic product. Because you believe that the product is not toxic, you do not wear personal protective equipment.

Sources to learn about poisonous and infectious materials include:
- the MSDS for the type(s) of hazardous products at your workplace
- local poison control center
- public health centers

Consequences

Potential consequences of exposure to poisonous or infectious materials include:
- immediate effects such as breathing difficulties, loss of consciousness, and death
- chronic and/or delayed effects such as asthma, eczema, cancer, and birth defects in children born to exposed workers
- infections and diseases such as HIV-AIDS, hepatitis, tetanus, anthrax, hantavirus, salmonella, rabies, ringworm, Lyme disease, Giardia (beaver fever), malaria

 SafeThink™

Strategies to reduce the hazards

When working with poisonous and infectious materials, you can use several strategies to reduce the hazards:

Eliminate or substitute—Where practical, replace a toxic material with a non-toxic or less toxic material. Use the lowest concentration of the material that can do the job effectively. Maintain the smallest inventory of the toxic material that meets the job demands.

Reduce atmospheric contamination—Materials in the form of gases, vapors, aerosols, mists, smokes, and dusts can contaminate the atmosphere. Use fume hoods where possible. Ventilate by opening windows and doors. Do **not** use toxic materials in poorly ventilated areas. Do **not** start internal combustion engines in a closed garage; carbon monoxide can quickly build up. To minimize exposing other workers to toxic materials, use the materials at a time when the least number of people will be in the area. Use warning signs and barriers to prevent others from entering the area. To remove dust, use a filter-equipped vacuum cleaner or wet mop instead of a broom.

Provide barriers—Personal protective equipment (PPE) is available to provide a barrier between the routes of entry and the hazard:
- specialized footwear, gloves, clothing, and face shields isolate the skin
- specialized goggles isolate the eyes
- respiratory protective equipment (RPE) isolates the nose, mouth, throat, and lungs

Personal protective equipment usually provides limited protection against skin punctures from infected objects. Use care and attention when working with sharp objects, including needles, to prevent skin punctures. In areas where snakes, rodents, and biting or stinging insects may be hidden, check closely before extending your hands. When working with pressurized equipment, check hoses and couplings for proper fit and damage. A high-pressure leak can cause the liquid to penetrate your skin. Refer to Part 5—*Non-Ambient Conditions* for more information about hazards associated with high-pressure liquids and gases.

Minimize transfer—Poisonous and infectious materials can be transferred **by** you or **to** you. Often workers, through their actions or inactions, transfer poisonous or infectious materials to themselves and others, for example:

- A worker wears protective gloves, coveralls, half-face respirator, and goggles when mixing poisonous chemicals. The worker wipes his or her forehead.
- A worker uses a rag to clean a washroom and then uses the same rag to wipe down handrails and water fountains.
- A worker has a cold. The worker touches his or her nose and then touches papers, the coffee pot, and shared work surfaces (e.g., door knobs).
- Workers share lip balm or a water bottle.
- A worker places raw meat on a plate, transfers the meat to a hot grill, and then puts the cooked meat back on the same plate.

When working with poisonous or infectious materials, always consider how, through your actions or inactions, you might transfer the hazardous material from the source to other objects.

There are many ways that poisonous or infectious materials can be transferred to you. In addition to the examples mentioned previously, some other ways of getting infected are:

- getting worms or other parasites from direct contact with soils, stagnant water, and animals
- directly contacting or inhaling mold spores and contaminated dust
- after spraying chemicals, storing contaminated coveralls and other personal protective equipment in the passenger compartment of a vehicle, in a motel room, or in your home

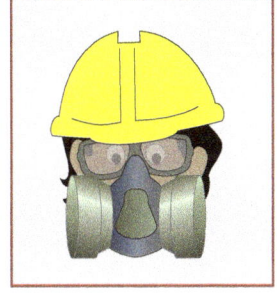

When working in an environment where poisonous and infectious materials may exist, always consider how the hazardous material could get transferred by you and to you.

> **Preventing the transfer of infectious diseases**
>
> One of the most effective controls to prevent the transfer of infectious diseases is to frequently wash your hands with soap and hot water.

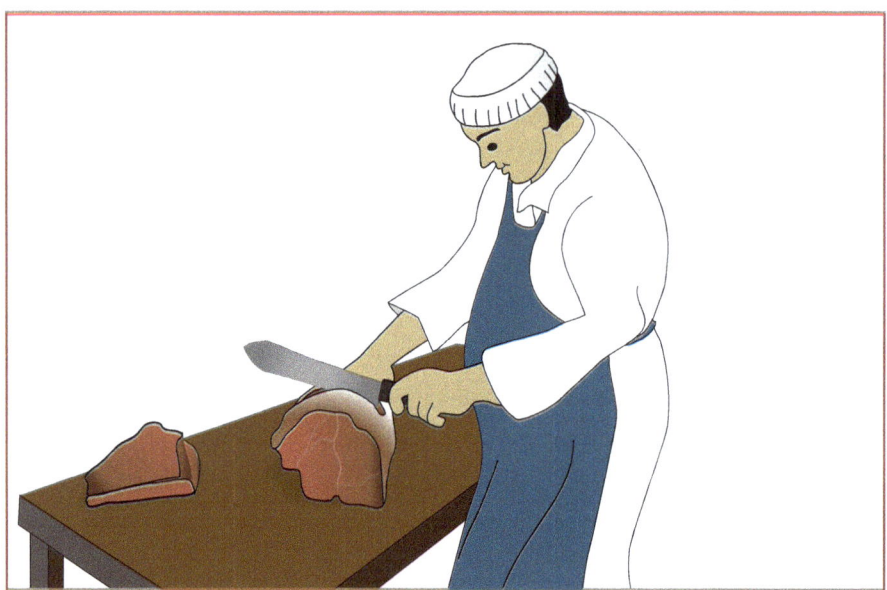

Early detection of poisonous gases

At some workplaces, there is a possibility of toxic gases being released to the atmosphere. Portable and fixed toxic gas detectors are used at these sites to detect and measure the concentration of toxic gases. Audible and visible alarms activate if concentrations of toxic gases reach specific levels. (Refer to Appendix 3 for a table describing types of exposure limits for toxic gases.)

When working at sites that have systems to detect the presence of toxic gases, make sure you know:
- the type of material that is being monitored
- the gas concentrations that trigger alarms
- the meaning of each type of audible and visible alarm
- your response to each type of alarm

Toxic effects of drugs, medications, and alcohol

Prescription and non-prescription drugs (e.g., over-the-counter medications such as antihistamines), alcohol, and banned substances can impair your thinking ability, judgment, alertness, senses, coordination, and reaction time. Some drugs can also affect your short-term memory. One of the dangers of drugs is that you may not be aware that your mental and physical performance is impaired. Some medications can also increase your sensitivity to sunlight and hazardous materials.

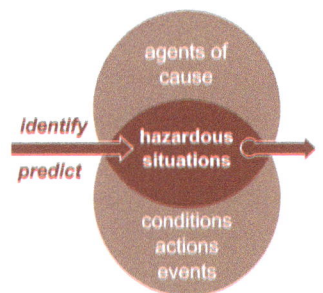

Consult your doctor and your pharmacist and read the literature supplied with the medication to find out about any adverse side effects. Inform your co-workers and supervisor if you are using medications so that they can be more vigilant in watching out for you. If your performance is being affected, you may have to be assigned less hazardous work.

Controls

Some controls you can use to prevent being harmed by poisonous and infectious materials include:

- Check all container labels, hazard symbols, and posted warnings before working with materials that may be toxic and/or before entering an environment that may be toxic. Follow site-specific procedures when working around or with toxic materials.

- Do not assume that an industrial product is as safe as similar domestic products. For example, industrial paints may contain lead; industrial-grade solvents may be more concentrated than domestic-grade solvents.

- If you disturb asbestos insulation around pipes and on building structures, leave the area immediately and inform your supervisor.

- Take the specialized training that is offered to you (e.g., confined space training if you enter trenches, cisterns, sumps, vessels, or holds of ships).

- Wear appropriate personal protective equipment and respiratory protective equipment. If you use a respirator, have it properly fitted. Always check the respirator seal before entering a potentially toxic environment.

- Make sure to select the right filter to protect you from types of toxic material to which you could be exposed. There is no universal filter that can protect you from all types of hazardous materials. Replace the filter if it becomes plugged and restricts breathing or if you smell the toxic material breaking through the filter.

- Work with a buddy—do not enter a potentially toxic environment alone.

- Always use the engineering controls provided (e.g., fume hood, isolation chamber).
- Do not pipette poisonous, corrosive, or infectious material by mouth; use automated pipettes.
- If you use portable equipment to monitor for toxic gas, learn how to use this equipment and how to respond to readings that indicate the presence of the gas.
- Take personal safety precautions when sweeping up, handling, and disposing of potentially poisonous or infectious wastes. Use gloves, respiratory protection, and the recommended disinfectant.
- Become informed of the harmful plants and animals (e.g., birds, rodents, snakes, insects) at your site that could harm you. Learn about their habitat, where they are likely to be encountered, and the protective measures to prevent contact.
- Apply the strategies (described earlier in this section) for reducing hazards associated with poisonous and infectious materials.

NOTE In many jurisdictions, workers potentially exposed to certain poisonous and infectious materials (e.g., arsenic, tuberculosis) must undergo regular medical tests.

Critical thinking questions

When working with or in an area where there are poisonous and infectious materials, ask yourself the following questions:
- What type of harm does the material pose?
- What recommended first aid should be used if I get exposed?
- What conditions, actions, and events could expose me to the hazard?
- What can I do to prevent exposure?
- How can I store the material safely?
- How can I dispose of the material safely?

3.5 Corrosive Materials

Corrosive Material

Corrosive materials may cause irreversible chemical burns to the skin, eyes, respiratory system, and digestive system. Corrosive materials commonly used in the workplace include:
- acids:
  - hydrochloric acid (e.g., for soldering)
  - sulfuric acid (e.g., vehicle batteries)
- bases (alkaline substances)
- potassium hydroxide (lye)
- sodium hydroxide (lye)
- halogens
- bromine (e.g., plastic manufacturing)
- chlorine

Hazardous situations

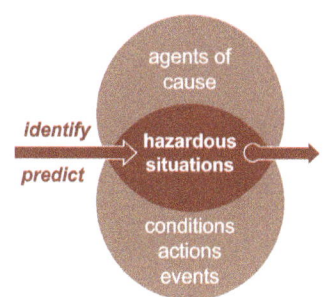

You could be exposed to corrosive materials when cleaning, etching, and removing paint and rust.

To learn about the corrosive materials that you could be exposed to at your workplace and the required safety measures, read the MSDSs for those materials.

Consequences

Potential consequences of exposure to corrosive materials include irritation and chemical burns to the skin, eyes, respiratory system, and digestive system. Corrosive materials may also damage metals, plastics, and other materials, causing equipment and materials to fail. When equipment and materials fail, workers may be injured or exposed to hazardous materials.

Controls

Controls you can use to prevent being harmed by corrosive materials include:
- Check the label and hazard symbols before using a product that may be corrosive. Follow site-specific procedures when working near or with corrosive materials.
- Check the MSDS for recommendations on personal protective equipment. The MSDS may recommend using

respiratory protection, particularly if the product will be used in a poorly-ventilated area.
- Store acids separately from bases (caustic or alkaline products).
- Know where the eyewash stations and emergency showers are located at your workplace, and know how to operate them.
- Keep pathways between tanks of corrosive materials and eyewash stations and emergency showers clear.
- Clean the work area thoroughly after a corrosive material has been used to remove corrosive residues.

Critical thinking questions

When working with or in an area where there are corrosive materials, ask yourself the following questions:
- What type of harm does the material pose?
- What recommended first aid should be used if I get exposed?
- What conditions, actions, and events could expose me to the hazard?
- What can I do to prevent exposure?
- How can I store the material safely?
- How can I dispose of the material safely?

3.6 Dangerously Reactive Materials

Dangerously Reactive Material

Dangerously reactive materials can burn or explode if they are exposed to heat or impact forces, or mixed with water or other chemical products. Dangerously reactive liquids and solids are extremely hazardous and may:
- react dangerously if they get wet or if humidity is high
- be highly toxic if inhaled, ingested, or absorbed
- undergo uncontrolled reactions that can cause a fire or cause sealed containers to rupture or explode

Part 3   Hazardous Materials

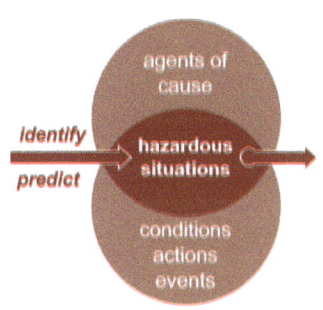

Hazardous situations

Dangerously reactive materials that can create hazardous situations include:
- self-reactive materials that are very unstable such as nitroglycerine, picric acid, or highly concentrated perchloric acid
- explosive charges
- substances that form polymers when heated such as acrylonitrile or vinyl acetate
- substances that condense rapidly such as acetaldehyde
- hardeners in fiberglass repair kits

Consequences

Potential consequences of mishandling dangerously reactive materials include:
- detonation, explosions, fires, and release of toxic gases
- irritation and chemical burns to the skin, eyes, respiratory system, and digestive system

Controls

Controls you can use to reduce the risk of harm from dangerously reactive materials include:
- Check the product label and hazard symbols to identify the hazards.
- Check the MSDS to identify the proper storage conditions (e.g., temperature, humidity), and personal protective equipment to use when handling the product.
- Take the specialized training offered if you handle or transport dangerously reactive materials.
- Use the appropriate personal protective equipment and follow the codes of practice and safe work procedures developed to protect you.
- Keep the area where dangerously reactive materials are stored and used meticulously clean. Residual powders may explode or react with water or other products. Turn on the ventilation system when using the product.
- Store the product in its original container.

Follow site-specific procedures for disposing of packaging and empty containers.

SafeThink™

Byproducts of some industrial processes are dangerously reactive. In the oil and gas industry, iron sulphide is formed when hydrogen sulphide reacts with iron piping and vessels. Iron sulphide can spontaneously ignite when exposed to air. When changing filters that may contain iron sulphide, care must be taken to prevent the used filter from drying out over time and exposing the iron sulfide to the air.

Precautions for handling the used filters include:
- immediately placing the used filters in an air-tight plastic bag
- placing the used filters in the box of the truck (not in the passenger compartment)
- disposing of the used filter according to site-specific procedures

Critical thinking questions

When working with or in an area where there are dangerously reactive materials, ask yourself the following questions:
- What type of harm does the material pose?
- What recommended first aid should be used if I am exposed?
- What conditions, actions, and events could expose me to the hazard?
- What can I do to prevent exposure?
- How can I store the material safely?
- How can I dispose of the material safely?

3.7 Waste Materials

Waste materials are an integral part of many industrial activities, for example:
- unwanted material from mining and oil operations (e.g., tailings from mining operations, salt water from crude oil processing)
- spent or used materials (e.g., batteries, filters, catalysts, solvents, engine oils, and coolants)
- contaminated materials from performing tasks (e.g., used rags, wastewater from washing shop floors). The contaminated materials may contain oils, solvents, glycols, or heavy metals.
- discarded or damaged materials (e.g., empty pesticide containers; metal filings and scrap pieces; wet moldy drywall; paper)

- urine and manure from animal feed lots and stockyards
- spoiled or leftover food, used cooking grease or oil

Waste materials may—or may not—be hazardous to health and safety and to the environment. Hazardous wastes may present one or more of the six types of hazard described previously. Waste materials can be classified in different ways, for example, non-hazardous or hazardous, depending on their:
- physical properties that make the material a fire hazard or contaminate the soil (e.g., paint cans with liquid paint could be a fire hazard and contaminate the soil; paint cans with dried paint are less hazardous)
- chemical properties (e.g., reactivity, corrosivity)
- impact to living organisms (including humans) and the environment (e.g., toxicity, persistence in the soil)

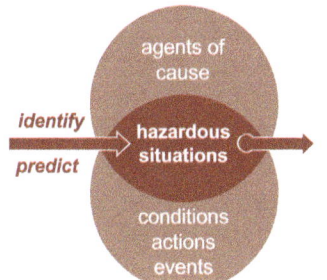

Hazards of waste materials—Non-hazardous products used in hazardous processes can become hazardous after use (e.g., used paint booth filters are hazardous if they contain liquid, flammable paint residues, and/or lead). Waste hazardous products typically have the same hazard properties as new hazardous products, but *other hazard properties may also be added during use.* For example, a cleaning solvent used to clean pipe threads is flammable before and after use; however, after use the solvent also contains toxic metals from pipe thread lubricant removed during cleaning.

Storage and disposal of waste materials—Various methods are used to store waste materials including bins, drums, pails, baskets, plastic and glass containers, floor sumps, and storage sheds. Separate waste containers are often used to store different types of waste. Some hazardous wastes must be kept separate to prevent hazardous chemical reactions (e.g., waste acid and waste caustic).

Some wastes can be recycled; other wastes must be disposed by incineration or landfilling. When waste containers are full, the waste is transported to an approved recycling or disposal facility. For wastes that are regulated, specific documentation is required to track the transportation and disposal process.

 SafeThink™

The unknown factor—A significant hazard for workers who handle wastes is the *unknown factor*; for example:
- Waste containers may not be labeled or the label may be illegible or misleading.
- Wastes from unknown activities that occurred years before may still be stored on site.
- Non-hazardous waste containers may unexpectedly contain hazardous wastes, particularly if the container is not in a secure area.
- Old drums used as waste containers may be leaking hazardous products.
- Water overflowing or leaking from uncovered waste containers (e.g., scrap metal bins) may be contaminating soil in the vicinity.
- Locations of hazardous waste containers may have changed; soil in the former storage area may unknowingly be contaminated.
- Washroom waste receptacles may contain infectious materials (e.g., used needles, blood-soaked paper towels or sanitary napkins).
- Containers that appear to be empty may contain toxic residues.
- Waste containers (e.g., drums) that are used for several different types of waste, resulting in a "toxic soup" of chemicals.

Waste bins should be in a secure area or equipped with a lid and padlock to prevent unauthorized access. Waste containers containing flammable products such as oily or solvent-soaked rags, spent filters, and flammable liquids should be tightly covered. The containers should be stored in a cool area, away from fuel tanks and lines, electrical panels, sources of ignition, and heavy traffic.

Controls

If you handle wastes at your workplace, protect yourself and the environment from the unknown factor:
- Find out what wastes are generated in your work area.
- Ask your supervisor to identify the precautions for handling the different types of wastes. If your supervisor is not sure,

investigate to determine the hazards, handling precautions, and storage requirements. Sources of information include the MSDS for the applicable product, government waste regulations, and industry associations.
- Use the recommended handling precautions; this may include using personal protective equipment and respiratory protective equipment.
- Ensure waste bins are properly labeled.
- Liquid wastes may have to be sampled and tested before disposal. Wear personal protective equipment and respiratory protective equipment if you are doing the sampling.
- When cleaning sludge from sumps or septic tanks, use personal protective equipment and respiratory protective equipment. The sludge may be poisonous or infectious.
- Do not pack down overflowing washroom waste receptacles; needles or razor blades (sharp and potentially infectious) may be concealed among used paper towels.
- Replace containers that are leaking, do not have lids, or are too small for the amount of waste generated. Waste containers that are overflowing or leaking contribute to soil contamination.
- Before cleaning up a spill, investigate to determine the composition of the spilled material and associated hazards.
- Store food wastes in closed containers and ship the wastes off site regularly. Wild animals, birds, and insects are attracted to the food and can pose a physical threat or may carry diseases.
- Be mindful of the possibility that wastes could drain into municipal sewer systems, lakes, or rivers.

Critical thinking questions

When working with or in an area where there are waste materials, ask yourself the following questions:
- What type of harm does the material pose?
- What recommended first aid should be used if I get exposed?
- What conditions, actions, and events could expose me to the hazard?
- What can I do to prevent exposure?
- How can I store the material safely?
- How can I dispose of the material safely?

3.8 What Can Go Wrong?

An important strategy to keep you and others from harm is to consider what can go wrong. However, the question *What can go wrong?* is too broad to help direct your thinking. The question needs to be focused on specific issues, for example, *What can go wrong with hazardous materials?* To further help focus your thinking, the work environment can be categorized or grouped into the following domains (abbreviated to PEMEO):

- **P**eople
- **E**quipment
- **M**aterials
- **E**nvironment
- **O**rganization

For each domain, ask *What if...?* questions about conditions, actions, and events that could occur and cause PEMEO to function poorly, behave abnormally, or fail. If there is a concern, determine the immediate effect.

This book focuses on consequences for people's health and safety. However if an incident affects people, there are often consequences for other PEMEO domains as well. For example, an acid leak puts people at risk of chemical burns. The acid leak could also harm equipment, damage materials, harm the environment, cost money to clean up, and harm the company's image.

The following table provides examples of using *What if...?* questions about what can go wrong with hazardous materials. Note that, in the examples, the worker may be performing a specific task or may be in the area that is affected.

What can go wrong with hazardous materials?		
Domain	What if…? *(conditions, actions, and events)*	Immediate effect
People	• What if I don't close the valve fully?	• Toxic gas will leak to the atmosphere.
	• What if I don't put enough neutralizer in the batch?	• The batch will still be caustic and corrosive.
	• What if I don't depressure and isolate the pump?	• Hot, pressurized toxic liquid will spray from the seal when I loosen the casing bolts.
Equipment	• What if the backup electric generator fails to start?	• Air circulation fans will shut down.
	• What if the motor starts when I am adjusting the conveyor?	• The steel safety pins will prevent the conveyor from moving but the shock will loosen the dust.
	• What if the valve develops a slow leak?	• The acidic solution will drip onto the gas pipe below and corrode the pipe.
Materials	• What if the raw material gets contaminated with a heavy metal?	• The heavy metal will separate out and deposit on the equipment.
Environment	• What if air circulation in the room is poor?	• Spray paint droplets will saturate the air.
	• What if a freezing rain causes an ice buildup on equipment?	• Standing and moving will be difficult.
	• What if mice invade the storage area?	• Shelves and supplies will be covered with infectious droppings.
Organization	• What if the maintenance department fails to check the condition of the overflow catch basin?	• Hazardous materials overflow into the catch basin which leaks, causing the material to run onto the floor.
	• What if the operations department fails to open an isolation valve slowly?	• The liquid surge will cause the pipes to vibrate and move.
	• What if the supplier replaces neoprene gloves with rubber gloves?	• The solvent will rapidly penetrate the gloves and contact the skin.

Having determined the possible immediate effects, you can ask additional questions:
- Could I or others become ill and/or injured?
- What should be my first response if an incident occurs?
- What can I do to minimize the possibility of an incident occurring and the severity of the consequences should an incident occur?

For a major incident such as a fire, follow your company's emergency response procedures. Companies also practice responding to simulated emergencies so that, if an incident occurs, the response will be effective.

For many of the incidents you identified by your *What if...?* questions, your response will be more effective when you:
- pre-determine the best response
- rehearse your response by imagining responding to the incident. Rehearsing increases the possibility that you will respond immediately and effectively.

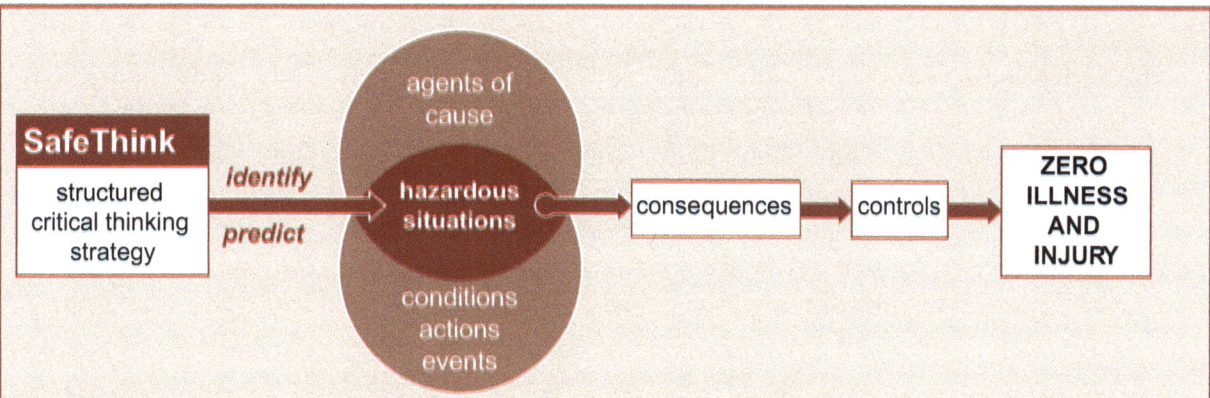

Using the SafeThink strategy

Does the work involve hazardous materials?

Certain conditions, actions, and events could expose you to hazardous materials. Whenever you see a material at your workplace, you need to determine whether or not the material is hazardous and whether or not you can get exposed to the materials (i.e., if you are at risk).

1. To determine if the material is hazardous, ask yourself the following critical thinking questions:
   - Is it a compressed gas?
   - Is it flammable or combustible?
   - Is it an oxidizing material?
   - Is it poisonous or infectious?
   - Is it corrosive?
   - Is it dangerously reactive?

With practice, when you think about the work or see a material in your workplace, you will automatically consider the six classes of hazardous materials to determine if the material is hazardous.

2. For every hazardous material you identify, ask and get answers to the following questions:
   - What type of harm does the material pose?
   - What recommended first aid should be used if I get exposed?
   - What conditions, actions, and events could expose me to the hazard?
   - What can I do to prevent exposure?
   - How can I store the material safely?
   - How can I dispose of the material safely?

Use the *SafeThink* strategy when you complete the learning activity for hazardous activities.

LEARNING ACTIVITY 3

Does the work involve hazardous materials? What conditions, actions, and events could expose me to the hazardous materials?

This learning activity will help you learn to identify and predict conditions, actions, and events that make hazardous materials potentially hazardous to workers.

1. List five hazardous materials in your workplace (manufactured products and/or naturally-occurring materials).

   _____
   _____
   _____
   _____
   _____

2. In the table below, list three **tasks** in your workplace that involve hazardous materials (e.g., changing the impeller of a pump used to transfer caustic soda, taking a sample of gas that could potentially contain hydrogen sulfide, removing ductwork containing mouse droppings). List the hazardous materials associated with each task.

Task	Hazardous Material
1.	
2.	
3.	

72

Part 3 Hazardous Materials

3. Select one of the tasks you listed in question 2. Identify one of the hazardous materials associated with that task and locate the Material Safety Data Sheet (MSDS) for that material.

Task _____

Hazardous material _____

3a. Identify some specific conditions, actions, and events that could expose you to the hazardous material.

_____
_____
_____
_____
_____

3b. Identify how the hazardous material can harm you.

_____
_____
_____
_____

3c. Identify the recommended first-aid response if you are exposed to the hazardous material.

_____
_____
_____
_____
_____

3d. For the task you have selected, list the precautions that you can take to reduce the risk of being harmed by the hazardous material.

before starting work _____

_____
_____
_____
_____

while doing the work

_____
_____
_____
_____
_____

after the work is complete

_____
_____
_____
_____
_____

3e. Identify safe methods to store the hazardous material.

_____
_____
_____
_____
_____

3f. Identify safe methods to dispose of the hazardous material.

_____

_____
_____
_____

4. Name the task used in question 3: _____

4a. Ask W*hat if...?* questions to identify what can go wrong in relation to hazardous materials and fill in the table below. To focus your thinking, consider conditions, actions, and events associated with each PEMEO domain. Identify the immediate effect. Because the mind thinks quickly, it is easy to go to the next level of effects and consider the consequences for people. Although the primary focus of *SafeThink* is on health and safety, knowing the root cause and the immediate effect are important for identifying effective controls and considering the impact of an event on the entire operation. (Part 9 uses the immediate effect to determine reasons for implementing comprehensive controls that would require a significant budget.)

What can go wrong with hazardous materials?		
Domain	**What if...?** *(conditions, actions, and events)*	**Immediate effect**
People		
Equipment		
Materials		
Environment		
Organization		

Here are some examples of conditions, actions, and events related to the Organization domain that can cause hazardous situations:

- poor scheduling (timing of activities)
- not following coordination plans
- a change in the work process
- shortage of staff
- lack of competent workers assigned to a specific task
- policy that can cause harm under certain conditions (e.g., wearing PPE in extremely hot environments can lead to heat stroke)
- work group introduces new hazard
- third party fails to maintain equipment/facilities
- supplier changes standards or composition of components or materials
- unpredicted large customer order
- cancellation or delay of large customer order (e.g., may have excessive inventory on site)
- failure to communicate priorities
- lack of documentation
- roles and responsibilities for work assignment not clear
- administrative process inadequate for maintaining inventory
- failure to carry out routine safety inspections
- lack of safety equipment
- failure to follow up on identified safety deficiencies

4b. From the table you have completed, select one immediate effect that may create or lead to a hazardous situation and answer the following questions:

Could I or others become ill and/or injured? What would be the consequences?

_____
_____
_____

Part 3 Hazardous Materials

What should be my first response if an incident occurs?

_____

_____

What can I do to minimize the probability of an incident occurring and/or the severity of consequences?

_____

_____

Questions 5 and 6 are to be answered individually.

5. From the following list of methods to learn the *SafeThink* questions, check three methods you will use to learn the questions.

Ways to learn the SafeThink questions

We all have preferred ways of learning. Using a combination of learning methods may help us learn more quickly and effectively. Here are some methods for learning the *SafeThink* questions:

- ☐ Memorize the questions (some people are good at memorizing, others are not).

- ☐ Use association. Think of a task and workplace and reason through the questions.

- ☐ Remember how many questions there are in a set.

- ☐ Highlight key words on the *SafeThink* Job Aid and memorize the words. Then use each word in the questions.

- ☐ Create personal anagrams. For the questions, anagrams are words that contain specific letters of other words or phrases.

- ☐ Practice learning the questions one set at a time.

- ☐ Break a set of questions into smaller groups, for example, three questions per group. Learn the first group well and then learn the second group, and so on.

☐ Use repetition. Make copies of the Participant's Job Aid and leave a copy in your vehicle, lunchroom, kitchen, and inside the door of your work locker. Keep reviewing the questions until you have learned all of them.

☐ Put the questions on small cards and practice.

☐ Say the questions aloud.

☐ Apply the questions on the job, at home, and while driving.

6. Of the three methods you selected for learning the *SafeThink* questions, which method do you prefer the most?_____

Option

Many participants have found that writing helps them learn and remember the questions. Write the critical thinking questions for hazardous materials in the box below. The questions are listed in the Job Aid.

■ FOOD for THOUGHT

■ Why the hazardous material category of SafeThink is more than WHMIS, GHS, or HAZMAT

SafeThink's self-instruction on hazardous materials is organized according to the main WHMIS (Workplace Hazardous Material Information System) categories of hazard. The five main WHMIS categories for classifying workplace hazardous materials are similar to the main GHS (Globally Harmonized System) categories. The *SafeThink* categories are not to be confused with the HAZMAT (Hazardous Materials) classification for transportation that has many specific classifications.

SafeThink uses WHMIS (soon to be replaced by GHS) as an organizational approach because many people have taken hazardous materials training and have a basic understanding about the types of hazards created by hazardous materials. For learning, it is useful to start with the learner's frame of reference. *SafeThink* training, however, goes beyond hazardous materials training. Whereas WHMIS focuses on careful labeling and controlling hazardous materials, *SafeThink* focuses on the interaction of hazardous materials with conditions, actions, and events to create hazardous situations and the controls to prevent exposure. Further, not every hazardous material can be labeled (e.g., infectious animals and their droppings or the janitor's rag used to clean a washroom). The composition of spilled materials and stored wastes may not be known... *SafeThink* addresses these concerns. *Most importantly, SafeThink* focuses on the conditions, actions, and events that can interact with hazardous materials to create a hazardous situation.

■ The specific SafeThink questions for hazardous materials include the six types of hazard created by hazardous material

The specific questions in the **Job Aid** address the six general categories of hazard because hazardous materials can pose more than one type of hazard. For example, a cleaning product may be flammable, toxic, and corrosive. When working with materials that are potentially hazardous, you must consider all the types of hazard associated with that material. By asking the six questions about the *types* of hazard associated with hazardous materials, you will not overlook any of the hazards.

■ The unknown factor

Hazardous materials can be in many different forms:
- unlabeled containers, substances, or biological agents
- spills
- dust
- vapor
- mist
- smoke

You may not be aware of the hazards posed by a material. When there is possible exposure to a material, a valuable question to ask yourself is, *Can this material be hazardous to my health?*

■ Consequences and causes

Consequences and causes are sometimes interchangeable. A consequence is caused by something. The cause may actually be a consequence of another cause. Here's an example:

Where is Jane today?

Oh, she's at home with a sprain. (cause or consequence?)

She fell. (cause or consequence?)

She lost her footing. (cause or consequence?)

She was getting out of her car and stepped on some ice. (cause or consequence?)

The ice is the *agent of cause*. In part, the ice caused Jane to fall. Jane's action of getting out of the car created the hazardous situation. It is often important to identify the root cause to select effective controls. Controls that may have prevented Jane from slipping include:
- removing the ice before Jane arrived at the parking area (the root cause)
- stepping on the ice in a way that maintains balance
- wearing footwear that reduces slipping on smooth surfaces
- parking the car at a location where there is no ice

Using PEMEO is a useful way to ask *What if...?* questions. PEMEO provides a structure to apply the *What if...?* questions so you do not overlook a potentially hazardous situation. *What if...?* questions are especially useful for identifying hazardous situations created by change.

Part 4
Objects, Motion, Force

Does the work involve objects, motion, or force that could cause harm?

What conditions, actions, and events could cause the objects, motion, or force to harm me?

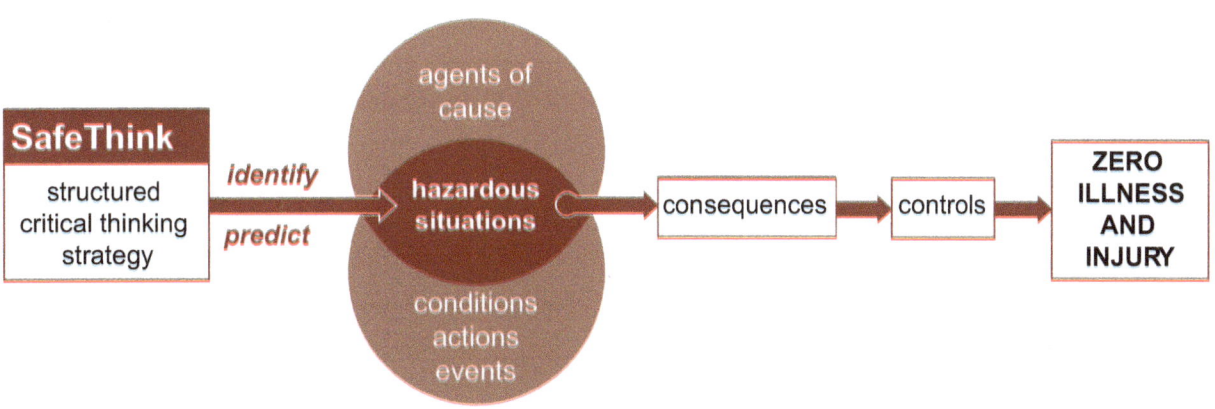

Training Objectives	Upon completion of this part, you will be able to identify and predict conditions, actions, and events that could make objects, motion, and force hazardous to workers.
	• Identify stationary objects, moving objects, and forces that could cause harm
	• Identify the harm the stationary objects, moving objects, and forces can cause
	• Identify conditions, actions, and events that could make objects, motion, or force lead to or create a hazardous situation
	• To prevent being harmed by objects, motion, and force, identify precautions that could be taken: – before starting a task – during the task – after the task is complete

The SafeThink Strategy		
Part	Category of hazard	Critical thinking question
Part 3	Hazardous Materials	Does the work involve hazardous materials?
Part 4	**Objects, Motion, Force**	**Does the work involve objects, motion, or force that could cause harm?**
Part 5	Non-Ambient Conditions	Does the work involve non-ambient conditions that could cause harm?
Part 6	Electricity	Is current or static electricity a factor in doing the work?
Part 7	Radiation	Is radiation present when doing the work?
Part 8	Changes	Could changes lead to or create a hazardous situation?

Part 4   Objects, Motion, Force

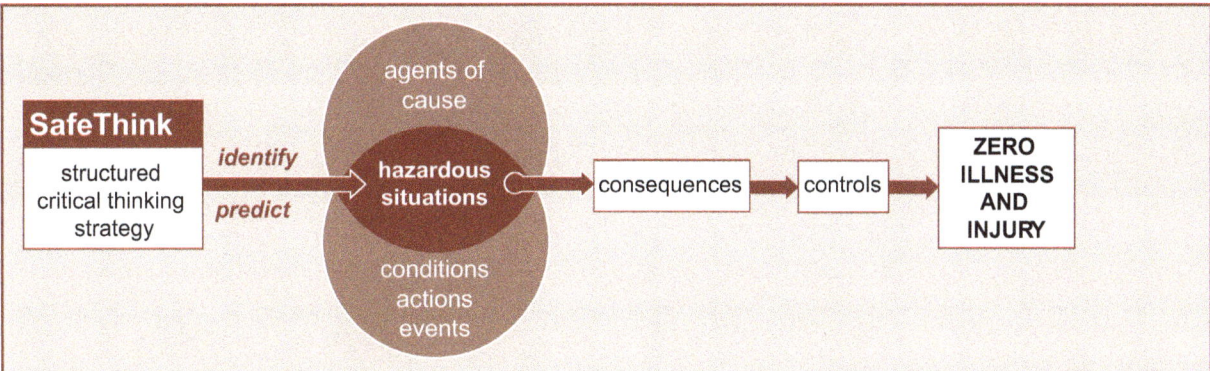

Using the SafeThink strategy

Does the work involve objects, motion, or force that could cause harm?

Ask:

- What type of harm does the object, motion, or force pose?
- What conditions, actions, and events could cause the object, motion, or force to
- harm me?
- What can I do to prevent being harmed by the object, motion, or force?

With practice, when you think about the work or see objects, motion, or force that could lead to or create a hazardous situation, you will automatically ask these questions.

A learning activity at the end of Part 4 helps you learn to apply the *SafeThink* strategy to your work and workplace. The goal is to identify the conditions, actions, and events which lead to hazardous situations involving objects, motion, and force.

4 Objects, Motion, Force

Physical injuries are often immediate and dramatic. Serious physical injury can result when people come in contact with objects. Three ways in which you can come into contact with objects are:
- stationary objects and a moving body (which could be you)
- moving objects and a stationary body (you)
- forces that have the potential to move either a body (you) or an object

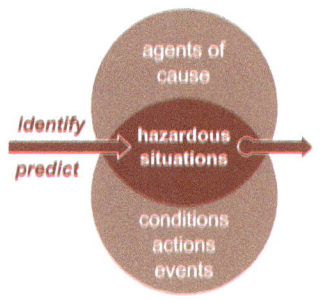

At workplaces, there are often conditions, actions, and events that can potentially cause you to come into contact with objects and become injured. Occupational health and safety regulations specify controls to prevent injury from some objects, motion, or force. For example:
- installing protective barriers (e.g., guards around rotating shafts, guardrails on stairs and gangways)
- shoring trenches and excavations
- using head protection (e.g., hard hats)

Potential harm due to objects, motion, and force include:
- strains, sprains, contusions, concussions, fractures
- splinters, punctures, cuts, severed digits, severed limbs
- death

Your workplace may not have the same stationary objects, moving objects, or forces that are listed in this part; the examples provided may not always have meaning for you. Nevertheless, it is important that you familiarize yourself with all of the contents of this part. The goal is to learn the thinking strategy and to determine the appropriate controls for a variety of work environments.

4.1 Stationary Objects

Stationary objects can cause injury if workers contact the objects. These objects may be materials, equipment, or structures which workers are exposed to during operation and maintenance, construction, or renovation. Hazardous objects can also be created by equipment and structural failures.

Seven common types of stationary objects, workplace examples, and controls are described in this section.

Obstructions

Obstructions caused by low hanging pipes, low doorways, and structural supports—particularly when located in traffic areas—can be hazardous. These objects should be marked with warning signs or tape.

Large equipment, bulk materials, structures

Large equipment, bulk materials, and structures can be hazardous. Operators, maintenance personnel, and construction workers performing tasks close to large stationary objects or in confined quarters can bump into the objects, or get caught on or punctured by sharp, protruding parts. Sometimes locating bulk materials and crates of equipment close to the work area, but out of the way of workers and mobile equipment, can reduce risk of injury. Materials must be stacked in a way that minimizes the risk of the stack collapsing.

Sharp edges

Sharp edges, including the edges of tools and cutting equipment and the edges of components formed during maintenance and construction (e.g., edges of steel plates) can cause injury. Hand tools for cutting, such as chisels, must be kept sharp to reduce the risk of injury. Sharp hand tools, which need less force to use, give the worker more control and reduce the possibility of the tool slipping during use. The cutting edges of power-driven tools and equipment must also be kept sharp to minimize binding and heat. Cut-resistant gloves and sleeves containing wire mesh can be used to handle sharp components such as cutters for wood chippers.

Sharp edges of broken tools and materials pose a safety hazard. Broken tools should never be used; broken materials such as glass, plastic, metals, and wood must be handled with care to prevent injury. During fabrication and material production, sharp edges of plastics, metals, and hardwoods pose a risk. Wherever possible, sharp edges should be rounded.

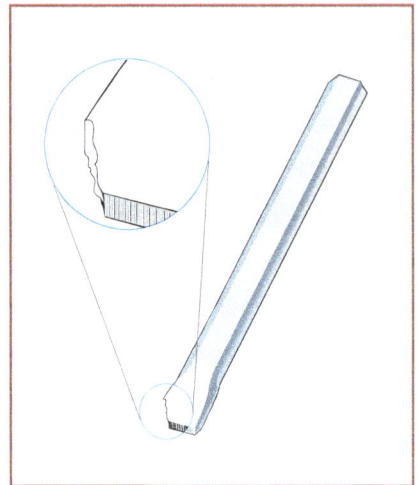

Pointed objects

Pointed objects are especially hazardous in poorly lit areas. Rods sticking out of disassembled equipment and rebar sticking out of concrete are difficult to see when looking directly at the ends of the objects. Walking, bending over, or falling on a pointed object could cause a puncture. When practical, remove the pointed object to eliminate the hazard. Several methods can

also be used to reduce the hazard. For example, pointed objects such as wooden stakes and wire markers can be painted or flagged with ribbon to make them more visible. A block of wood with a hole in it, or a plastic cup (e.g., blue plumbing cap) can be placed on the end of a pointed object to prevent injury and make the object more visible.

Part 4   Objects, Motion, Force

Objects lying on the floor or ground

Objects lying on the floor, including extension cords, temporary electric cables, parts, materials, and tools, could cause you to become caught, trip, or fall. Often, poor housekeeping causes these hazardous conditions.

Slippery surfaces

Slippery surfaces can cause you to fall or injure your back while trying to prevent falling. Wet floors, oil spills, grit, and dust can create very slippery conditions. Warning signs and good housekeeping practices are common preventive measures. Rainwater and snow on metal and smooth concrete surfaces can be treacherous both to people on foot and to operators of mobile equipment (e.g., a warehouse forklift operator).

Suspended or elevated objects

Suspended or elevated objects can fall, injuring people and damaging equipment on lower levels. Safety regulations specify load limits, standards, and operating procedures for cranes, rigging, scaffolding, and ladders. Regulations also specify when guard rails and fall arrest equipment must be used. These regulations, standards, and procedures are designed to prevent objects and people from falling.

Sometimes scaffolding must be used. The scaffolding must be strong enough to carry the combined weight of materials and workers and stable enough to prevent tipping. An inspection tag placed on the scaffolding indicates whether or not the scaffolding is safe to use. Before mounting scaffolding, check the tag for safety status and the inspection expiry date. Depending on the height and design of the scaffolding, you may also require fall protection (a safety harness and safety lines).

 If you are suspended in a safety harness, do **not** remain in a motionless upright position for more than five minutes. This position causes pooling of blood in the legs and can lead to dizziness, rapid heartbeat, and loss of consciousness.

If a person experiences these symptoms, do **not** lay the person down immediately—bring him/her to a horizontal position gradually (e.g., over a 30 minute period).

On scaffolding, organize tools and materials to reduce tripping, especially when wearing respirators. Respirators hamper your ability to see your feet and nearby objects.

Part 4 Objects, Motion, Force

During the installation and removal of components such as valves and lighting fixtures located near ceilings, the components could accidentally fall. A rope connecting them to a structural support will prevent components from falling. Small components and tools should be contained in a tray or pouch to prevent them  from falling. Place barriers and ribbon (tape) around the work area below to prevent people from entering the fall zone.

 Tools, small components, and materials located near an opening in a floor (e.g., second floor of an atrium) can be hazardous should they be accidentally kicked over the edge. Locate objects away from openings and follow good housekeeping practices to reduce the danger of objects falling to the level below.

Toeboards and guardrails must be installed at the edges of mezzanine floors to prevent objects from rolling or being kicked over the edge. Barricades must be provided around open pits and excavations, and restraining grids made of steel bars (grizzly bars) must be provided over open hoppers, chutes, and bins.

Other examples of stationary objects that may be hazardous are listed in Appendix 4—*Table 3: Stationary Objects that May be Hazardous.*

Controls for stationary objects that may be hazardous

Controls you can use to reduce the risk of being harmed by stationary objects include:

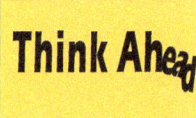

- Put objects back in their proper storage location after use.
- Keep your work areas clean and tidy.
- Conduct a workplace inspection to identify and mark hazardous objects (including glass doors and windows that may be difficult to see). Turn on lights before retrieving objects from storage sheds.
- Post hazard warnings.
- Block off areas around hazardous objects (e.g., hot kilns, open pits).
- Use the handrail when ascending or descending stairs.
- When working at heights, instead of carrying tools up the ladder, use a rope and bucket to hoist the tools.
- Make sure railings and toe boards are installed or use other means to prevent objects from falling from elevated work surfaces.
- Use PPE (e.g., fall protection, hard hats, gloves, eye protection, wrist and back supports).
- Do not stand below the edges of mezzanines and openings in the floor above.
- Stay away from the edges of excavations and open tanks.
- Modify components, materials, or surfaces to reduce the hazard. For example, round sharp edges, place protective shields on points, nail or tape carpet edges, grade uneven storage yards, raise or lower shelving, provide anti-fatigue mats.
- Remove or clean up surface spills, ice, or snow.
- Raise crane hooks when the cranes are not in use.
- Reroute electrical cords around traffic areas.
- Cover (permanently or temporarily) open chimney holes, sampling pits, sumps, trenches, and manholes.
- Pile soil and rocks well back from the edges of excavations.
- Collect and dispose of surplus or waste materials.
- Tag and repair broken equipment or fixtures.

- Use personal protective equipment (PPE) (e.g., coveralls, gloves, hard hats, safety glasses, fall protection, life jackets, safety footwear).

Summary of generalities—stationary objects

To summarize, the generalities of hazards relating to stationary objects are:
- obstructions
- large equipment, bulk materials, structures
- sharp-edges
- pointed objects
- objects lying on the floor or ground
- slippery surfaces
- suspended or elevated objects

4.2 Motion (Moving Objects)

Eleven different types of hazardous conditions are described under the category of motion.

Rotating equipment

Rotating equipment parts can cause you to become caught or injured. Rotating shafts, belts, pulleys, chains, gears, augers, and conveyor belts must be equipped with guards to prevent injuries. However, during equipment maintenance and inspection, guards may have to be temporarily removed and the equipment started, exposing you to a potential injury.

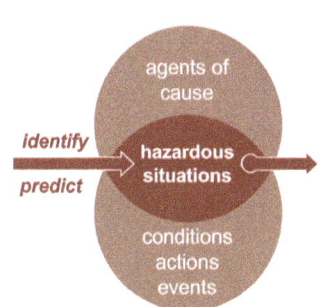

Cutting equipment such as chain saws, lathes, shapers, milling machines, mowers, and chippers have high-speed rotating cutters that are difficult to guard. Your best way of preventing an injury is to stay clear of the moving parts and wear eye and face protection to protect yourself from flying particles and chips. Rotating components such as lawnmower blades can cause stones to fly at high speeds in any direction. When using equipment where there is the potential for flying particles or objects, keep others away from the work area. If materials plug or jam equipment, for example grass in a lawnmower chute, always stop the equipment and, if possible, unplug or lock out the equipment before removing the materials.

 SafeThink™

When using power tools to cut materials (e.g., radial arm saws, portable electric saws), do not place your hand(s) in line with the direction of the cut. The rotating or reciprocating blade can suddenly and rapidly move towards your hand if the material breaks or the cutting tool climbs over the material.

When supporting material and one hand is *out of sight*, check to ensure that your hand is not in line with the direction of the cut, drill bit, or fasteners (e.g., screws, staples, nails).

The contact point between a set of rotating gears or rollers creates a *pinch point* where fingers and hands can be caught and crushed. When fingers or a hand gets caught, the rotating gears or rollers continue to pull the fingers and hands through the equipment. Roller equipment may have an emergency release. When the emergency release is activated, the pressure on the rollers is released to minimize injury.

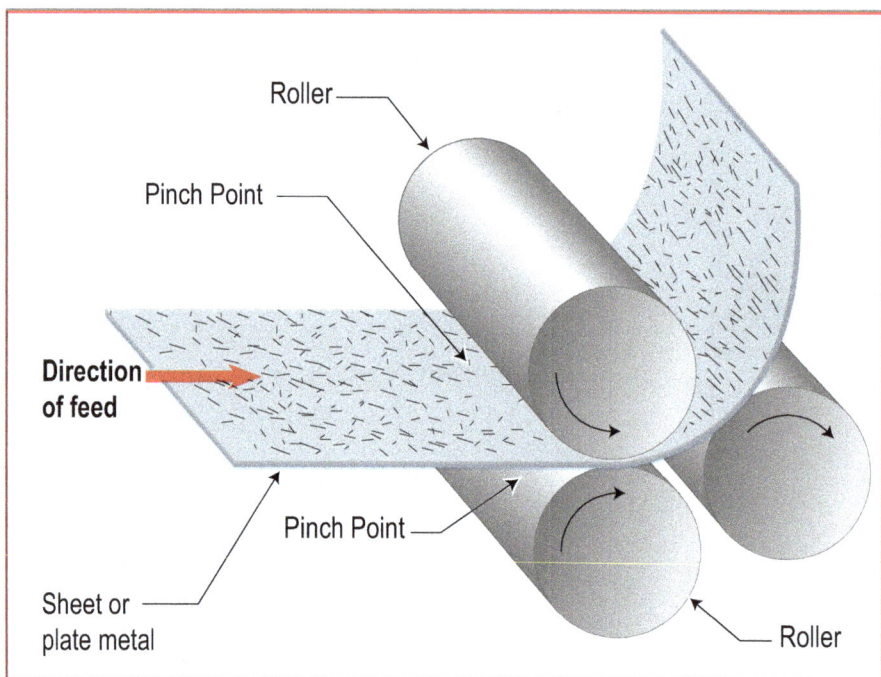

Rotating components such as chains and sprockets, belts and pulleys, gears, and rollers have pinch points where fingers, hands, hair, and clothing can get caught. Keep your hands clear of rotating components. Make sure long hair is tied back and do **not** wear jewelry or loose clothing.

Part 4 Objects, Motion, Force

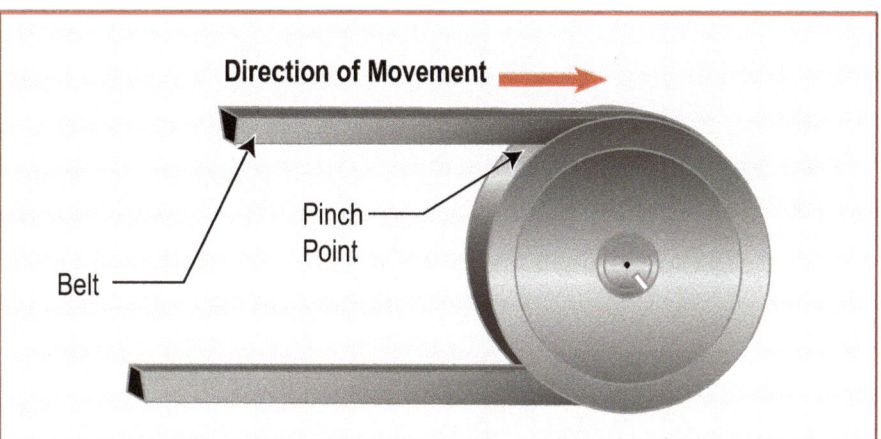

Pinch Points
The term pinch points refers to locations on equipment or between equipment where a worker can be pinched or crushed.

Feeding materials into and removing materials from moving equipment (e.g., sweeping up metal filings from under a lathe) is hazardous. Controls you can use to prevent injuries from rotating equipment include:
- Use push sticks to feed material through cutting equipment (e.g., table saw).
- Shut down and electrically and/or mechanically lock out the equipment before removing materials.
- Use special grasping tools (not your fingers) to remove jammed materials.

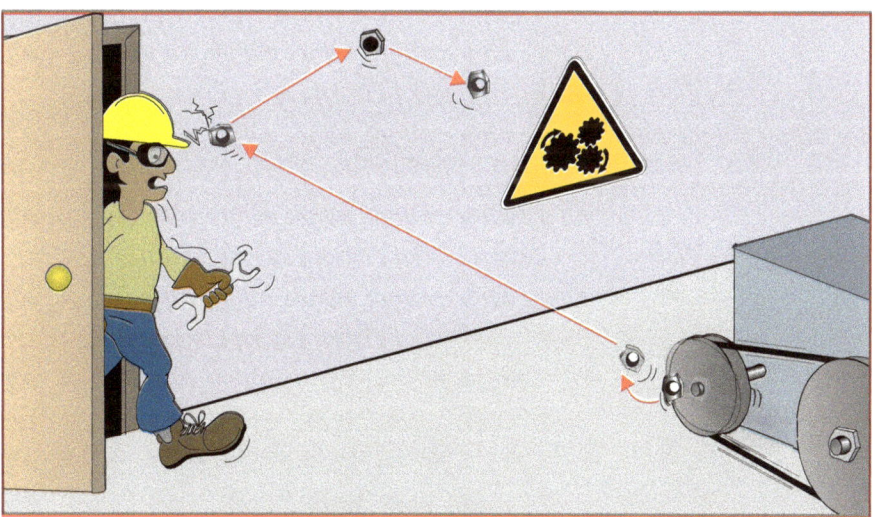

On *high speed rotating equipment*, temporary counterweights for balancing equipment and coupling bolts to connect shafts can loosen and fly off at very high speeds. To minimize risk, stand out of the *line of fire*.

95

Reciprocating parts

Reciprocating parts (such as those found on presses and automatic cutoff saws) and moving materials (such as manufactured board) often come close to or contact stationary structures. Fingers and hands can be crushed between the contact points (pinch points). To prevent injury from reciprocating cutting and shaping equipment, use a push stick (push block) to feed material into the equipment and keep your hands clear.

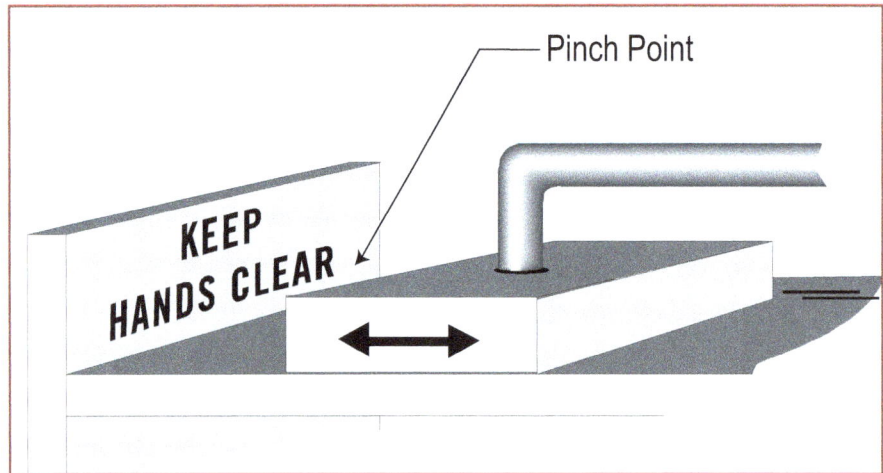

Cabinet doors and drawers create pinch points. Use the hardware provided to close them.

Abrasive surfaces

Abrasive surfaces on power-driven grinders and sanders can instantly remove flesh on contact. Operators of portable grinders and sanders can lose control of the equipment if the abrasive surface makes too fast a contact with the material. The removed material forms a fine dust that can affect breathing, irritate eyes, and can be hot enough to burn the skin. The surface of the material being ground or sanded can become very hot.

Controls you can use to prevent being injured by abrasive surfaces include:
- Wear protective equipment (e.g., gloves, face shield and goggles).
- Do not make direct contact with the abrasive surface. The abrasive surface can remove flesh very quickly.

- Use both hands to control portable power tools that are designed for two handed use.
- When the equipment is stopped, be careful not to take action that could cause your hand or another part of your body to skid across the abrasive surface.
- Grinding and cutting metals heat the metals. To prevent burns, use gloves or wait for the materials to cool before handling.

Vibration

Vibration can be hazardous; for example:
- Over time, vibration can cause fasteners to loosen; structures and components can fail.
- Vibrating surfaces can cause loose objects to move and fall.
- Vibration can cause equipment to move out of alignment.
- Vibration can cause excessive noise that can irritate workers and impair hearing.

Workers who regularly use tools that vibrate (e.g., angle grinders, chainsaws, jackhammers) can develop impaired blood circulation in their fingers (white finger disease). Fingers become highly sensitive to cold and minor cuts ulcerate quickly. Whole-body vibration and mechanical shock, experienced by vehicle and machine operators, can cause damage to soft tissues, joints, and spinal discs.

Excessive vibration can cause some types of high-speed rotating equipment (e.g., turbines) to self-destruct. The potential for excessive vibration is highest at startup. Barriers may be provided for the operator's safety; stay behind the barrier when starting the equipment and, if possible, when observing the operating equipment. Stay out of the operating equipment area when possible.

Loose objects

Loose objects such as tools, components, and materials can fall into moving parts and be propelled at high speeds. Before equipment is started, especially after repairs have been done, inspect the equipment to ensure no loose objects are resting on or near the equipment. Position loose objects, including hand-held objects, so that they will not fall into moving parts or hit someone.

When equipment is operating, electrical cords, cables, ropes, hoses, and loose clothing can be dragged accidentally into or dangled over moving parts. You can be pulled into the moving parts or be lashed by the whipping cord. To prevent injuries, secure cords, cables, and ropes away from the equipment and, if you are an equipment operator, wear close-fitting clothing.

Projectiles

Projectiles can be created by hand and power-operated tools such as hammers, chisels, and picks used to shape or break up materials. Wear eye protection and stay clear of the work to reduce your risk of injury.

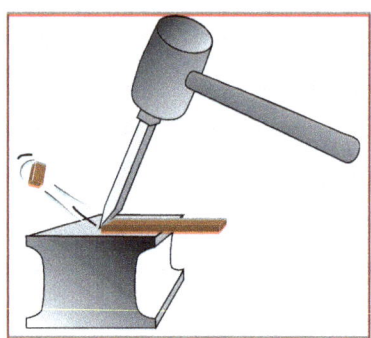

Mobile equipment and vehicles

Using mobile equipment in areas where people must work is hazardous. In warehouses and factories, floors are often marked to indicate separate areas for equipment traffic and pedestrian traffic. Often, the mobile equipment has the right-of-way.

Mobile equipment typically sounds a high-pitched, beeping alarm when backing but do not rely on the alarm to warn you of approaching equipment. The alarm can be hard to hear in noisy areas or may not be working. Some mobile equipment may have blind spots; the operator may not be able to see you in the blind spot. If you must be in the area, make eye contact with the equipment operator before walking near the equipment. Always monitor your immediate environment for changes or impending changes that could cause you harm.

Backing into or over a stationary object located behind the vehicle is one of the most common vehicle accidents. Before backing up, always check behind the vehicle to ensure there are no people or objects in your path.

In parking lots, accidents commonly occur when backing out of the parking stall. It is safer to back into and drive out of parking stalls.

Carrying materials

Carrying long materials or large sheets of material can be hazardous; the materials can strike other workers, ladders, other materials, and structures. The potential for unintended contact increases when you are:
- rotating the material
- maneuvering around corners

- passing through doorways
- working in tight spaces

Precautions to follow when carrying long materials or large sheets include:
- Examine the route before carrying the materials.
- If others are near, let them know you are about to move the materials. Wait until others are out of the way.
- Move slowly when rotating materials and going around corners, checking both ends of the materials continually to prevent contact.
- Let others know you are about to enter a doorway and move slowly.
- Angle long pieces upwards to prevent striking anyone.
- Use a cart designed for moving materials.
- Ask for help.

Pay careful attention to workers who are carrying long materials or large sheets of materials. They may not see you or unintentionally hit you or other objects near you.

People

The potential for physical injury increases as the number of people working in a small area increases. Potential for an injury occurring increases further if the workers are doing unrelated tasks, for example, plumbing, electrical, heating, and drywall. The best way to reduce the hazards caused by people working in close quarters is to reduce the number of people working in that area. Letting others know of the activity about to take place and coordinating work can also reduce the potential of an injury.

Strobe lights

Strobe lights used to analyze and refine equipment operation make moving objects such as rotating pulleys appear to stand still (stroboscopic effect). When working in an area where a strobe light is operating, be careful not to touch objects that are capable of movement.

Animals

Large animals, both domestic and wild, can pose a hazard. Hazards associated with large domestic animals include:
- being crushed between the animal and solid structures
- being kicked, stepped on, or bitten

Precautions include being vigilant, staying away from the danger zones, and restricting the animal's movements.

On highways, wild animals such as deer, moose, and elk pose a collision hazard. Often these animals do not have a natural instinct that there is danger from moving vehicles; they may walk slowly across the highway. At times they become startled and act in unpredictable ways. For example, they may run across the highway in front of a moving vehicle and then turn around and run back. Large, wild animals are more likely to be active at dawn and dusk when visibility is limited. Precautions include watching the ditches for wild animals and slowing down. When you spot an animal in the ditch, slow down, and be prepared to stop suddenly. Do not get out of your vehicle to approach wild animals. Wild animals can become aggressive and may charge.

Other workplace examples of moving objects that may be hazardous are listed in Appendix 4—*Table 4: Moving Objects That May be Hazardous.*

Controls for moving objects that may be hazardous

Some controls you can use to prevent injuries from moving objects include:
- Read and follow hazard warnings.
- Hold pre-job meetings to identify hazards.
- Provide a flag person.
- Pay attention to audible and visible alarms on mobile equipment.
- Leave guards on machinery intact.
- Use push sticks and grasping tools for manually feeding material.
- When your hand is out of sight, check to ensure that it is not in line with the direction of cut, drill bit, or fasteners.
- Cautiously carry materials to prevent hitting other workers.
- Stay out of the line of fire when starting equipment, keeping your hand away from rotating equipment.
- When grinding and cutting metal objects, wear gloves to protect your hands from contacting the hot metal or let the metal cool.
- Do not touch any objects when strobe lights are operating.
- Check to make sure all components are properly tightened before starting equipment.
- Do walk-around inspections before starting equipment to ensure tools and spare parts cannot fall into moving components.
- Start equipment cautiously.
- Use blocks and parking brakes when parking mobile equipment and vehicles.
- Use PPE (e.g., eye protection, hard hat, safety footwear, hearing protection, fall protection).

NOTE

When practical, do **not** store materials such as portable computers, briefcases, boxes, books, or parts in the passenger compartment of a vehicle. If you have a collision or rollover, flying objects can cause serious injury.

Summary of generalities—motion

To summarize, the generalities of hazards relating to motion are:
- rotating equipment
- reciprocating parts
- abrasive surfaces
- vibration
- loose objects
- projectiles
- mobile equipment and vehicles
- carrying materials
- people
- animals

4.3 Force

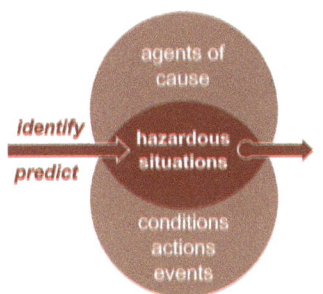

The application of physical force, either by equipment or by a worker, can lead to a serious injury. This section describes the following issues related to force that can cause harm:
- direction of applied force
- direction of force applied to sharp or pointed tools
- chains, cables, straps, and ropes
- material failure
- sudden uncontrolled release of high-pressure liquids and gases
- excessive physical exertion

> **Two General Rules**
>
> The two general rules about force to remember are:
>
> **Always** apply force in the safest fall direction in case the material slips or breaks.
>
> **Never** put force on tools and objects in the direction of any body part (i.e., direct the force away from your body).

Direction of applied force

Force applied to wrenches, levers, and objects can be hazardous if the force is directed towards stationary objects and guardrails. As an example, a worker, standing on a catwalk three m (10 ft.) above the floor, is applying force

to a 1½ m (4.5 ft.) wrench to loosen bolts on a compressor discharge valve. Should the bolt or wrench break or the wrench slip off the bolt, the worker will be propelled in the direction of the force he or she is applying. Force must be applied so that the worker will not be propelled over the guardrail or into the equipment. When pushing or pulling on tools and materials, place one foot behind the other to brace yourself from falling in case the tool or material suddenly gives way.

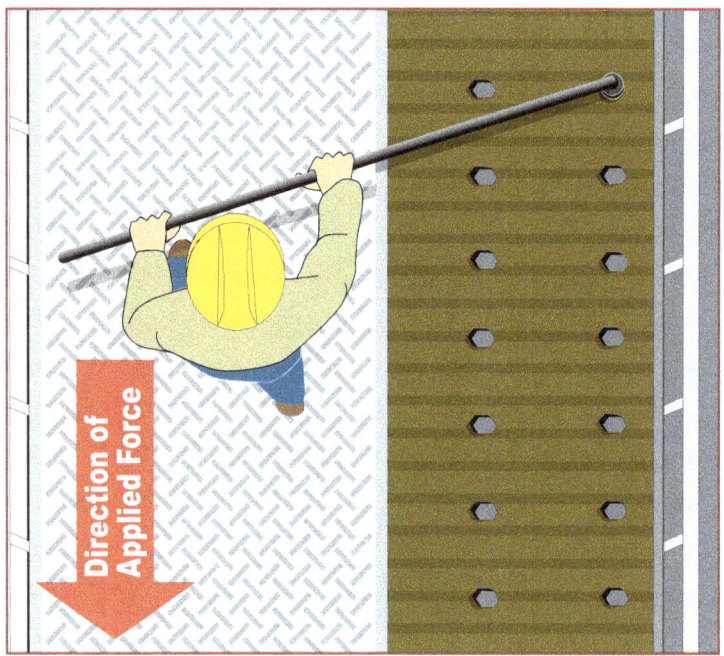

Direction of force applied to sharp or pointed tools

Force applied to sharp or pointed tools should never be directed towards any body part. If the tool slips or the object breaks, the tool will puncture your body. Apply force away from your body. The following are examples of situations that can cause harm.

You are using a screwdriver to open a paint can. You put one hand on the top of the can and position the screwdriver on the opposite side of the can, pointing in the direction of your hand. The screwdriver slips off the lid while you apply force, driving the screwdriver into your hand. A safer way to open a paint can is by using a proper hook-type opener that catches on the side of the container.

When you use a wood chisel by hand to shape materials, the chisel should never be pointed towards your body. If the chisel slips or the material suddenly breaks, the chisel can puncture you.

Reaction forces are exerted by power tools. Hand-held power tools may react with sudden, unintended motion if used or held incorrectly. The impact of this motion can injure you. Use both hands to control portable power equipment designed for two-handed use.

Rotational kickback is a sudden, violent, backward motion. Using a chainsaw as an example, kickback can occur if the kickback zone—the upper tip of the guide bar—touches an object such as a tree trunk, branch, or other object. Pinching the saw chain along the top of the guide bar may push the saw far enough back so that the kickback zone hits an object and kicks back at the operator. To prevent chainsaw kickback, the operator must follow specific operating procedures.

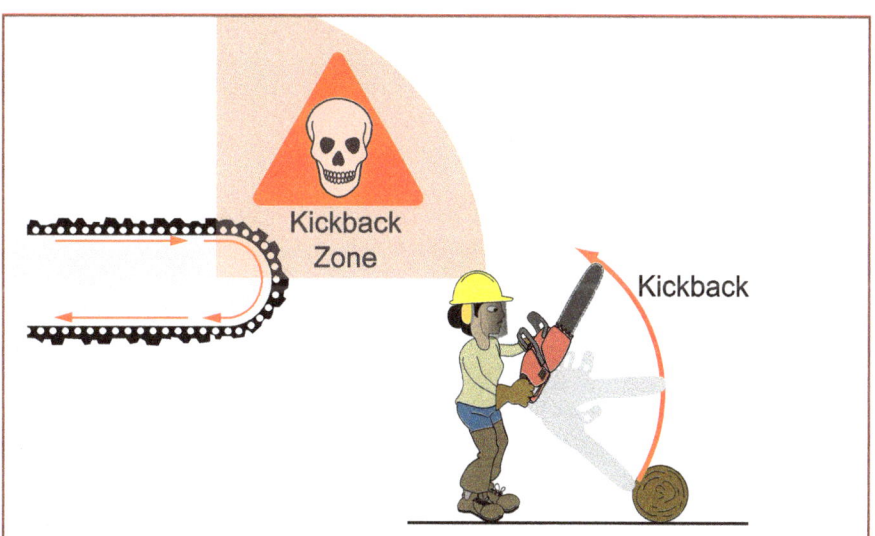

Sometimes tools have to be used near moving parts. For example, in industries which handle wood fiber (pulp or board manufacturing), an air lance is used to blow clean equipment while it is in operation. The air lance is a 1.3 m (4 ft.) long pipe on the end of a compressed air hose and must be held carefully to avoid contact with the operating equipment being cleaned. Inadvertent contact can cause the air lance to recoil or be drawn into the equipment.

Force applied to chains, cables, slings, and ropes

Chains, cables, slings, and ropes used to secure, transport, lift, or position objects can be subjected to extreme forces. Should a chain or cable break under force, the load can dislodge, fall, and crush a worker. A broken cable twists and snakes through the air and can severely injure nearby workers. When using chains and cables to move or position objects, the applied force must not exceed the rated capacity. The correct size of chains, cables, hooks, and shackles must be selected for the job

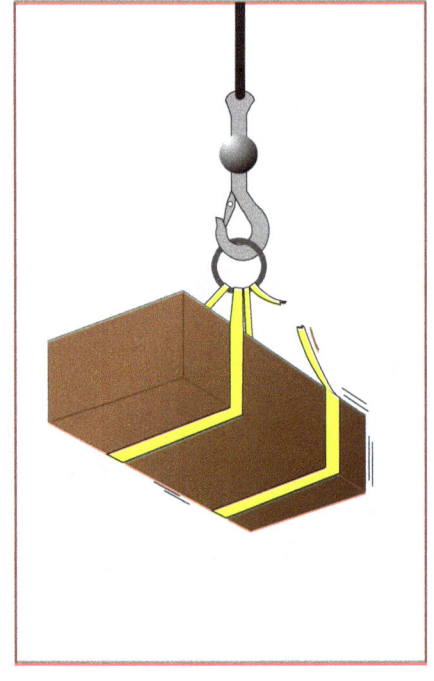

and inspected for damage before use. When possible, workers should position themselves to minimize the risk of being hit, either by the chain, cable, or the object under force, should one of the attaching components fail.

Use a tag line to control and guide a suspended load so that you can stay clear of the fall zone. Do not walk or stand under the suspended load.

Material failure

Material failure can occur as a result of weakening through prolonged use, exposure to degrading environments, or excessive forces. The applied force should not exceed the load-bearing capabilities of the materials. Materials such as wood are often temporarily used as levers, braces, and load supports. Under excessive force, the wood can break, either with the grain, creating a long, sharp splinter (a piercing hazard), or across the grain in several places (a projectile hazard). If the support or lever breaks, the load could shift (hazardous motion).

Sudden uncontrolled release of high-pressure liquids and gases

The sudden uncontrolled release of high-pressure liquids and gases from pipes, hoses, and vessels can pose a serious risk to workers. Part 5—*Non-Ambient Conditions* provides a detailed description of the hazards associated with pressurized components and describes how you can protect yourself.

Excessive physical exertion

Ergonomic hazards include:
- applying a large force on a small surface
- repetitive motion
- forces exerted by or impacting on the body

Ergonomic hazards can cause injuries to muscles, tendons, ligaments, nerves, cartilage, joints, and spinal discs (musculo-skeletal injuries). If not controlled, ergonomic hazards can cause short-term discomfort; they can also have cumulative effects leading to temporary or long-term disabilities.

Incorrect manual lifting is one of the most common ergonomic hazards. Injuries include strains, sprains, hernias, and serious damage to the back. Whenever you need to lift something heavy or awkward:
- Get help.
- Use a dolly, hand crane, or forklift.

- If you must lift an object unaided, do not twist while lifting and use your leg muscles rather than your back muscles. Your back, which is not as strong as your legs, is more easily injured.

Some companies have policies limiting the amount of weight a worker can lift manually.

Other types of injury caused by physical exertion are:
- Workers who continually lift their arms to reach objects and to exert force (e.g., hang plants, drywall ceilings, install electrical light fixtures) can develop painful rotator cuff injuries, which can permanently restrict shoulder movement.
- Workers who perform repeated physical movements can develop repetitive strain injuries, including damage to tendons, nerves, muscles, and other soft tissues.
- Workers who stand or walk on slippery surfaces (e.g., ice, ceramic tile floors) can damage tendons and ligaments in their feet (a result of continually flexing their toes to maintain balance). Standing in one spot on hard surfaces can cause heel injuries (e.g., plantar fasciitis).
- Workers who exert a large force on a small surface area of their body can damage soft tissue and bone. Examples of this type of activity are:
  - lifting heavy objects that have a limited surface area (e.g., small handle on a heavy tool box, edge of a sheet of plate metal)
  - putting force on small-handled pliers
  - pounding with the palm of the hand to move objects into place
- Workers who become fatigued are more likely to be injured. The likelihood of injury increases because workers become less attentive and their coordination and strength drop.

Ways to prevent injuries from ergonomic hazards include:
- Use ergonomically designed tools that are sized appropriately for you.
- Use anti-fatigue mats when standing for long periods.
- Use chairs and workstations adjusted to fit your body.
- Use specialized work wear (e.g., anti-vibration gloves).

- Use lifting, carrying, and reaching devices (e.g., handcarts, trolleys, pole hooks).
- Vary tasks, take breaks, and pace yourself to reduce fatigue.

Other workplace examples of forces that may be hazardous are listed in Appendix 4—*Table 5: Forces That May be Hazardous*.

Controls for forces that may be hazardous

Some controls you can use to reduce the risk of harm from forces include:
- Use the right tool for the job.
- Restrict access (e.g., involving as few people as necessary in jobs that involve forces that could cause harm).
- Notify others that hazardous operations such as pressure testing are about to take place. Use signals if necessary.
- Inspect tools to identify defects before use.
- Follow safe work procedures for cranes, hoists, manual lifting, stacking materials, and other tasks involving the use of force.
- Use a tag line to control and guide suspended loads.
- Use hoists or other lifting equipment instead of manually lifting or moving heavy or awkward objects.
- Make sure railings and toe boards are installed or use other means to prevent objects from falling from elevated work surfaces.
- Use PPE (e.g., fall protection, hard hats, gloves, eye protection, wrist and back supports).

Summary of generalities—force

To summarize, the generalities of hazards relating to force are:
- direction of applied force
- direction of force applied to sharp or pointed tools
- force applied to chains, cables, straps, and ropes
- material failure
- sudden uncontrolled release of high pressure liquids and gases
- excessive physical exertion

4.4 What Can Go Wrong?

An important strategy to keep you and others from harm is to consider what can go wrong. For objects, motion, and force, ask *What if...?* questions about conditions, actions, and events that could occur and cause PEMEO to function poorly, behave abnormally, or fail. If there is a concern, determine the immediate effect.

The following table provides examples of using *What if...?* questions about what can go wrong with objects, motion, and force. Note that, in the examples, the worker may be performing a specific task or may be in the area that is affected.

NOTE

PEMEO stands for:
People
Equipment
Materials
Environment
Organization

What can go wrong with objects, motion, and force?		
Domain	**What if...?** (conditions, actions, and events)	**Immediate effect**
People	• What if I put the crates in the alleyway?	• Workers on the other side would have their escape route blocked.
	• What if I wait until the job is finished to clean up the sawdust?	• My footing will be poor.
	• What if the drywaller tries to remove the drywall board while I am standing on the ladder?	• The board could hit the ladder and knock it over.
Equipment	• What if the brake on the hoist fails?	• The load will drop to the ground.
	• What if the conveyor starts?	• My arm would be caught in the drive chain.
	• What if the truck driver fails to stop when I make the stop signal?	• I will be caught between the truck and the trailer.

(continued)

What can go wrong with objects, motion, and force?		
Domain	**What if...?** (conditions, actions, and events)	**Immediate effect**
Materials	• What if the wooden pry lever breaks?	• I will fall backwards. • The wood will split into two long sharp points.
	• What if bolts for the frame are of lower grade than recommended?	• The bolts could break.
	• What if the small block of wood slips when sanding it with the stationary sander?	• My hand will make contact with the sanding disk.
Environment	• What if I step out of the vehicle onto the icy pavement?	• I could slip.
	• What if the wind gets stronger while erecting the wall for the house?	• The wall could fall.
Organization	• What if the roofers start work?	• Materials and tools could fall off the roof and hit me.
	• What if the electrical power fails?	• The lights in the work area would fail.

Having determined the possible immediate effects, you can ask additional questions:
- Could I or others become ill and/or injured?
- What should be my first response if an incident occurs?
- What can I do to minimize the possibility of an incident occurring and the severity of the consequences should an incident occur?

For many of the incidents identified by the *What if...?* questions, your response will be more effective when you:
- pre-determine the best response
- rehearse your response by imagining responding to the incident. Rehearsing increases the possibility that you will respond immediately and effectively.

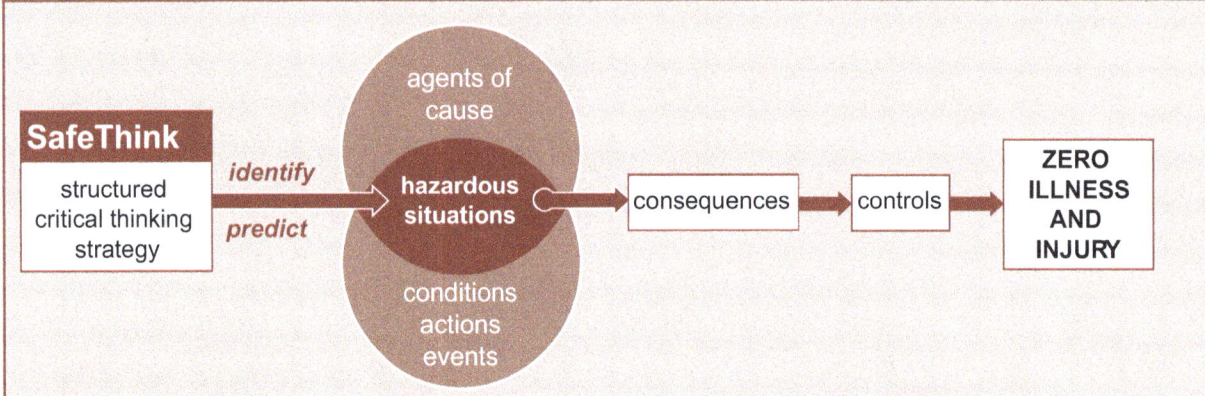

Using the SafeThink strategy

Does the work involve objects, motion, or force that could cause harm?

Whenever your work involves objects, motion, or force, you need to determine whether or not you are at risk. In the workplace, specific conditions, actions, and events can create situations that make objects, motion, and force hazardous. Ask yourself the following questions:
- What type of harm does the object, motion, or force pose?
- What conditions, actions, and events could cause the object, motion, or force to harm me?
- What can I do to prevent being harmed by the object, motion, or force?

With practice, when you think about the work or see objects, motion, or force in your workplace, you will automatically consider the possibility of being harmed.

Use the *SafeThink* strategy when you complete the learning activity for objects, motion, and force.

Does the work involve objects, motion, or force that could cause harm? What conditions, actions, and events could cause the objects, motion, or force to harm me?

This learning activity will help you learn to identify and predict conditions, actions, and events that make objects, motion, and force hazardous to workers.

1. There are thousands of agents of cause. One of the powerful features of *SafeThink* is that it identifies agents of cause as *generalities* to make the thinking process manageable. Some agents of cause for objects,

motion, and force are listed in the table below. For each agent of cause, provide an example from your workplace or personal life. For example:

- a wet floor is a slippery surface
- force on the cable of a winch between a rail car and winch

Agents of Cause	Specific Example
Objects	
Obstructions	
Large equipment, bulk materials, structures	
Sharp objects	
Pointed objects	
Objects lying on the floor or ground	
Slippery surfaces	wet floor
Suspended or elevated objects	
Motion	
Rotating equipment	
Reciprocating parts	
Abrasive surfaces	
Vibration	
Loose objects	
Shrapnel/projectiles	
Mobile equipment and vehicles	
Carrying materials	
People	
Animals	
Force	
Direction of applied force	
Direction of force applied to sharp or pointed tools	
Chains, cables, straps, and ropes	force on the strap between a rail car and winch
Material failure	
Sudden release of high pressure liquids and gases	
Excessive physical exertion	

2. List three *stationary* objects (including surfaces and materials) in your work area that are potential hazards. Describe the precautions you can take to keep from being injured when you work in the vicinity of the three objects.

Stationary Objects	Precautions
1.	
2.	
3.	

3. List three tasks that you perform that involve **objects, motion, and force** that have the potential to cause injury to you or others. For each task, identify the three most critical conditions, actions, and events that could make the objects, motion, and force hazardous to you or others.

Task	Conditions, Actions, Events
1.	
2.	
3.	

Many tasks are complex, making it difficult to think of all the hazardous situations associated with the task and work environment. To make identifying and predicting hazardous situations easier and more rigorous, break the task into two to seven parts or major steps. A major step has a logical beginning and end and is a significant accomplishment towards completing the task. The table on the next page shows examples of breaking tasks into major steps.

Part 4 Objects, Motion, Force

Breaking Tasks into Major Steps

Task: Replace a linoleum floor
Major Step 1: Remove old linoleum.
Major Step 2: Prepare floor.
Major Step 3: Install new linoleum.

Task: Start a pipeline pump station
Major Step 1: Carry out pre-start checks.
Major Step 2: Start booster pumps.
Major Step 3: Start main pumps.
Major Step 4: Increase throughput.
Major Step 5: Monitor station operation.

Task: Replace a pump and motor
Major Step 1: Isolate pump and lock out motor.
Major Step 2: Disconnect attachments & skid.
Major Step 3: Remove old pump and motor and position new pump and motor.
Major Step 4: Bolt down skid and connect attachments.
Major Step 5: Prepare pump and motor for startup.
Major Step 6: Start pump cautiously.
Major Step 7: Clean area and document work.

Task: Start a compressor
Major Step 1: Carry out pre-start checks.
Major Step 2: Configure valves.
Major Step 3: Start compressor.
Major Step 4: Load compressor.
Major Step 5: Monitor compressor operation.

To develop a procedure, each major step is expanded to provide 5 to 9 specific action steps. Here is a partial example of a procedure for unloading a railcar (railway tank car).

Task: Unloading a Railcar
Major step 1—Prepare railcar for unloading 1. 2. etc.
Major step 2—Connect lines between railcar and unloading rack 1. 2. etc.
Major step 3—Connect unloading instrument air to railcar 1. Break metal seal on railcar dome. 2. Open dome to reveal air connections. 3. Remove plug from 1-inch air manual valve. 4. Install Chicago fitting and nipple. 5. Connect unloading platform instrument air line to installed Chicago fitting.
Major step 4—Unload railcar 1. etc.
Major step 5—Depressurize and disconnect unloaded railcar 1. etc.

To use the structured critical thinking strategy effectively to identify and predict hazardous situations, you must:
- break the task into major steps
- for each major step, think about the specific action steps and the associated conditions, actions, and events that could cause a hazardous situation

4. Select one of the tasks from question 3. First, break the task into major steps; then complete questions 4a, 4b, and 4c. You may want to refer to tables A3, A4, and A5 in the appendix for examples of objects, motion, and force that can be hazardous.

Task _____

Major step 1 (before working) _____

Major step 2 (while working) _____

Major step 3 (while working) _____

Major step 4 (while working) _____

Major step 5 (while working) _____

Major step 6 (while working) _____

Major step 7 (after work is complete) _____

4a. Identify conditions, actions, and events involving stationary objects, motion, and force that exist **before** doing the work that could cause harm to you or others (for example, a low overhang). Identify possible controls to reduce the risk of an incident.

_____
_____
_____
_____

4b. Identify conditions, actions, and events involving stationary objects, motion, and force that exist or develop **while** working that could cause harm to you or others (for example, a truck delivering materials is temporarily parked in a work area). Identify possible controls to reduce the risk of an incident.

_____
_____
_____
_____
_____

4c. Identify conditions, actions, and events involving stationary objects, motion, and force that exist **after** the work is complete that could cause harm to you or others (for example, supplies and waste left on the floor). Identify possible controls to reduce the risk of an incident.

_____
_____
_____
_____
_____

5. Name another task that involves objects, motion, and force: _____

5a. Ask *What if...?* questions to identify what can go wrong in relation to objects, motion, and force and fill in the table. To focus your thinking, consider conditions, actions, and events associated with each PEMEO domain.

What can go wrong with objects, motion, and force?		
Domain	**What if . . . ?** (conditions, actions, and events)	**Immediate effect**
People		
Equipment		
Materials		
Environment		
Organization		

Examples of conditions, actions, and events related to the Organization domain that can cause hazardous situations:

- poor scheduling (timing and/or sequence of activities)
- not following plans
- lack of communication equipment (e.g., cell phones)
- a change in the work process
- shortage of workers/competent workers
- another work group introduces new hazard
- poor maintenance of equipment/facilities
- increased anxiety resulting from market and weather uncertainties
- inadequate training for workers
- failure to communicate priorities
- insufficient or incorrect documentation
- roles and responsibilities for work assignment not clear
- failure to carry out routine safety inspections
- lack of safety equipment
- failure to follow up on identified safety issues
- financial priorities do not include safety

5b. From the table you have completed, select one effect that may create or lead to a hazardous situation and answer the following questions:

Could I or others become ill and/or injured? What would be the consequences?

_____

_____

What should be my first response if an incident occurs?

_____

_____

 SafeThink™

What can I do to minimize the probability of an incident occurring and/or the severity of consequences?

_____

_____

_____

The SafeThink Strategy

The *SafeThink* strategy to identify and predict hazardous situations caused by one category of hazard is as follows:

1. Identify the task.

2. Break the task into two to nine **major steps**.

3. Break **major step** 1 into **action steps**.

4. For each **action step**, ask the general *SafeThink* question for the specific category of hazard.

5. If you answer **yes** at step **4**, then ask *Are there any conditions, actions, and events that will lead to or create a hazardous situation?*

6. If you answer **yes** at step **5**, then ask the remainder of the follow-up questions and select effective controls.

7. Repeat steps **4**, **5**, and **6** for the remaining **action steps**.

8. Repeat steps **3** to **8** for each of the remaining major steps

Before starting work, apply the *SafeThink* strategy to the entire task (major steps and action steps) to prevent illness and injury. While working, focus on completing one major step at a time. Apply the *SafeThink* strategy before starting a general step and before carrying out each action step. Later in this book you will learn ways to make the thinking process more efficient.

Part 4 Objects, Motion, Force

Option

Many participants have found that writing helps them learn and remember the questions. Write the critical thinking questions for objects, motion, and force in the box below. The questions are listed in the Job Aid.

FOOD for THOUGHT

■ A limited number of agents of cause created by tools and equipment

There are thousands of tools and many types of equipment but only a limited number of agents of cause that can create harm. For example, *rotating* equipment can be hazardous regardless of the type: rotating shafts, fans, saws, grinders, blenders. *Reciprocating* equipment such as jigsaws and presses can cause harm. Rotating and reciprocating are *generalities* of agents of cause. By using generalities, you can quickly identify agents of cause without having to memorize every type of equipment and specific agents of cause.

NOTE The agents of cause for tools and equipment also include categories of hazard other than objects, motion, and force. For example, non-ambient conditions, electricity, and radiation may also be involved.

■ Breaking tasks into small chunks or steps

For many tasks, there are no written procedures to refer to when performing the work. When a task consists of many action steps, it is very difficult to think through all the steps to identify and predict hazardous situations without a written procedure. To make the thinking process manageable, break the task into major steps consisting of five to nine action steps. Often there are natural points in the task where work can stop temporarily (e.g., for a rest break). Major steps can begin and end at these natural points. Refer to the examples in the Learning Activities to identify the natural points for breaking a task into major steps. For each major step, think about each action step to identify the agents of cause and the conditions, actions and events that can lead to or create a hazardous situation. Use *What if...?* questions to determine what can go wrong.

Many people find that the process of breaking tasks into major steps or specific steps and then identifying and predicting hazardous situations is difficult. Yet, the thinking process should come naturally because it is used every day. For example, a pre-job hazard assessment uses the thinking process to some degree. When people stop work for a moment and think through what they are going to do next, how they are going to do it, and the safety issues, they are applying the thinking strategy. For most tasks, you first need to think through how you are going to do the work effectively and efficiently to be able to identify and predict hazardous situations. Breaking the task into smaller chunks and then into specific action steps for each chunk makes the thinking process easier and more effective.

SafeThink is a rigorous strategy to identify and predict hazardous situations before working, while working, and after work is complete. To be effective at preventing illness or injury, you need to practice applying *SafeThink* until it becomes a natural part of the way you think about work, plan work, do work, and ensure the workplace is safe for others after you have completed your work.

■ Higher level learning

Learning a new strategy or refining an existing strategy takes effort. Learning to apply the strategy effectively requires personal commitment and practice.

SafeThink uses many educational methods to make the learning easier and the thinking strategy effective and efficient. One of the most powerful methods is the use of generalities. Refer to Appendix 1 for an explanation of generalities.

People often learn generalities through experience. While learning, the information is stored in the brain. Pathways are formed to access the information. As more information is acquired, the brain groups the information and establishes links between the groups. For example, transportation machines can be grouped into air, land, and water. Grouping information gives meaning and makes processing information more efficient and less stressful.

Have you ever taken a course where the instructor provided a great deal of information and you initially felt overwhelmed but, after struggling with the information, you suddenly understood? Eureka! What happened was that your brain grouped the information you learned so you can quickly access it. Pathways between the groups enable you to relate one type of information to another so that the information is meaningful.

SafeThink is structured to make learning easier for you. Much of the information is presented as generalities:
- The six general questions are generalities.
- The three generic questions are generalities (conditions, actions, events; consequences; and control).
- The agents of cause are generalities that are common to most workplaces and personal environments.

All these generalities make the strategy easier to use and more flexible because the strategy can be used in unfamiliar surroundings.

In the Job Aid, the three generic questions are repeated in each set of the specific questions. Keep this concept in mind when learning the specific *SafeThink* questions even though the wording may be different. It will help you to reason through the questions for each category of hazard and ensure that you don't miss any questions.

Historically, many workers have learned about hazardous situations through trial-and-error, in some cases, with unfortunate consequences. Over time, they have created their own generalities to prevent being harmed. It is no longer acceptable to learn by trial-and-error. *SafeThink* provides the generalities of agents of cause and a strategy to apply the knowledge to identify and predict hazardous situations.

■ Ways to learn the SafeThink questions

We all have preferred ways of learning. Using a combination of learning methods may help us learn more quickly and effectively. Here are some methods for learning the *SafeThink* questions:

- Memorize the questions (some people are good at memorizing, others are not)
- Use association. Think of a task and workplace and reason through the questions.
- Remember how many questions there are in a set
- Highlight key words on the *SafeThink* Job Aid and memorize the words. Then use each word in the questions.
- Create personal anagrams. For the questions, anagrams are words that contain specific letters of other words or phrases.
- Practice learning the questions one set at a time.
- Break a set of questions into smaller groups, for example, three questions per group. Learn the first group well and then learn the second group, and so on.
- Use repetition. Make copies of the Job Aid and leave a copy in your vehicle, lunchroom, kitchen, and inside the door of your work locker. Keep reviewing the questions until you have learned all of them.
- Put the questions on small cards and practice.
- Say the questions aloud.
- Apply the questions on the job, at home, and while driving.

Part 5
Non-Ambient Conditions

Does the work involve non-ambient conditions that could cause harm?

What conditions, actions, and events could expose me to non-ambient conditions?

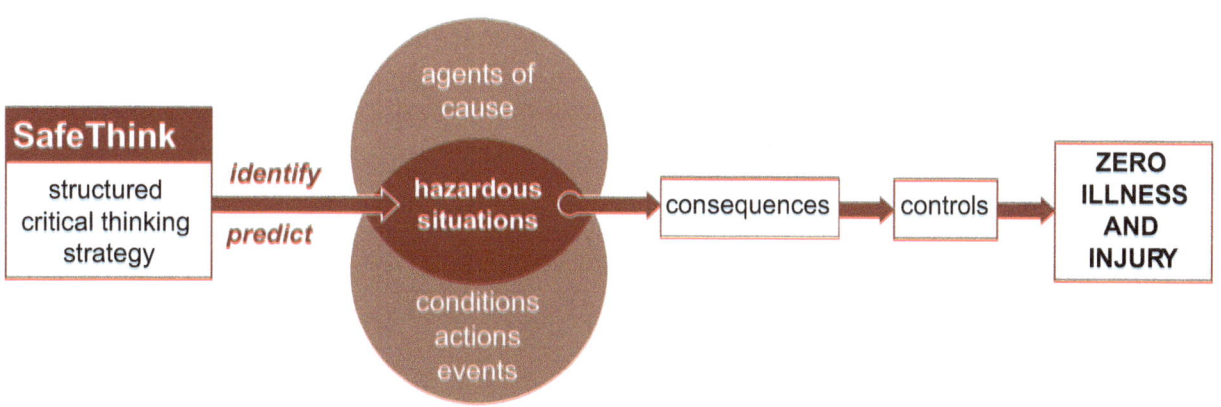

Training Objectives	Upon completion of this part, you will be able to identify and predict conditions, actions, and events that could make non-ambient conditions hazardous to workers.

- Identify non-ambient conditions in your workplace
- Identify the harm the non-ambient conditions
- can cause
- Identify the conditions, actions, and events that could expose you to non-ambient conditions
- To prevent being harmed by non-ambient conditions, identify precautions that could be taken:
  - before starting a task
  - during the task
  - after the task is complete

The SafeThink Strategy		
Part	Category of hazard	Critical thinking question
Part 3	Hazardous Materials	Does the work involve hazardous materials?
Part 4	Objects, Motion, Force	Does the work involve objects, motion, or force that could cause harm?
Part 5	**Non-Ambient Conditions**	***Does the work involve non-ambient conditions that could cause harm?***
Part 6	*Electricity*	Is current or static electricity a factor in doing the work?
Part 7	*Radiation*	Is radiation present when doing the work?
Part 8	*Changes*	Could changes lead to or create a hazardous situation?

Part 5 Non-Ambient Conditions

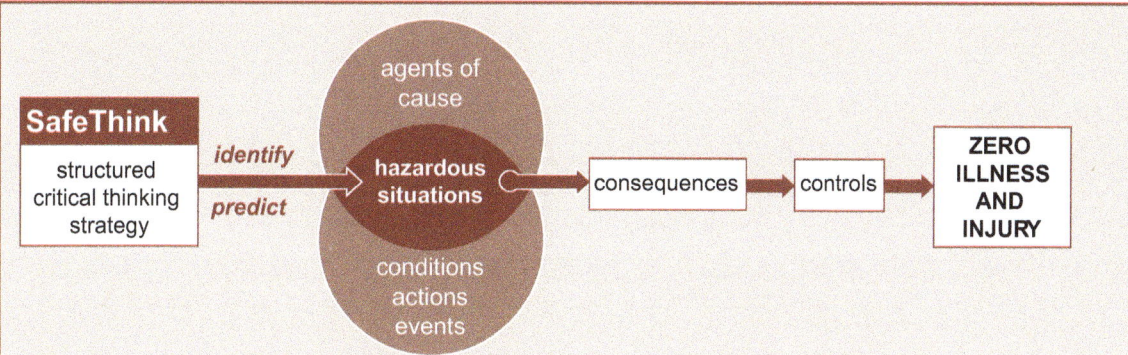

Using the SafeThink strategy

Does the work involve non-ambient conditions that could cause harm?

Ask:

- Is pressure involved?
- Is temperature involved?
- Are there unusual light conditions?
- Will noise be excessive?
- Will there be hazardous emissions?
- Will there be an oxygen-deficient (or excessive oxygen) atmosphere?
- What type of harm does the non-ambient condition pose?
- What conditions, actions, and events could expose me to non-ambient conditions?
- What can I do to prevent being harmed by non-ambient conditions?

With practice, when you think about the work or see a non-ambient condition that could lead to or create a hazardous situation, you will automatically ask these questions.

A learning activity at the end of Part 5 helps you learn to apply the *SafeThink* strategy to your work and worksite. The goal is to identify the conditions, actions, and events which lead to hazardous situations involving non-ambient conditions.

5 Non-Ambient Conditions

For *SafeThink*, ambient conditions are defined as conditions, such as air quality and temperature, which provide a physically comfortable environment for people. *Non-ambient* conditions are often uncomfortable and exposure to these conditions may be hazardous. Non-ambient conditions can be caused by changes in pressure, temperature, light, noise, dust, fumes, smoke, and vapors. Whenever you encounter environments where non-ambient conditions exist or could occur unexpectedly, you should immediately consider the potential for harm.

Some of the conditions, actions, and events that fall under the category of non-ambient conditions also apply to other categories. An example is pressure (which was described in Part 4—*Objects, Motion, Force*). Nevertheless, thinking about non-ambient conditions is an excellent strategy for identifying situations that could cause you harm.

5.1 Pressure

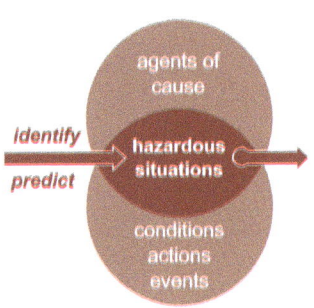

Liquids and gases under high pressure can suddenly be released, causing physical injury. If the released materials are hazardous, they can affect your health. Potential consequences of the sudden release of high-pressure liquids and gases include:
- physical injuries such as amputated limbs or liquids penetrating the body (injection)
- poisoning
- asphyxiation
- burns
- abrasions

High-pressure liquids

The sudden, uncontrolled release of high-pressure liquids from pipes, hoses, and vessels can result in a stream of liquid with enough energy to penetrate or cut metals—or injure a worker. High-pressure liquids are contained in equipment such as paint sprayers, hydraulic hoses, and high-pressure water jetting equipment such as hydrovacs. At gas plants, chemical plants, and refineries, high-pressure liquids are contained in vessels and piping. Liquids pipelines also contain high-pressure liquids.

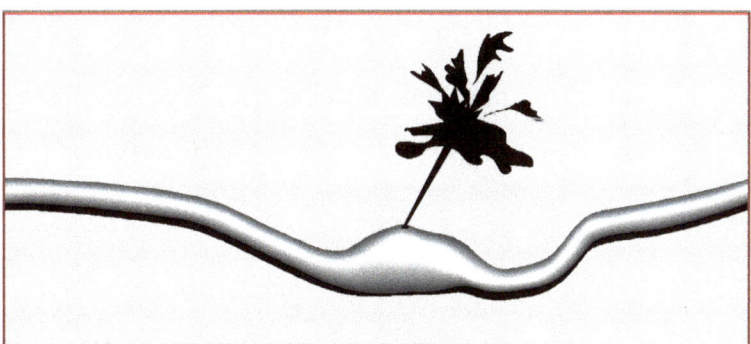

High-pressure equipment and systems (both liquid and gas) are designed to withstand excess pressure:
- High-pressure equipment has safety devices such as pressure relief valves that relieve pressure if pre-set limits are exceeded.
- Equipment is designed to withstand considerably more pressure than usual under normal operating conditions (e.g., failure pressure may be one and one-half times or two times greater than operating pressure).

If you work with equipment that contains high-pressure liquids, take the following precautions to protect yourself:
- Check all hoses for damage or leaks before using the equipment and make sure hose connections are secure.
- Wear eye protection.
- Follow manufacturer's recommendations when installing components.
- Tighten bolts to the recommended tightness using a torque wrench.
- Don't let hoses come into contact with heat sources, welding arcs, or other equipment that could damage the hose.
- Identify the maximum operating pressure (MOP) for pipelines or pressure equipment and find out what to do if pressure exceeds MOP, the safety relief valve malfunctions, or the line does not shut down.
- Follow your site's safe work procedures when starting pressurized equipment.

High-pressure gases

High-pressure gases can be very hazardous. If the equipment containing the high-pressure gas ruptures or explodes, gases will escape and expand, causing shrapnel to travel at very high speed. High-pressure gases are contained in equipment such as air hoses and welding equipment. At gas plants, chemical plants, and refineries, high-pressure gases are contained in vessels and piping. Gas pipelines also contain high-pressure gas.

High-pressure gases from air hoses, blowers, and welding equipment can stir up dust and drive particles into your skin and eyes. A stream of high-pressure gas directed at components can cause overheating. Depending on the gas, a sudden release can either raise or lower temperatures. A line break and the sudden release of gas can cause freezing or asphyxiation. For safety, move across wind or upwind of the break.

If you work with equipment containing high-pressure gas, take the precautions recommended above for high-pressure liquids, and also the following precautions:
- Do not use compressed air to clean your work clothes.
- Use vacuum hoses, not compressed air, to clean parts and work areas.
- Never use oxygen (e.g., from gas welders) to clean parts. Oxygen can cause oil and grease to spontaneously ignite.

5.2 Temperature

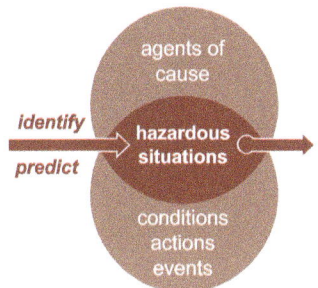

High or low temperatures are associated with many industrial processes and worksites. Exposure to high or low temperatures can injure you if you are not properly equipped. The danger increases when hazardous materials or other hazardous non-ambient conditions are also present. Workers with chronic health problems (e.g., diabetes), older workers, and workers who are not physically fit are at higher risk for temperature-related illnesses and injuries.

Potential consequences of high and low temperature conditions include:
- High temperatures can cause burns, dehydration, heat stress, heat stroke, and death.
- Low temperatures can cause burns, frostbite, hypothermia, and lung damage.

High temperatures

Many industrial processes involve high temperature materials, equipment (such as kilns, reboilers, and heat exchangers) and hot pipes that can burn your skin. Sometimes it is difficult to prevent contacting a hot surface, especially if you are in a very small space. Adjacent equipment may be very hot; when you are in close quarters, you could back into the equipment.

When materials are being cut, ground, or shaped, the materials and some equipment components can become very hot. You may need to allow time for materials to cool before handling them.

Laboratory equipment for analyzing, testing, or calibrating can often be very hot. Be careful not to contact baths (oil or glass bead) or the components being tested. Use PPE, gloves, and tongs to handle hot material.

Working near hot materials, equipment, or pipes can also cause heat stress. The effects of heat stress range from minor discomfort or skin rashes to fainting, heat stroke, and death.

Controls for high temperatures

Some controls you can use to prevent being harmed by exposure to high temperatures include:

- If you work with very hot materials, equipment, or processes, wear appropriate PPE (e.g., insulated gloves, coveralls, aprons) to prevent burns. Protective clothing with internal cooling systems (air flow systems or cold packs) is available.
- Make sure all ventilation systems are operating before starting the work; poor ventilation increases the risk of heat stress.
- If you must work in hot areas for prolonged periods, drink small amounts of water frequently to prevent dehydration, and take breaks as often as you can.
- If you work outside, wear a hat to minimize your exposure to the sun.
- Do not leave animals or children in a vehicle unattended in hot weather. If the air conditioner or engine fails, the interior will get very hot. Always leave a window partially open if leaving animals unattended in a vehicle.

Low temperatures

Very low temperatures are encountered:

- at process equipment, piping, and laboratory equipment in plants and factories which use low temperature processes
- in refrigerated spaces such as packing plant coolers
- during outdoor work on very cold winter days

Working outside on very cold winter days, particularly in windy conditions, increases your risk of frostbite and hypothermia.

Working in refrigerated spaces or cold, wet environments increases your risk of sustaining repetitive strain injuries (e.g., tendonitis) and muscle strains.

Continuing exposure to cold temperatures can cause blood vessels in the extremities to constrict painfully. Very cold temperatures can also cause severe thermal burns.

Wear properly insulated winter clothing, including hats, gloves, and footwear. If you collect samples from cold bodies

Part 5 Non-Ambient Conditions

of water, you may need a drysuit or insulated wetsuit as well as a life jacket.

If you work in unusually hot or cold environments, maintain contact/communication with co-workers or work in pairs. When you work outside, check for the white skin patches that indicate frostbite. Confusion, slurred or incoherent speech, dizziness, or fainting could indicate heat stress or hypothermia. If you work alone, arrange to check in with someone at regular intervals and determine what is to be done if you fail to make contact.

Cryogenic liquids

Cryogenic liquids are gases that have boiling points lower than –150°C (–238°F). Cryogenic liquids are most commonly encountered in process equipment and piping at gas plants, refineries, and chemical plants. The cryogenic materials you are most likely to encounter are natural gas liquids (NGLs), liquid nitrogen, argon, helium, hydrogen, and liquid carbon dioxide.

Cryogenic liquids at industrial worksites are usually contained in thermally insulated flasks, cylinders, pipes, or tanker trucks.

Cryogenic liquids can cause thermal burns to the skin and asphyxiation. Other workplace examples of hazards and controls are listed in Appendix 4—*Table 6: Cryogenic (extremely cold) Liquids—Hazards and Controls*.

5.3 Light

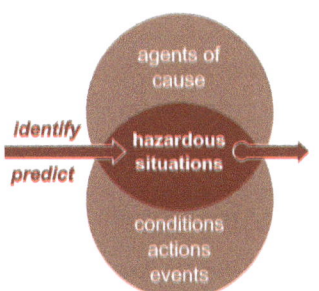

Inadequate light, extremely bright light, and the transition between the two conditions can be hazardous. If lighting is inadequate, your risk of being injured from trips, slips, and falls or contacting moving objects increases. Glare from bright sunlight increases your risk of a vehicle accident. Too little or too much light can lead to eyestrain. Exposure to welding flashes (direct or reflected off the walls) can injure your eyes. Some testing equipment (e.g. strobe lights) can create perception difficulties that could then cause you to be injured from moving equipment.

Potential consequences of excessive exposure to non-ambient light conditions include:
- eye injuries
- blindness

Controls

Some controls you can use to reduce the risk of harm from light include the following:

- If light levels in your work area are inadequate, notify your supervisor. Employers must provide adequate lighting for workplace tasks.
- Erect portable welding screens between welding equipment and other work areas.
- Wear approved eye protection in welding areas.
- When you come into a building from outside, your eyes take a few moments to adapt to the change in lighting. Pause inside the doorway until your eyes adjust. If there are hazardous objects or fall hazards (e.g., dangling crane hooks, a pile of pallets, or a stairwell) near the entrance, you could be harmed if you proceed inside too quickly.

5.4 Noise

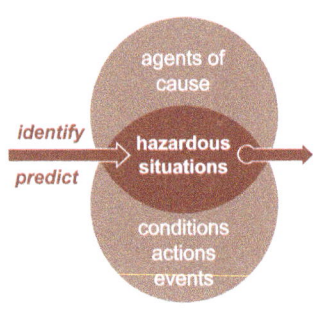

Operating equipment such as jackhammers, grinders, riveters, compressors, or mobile equipment such as forklifts, loaders, and mowers, expose unprotected workers to high noise levels. Some jobs may involve exposure to short, high-noise periods, or sudden bursts of noise. For example:
- installing sheet metal air ducts
- erecting metal scaffolding in warehouses
- sounding a ship's whistle
- firing a gun

Consequences

Potential consequences of working in continuous or intermittent noise conditions include:
- temporary and/or permanent hearing impairment or loss. Hearing loss often occurs over time and workers may not be aware that their hearing is degenerating.
- increased stress levels

- impaired communication, which can result in accidents
- startle reaction to sudden noises could result in an injury

Controls

Occupational health and safety regulations set exposure limits for noise in the workplace. The legislation requires employers to post hazard warnings in high noise areas and specifies the types of hearing protection required for different noise levels. If you work in a high-noise area, protect your hearing by using the appropriate hearing protection. If you test signal devices and alarms, warn workers that the equipment will be sounding to prevent them from being startled.

Hearing protectors that look similar can provide different levels of noise reduction. If noise causes you to experience discomfort or ringing in the ears, or if you find yourself talking loudly after leaving a noisy area, consider increasing the level of hearing protection you are using. In very high noise conditions, both ear plugs and ear muffs may be required.

In many jurisdictions, workers potentially exposed to high noise levels must undergo regular hearing tests.

5.5 Hazardous Emissions

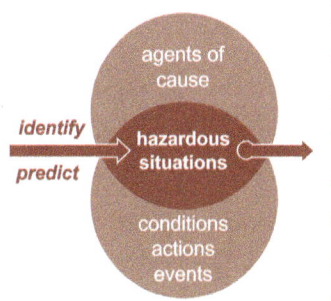

Hazardous materials may emit hazardous vapors or gases (refer to Part 3—*Hazardous Materials*). Many industrial activities can discharge potentially hazardous materials into the air, reducing air quality:
- dusts and fibers
- aerosols
- mists
- vapors
- fumes
- smoke

Dusts and **fibers** are fine, dry particles of organic or inorganic materials. The particles are generated from moving, cleaning, cutting, and milling materials such as wood, grain, and textiles and from sanding and sandblasting operations. The

fire and explosion hazard may be high in areas where there are excessive amounts of dust and fibers. Inhaling dusts and fibers can affect the lungs and respiratory system. In many jurisdictions, workers potentially exposed to certain dusts and fibers (e.g., asbestos) must undergo regular medical tests.

Aerosols are large liquid droplets or solid particles generated when aerosol applicators are used to spray products such as paints and pesticides. Aerosols can remain suspended in the air for long periods.

Mists are small liquid particles generated when vapors condense to form liquids and when liquids are dispersed by splashing or atomizing. Acid mists are formed during operations such as electroplating and pickling; oil mists are formed during cutting, grinding, and machining operations.

Vapors are the gaseous form of a substance. Solvents used for cleaning can be harmful if their vapors are inhaled or absorbed through the skin or eyes. When two-component paints and epoxy sealants and grouts are applied, a chemical reaction takes place that can produce toxic vapors.

Commercial cleaning products may give off vapors that can be harmful if inhaled. Commercial cleaners should never be mixed. These products may contain acids, bases, and bleaches that can react with each other to produce toxic vapors and excessive heat.

Fumes are airborne particulate formed by the condensation of metal gases. Often fumes are generated during welding and metallizing. Metal fumes are a health hazard, particularly fumes from galvanized metals and metals that have chromium or lead-based paints, coatings, and lubricants.

Smoke is produced as a result of incomplete combustion of organic materials (e.g., wood, oil, plastic). Usually smoke contains both dry particles and droplets.

Consequences
Potential consequences of hazardous emissions include:
- respiratory tract (lung) damage
- eye injury
- restricted visibility which can cause accidents.

The table below lists the various types of hazardous emissions and provides industry examples.

	Hazardous Emissions on Industrial Worksites		
Type	**Definition**	**Type of hazard**	**Industry example**
Dust	Solid particles or fibers generated by handling, crushing, grinding, impacting, detonating, or otherwise processing solid materials. Gravity causes dust to settle.	• Fire/explosion • Respiratory hazard • Eye injury	• Grain dust in a grain elevator • Coal dust in a mine loading tipple • Silica dust from sandblasting • Dust from a building demolition site (including wood, plaster, and cement particles, asbestos fibers)
Aerosol	Liquid or solid particles dispersed in air. The droplets or particles remain suspended for some time.	• Fire/explosion • Respiratory hazard • Eye injury	• Paint application using an electric sprayer or aerosol bomb
Mist	Suspended liquid droplets usually produced when a liquid is dispersed by splashing, foaming, or atomizing.	• Fire/explosion (flammable or combustible mists) • Respiratory hazard • Eye injury	• Acid mists from heated acid dip tanks • Oil mists produced during grinding and machining operations • Solvent mists from tool or parts cleaning
Vapor	The gaseous form of substances that are normally in the solid or liquid state at room temperature and pressure.	• Fire/explosion (flammable or combustible gases) • Respiratory hazard	• Water vapor emitted when an autoclave is opened • Fuel vapors leaking from defective valves, seals, and when fueling equipment and vehicles
Fume	Airborne particles formed by the condensation of metal gases.	• Respiratory hazard	• Metal fumes from welding (e.g., zinc fumes)
Smoke	A suspension of particles from combustion of organic materials. Usually smoke contains both dry particles and droplets.	• Respiratory hazard • Eye injury • Reduced visibility	• Wood smoke, which contains incompletely burned wood particles and hydrocarbon droplets

Refer to the product MSDS for specific hazards and preventive measures.

Controls

Occupational health and safety regulations set occupational exposure limits for hazardous emissions (gases, vapors, and particulate emissions).

Some controls you can use to prevent being harmed by hazardous emissions include:
- Review the product MSDS and your company's emergency procedures so that you know:
  - what hazardous emissions may occur or already exist at your worksite
  - how to protect yourself from the hazardous emissions
- Use the PPE specified in the MSDS (especially respiratory protection with the correct filter for the emission).
- Use paint booths and fume hoods, turn on ventilation fans, or open as many windows and overhead doors as possible to improve ventilation.
- Use gas monitoring equipment throughout the work activity.
- Change the sequence of work activities to allow time for the air to clear.
- Carry out emissions-generating activities at times when most people are away from the area.
- Cover the area with shrouds to contain hazardous emissions (e.g., dust from sandblasting) to prevent contaminating adjacent areas.

5.6 Oxygen-Deficient Atmospheres

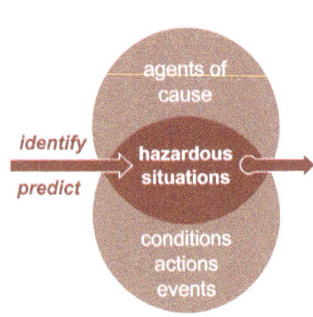

Entering confined spaces such as vessels, sumps, ditches, and trenches is hazardous. Two distinct hazards may exist in confined spaces:
- toxic gases may be present
- low oxygen concentrations can cause asphyxiation

Oxygen-deficient atmospheres can occur in:
- poorly ventilated areas (e.g., confined spaces such as vessels, silos, mines, tunnels, cisterns, and holds of ships)
- locations where equipment can absorb oxygen (e.g., carbon filter beds, or inside a marine barge where rust has used up the oxygen)

- places where the normal atmosphere (which usually contains 21% oxygen) has been diluted or displaced by a toxic gas (e.g., a low spot on an oil lease where there is a high concentration of hydrogen sulfide gas, a shop in which a faulty furnace emits carbon monoxide gas, or operating an internal combustion engine in a confined space)
- atmospheres where nitrogen used for purging has replaced the oxygen (e.g., inside tanks or vessels)
- liquid reservoirs or water bodies (e.g., lagoons, open tanks, or pits) in which a worker could drown

Potential consequences of oxygen-deficient atmospheres include:
- disorientation and impaired judgment at slightly reduced oxygen levels
- mental failure and fainting at more severely reduced oxygen levels
- breathing difficulty and death at very low oxygen levels

Controls

Some controls you can use to prevent being harmed from oxygen-deficient atmospheres include:
- Learn and follow your company's written codes of practice, work plans, step-by-step job procedures, and emergency procedures.
- Take specialized training, including respirator use, work procedures, and emergency and first aid procedures.
- Hold or attend pre-job safety meetings.
- Use the appropriate PPE (including supplied air respirators and safety lines).

Wearing PPE can create difficulties:
- heat stress
- restricted vision
- restricted movement
- respiratory discomfort

Adjust your work to accommodate these difficulties.

- Monitor the oxygen, toxic gas, and flammable gas concentrations in the atmosphere before, during, and after the work is completed.

- Pipe in fresh air but continue to monitor the oxygen level (see the notes).
- Post a qualified safety watch outside the potentially hazardous area.

NOTE A normal atmosphere contains approximately 21% oxygen. When the oxygen level falls below 19.5%, you will begin to experience the effects of oxygen deficiency. Always:
- monitor the oxygen level when you work in a poorly-ventilated area (e.g., a confined space)
- use a supplied air respirator when entering an atmosphere that could contain less than 19.5% oxygen

If you are **not** using a supplied air respirator and the oxygen level falls below 19.5%, you are in *imminent danger of asphyxiation. Immediately* escape from the area.

NOTE Excessive oxygen can also be hazardous. Air that contains more than 23% oxygen is a significant fire and explosion hazard, particularly when ignition sources and/or combustible gases are present:
- Always monitor the oxygen level when you work in a poorly-ventilated area (e.g., a confined space).
- If the oxygen level is greater than 23%, you are in danger from a fire or explosion. Immediately turn off all ignition sources and escape from the area.

5.7 What Can Go Wrong?

An important strategy to keep you and others from harm is to consider what can go wrong. For non-ambient conditions, ask *What if...?* questions about conditions, actions, and events that could occur and cause PEMEO to function poorly, behave abnormally, or fail. If there is a concern, determine the immediate effect.

The following table provides examples of using *What if...?* questions about what can go wrong with non-ambient conditions. Note that in the examples, the worker may be performing a specific task or may be in the area that is affected.

What can go wrong with non-ambient conditions?		
Domain	**What if…?** (conditions, actions, and events)	**Immediate effect**
People	• What if I use a glove with a hole in the thumb to handle the welded metal?	• The hot metal will make contact with my skin.
	• What if I weld materials that are covered with old paint?	• The paint could give off toxic fumes and vapors.
	• What if I operate the impact drill in an area where other people are working?	• The drill will create excessively high noise, affecting workers.
Equipment	• What if the coupling on the airless paint sprayer comes loose?	• Paint will spray out with high velocity and force.
	• What if the engine has been shut down just before I work on it?	• The engine will be hot.
	• What if the dust collector bag is full?	• Dust will not be collected properly and will contaminate the atmosphere.
Materials	• What if the materials are very shiny?	• The materials will reflect bright light onto workers, causing glare.
	• What if the materials can easily disintegrate?	• Dust will contaminate the atmosphere.
Environment	• What if trash is burned near a building under construction?	• Workers nearby will be affected by the heat and smoke.
	• What if, in winter, the equipment outside is at the same temperature as the atmosphere?	• During maintenance, using bare hands to handle small equipment parts could cause frostbite.
Organization	• What if the renovators are painting?	• The vapors will get into the ventilation system and travel to other areas of the building.
	• What if the department has a policy that all workers near the furnace must wear flame-resistant vests, coveralls, and long sleeve shirts?	• On very hot days, workers could experience heat stress.

Having determined the possible immediate effects, you can ask additional questions:
- Could I or others become ill and/or injured?
- What should be my first response if an incident occurs?

- What can I do to minimize the possibility of an incident occurring and the severity of the consequences should an incident occur?

For many of the incidents you identified by your *What if...?* questions, your response will be more effective when you:
- pre-determine the best response
- rehearse your response by imagining responding to the incident. Rehearsing increases the possibility that you will respond immediately and effectively.

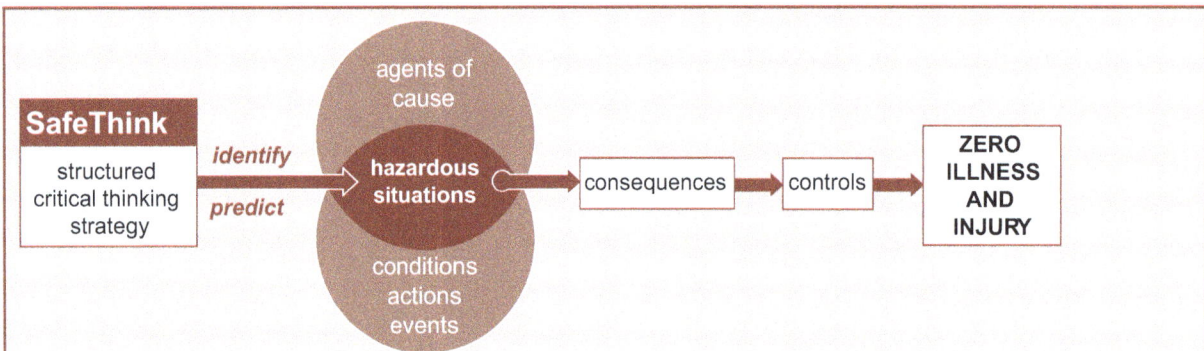

Using the SafeThink strategy

Does the work involve non-ambient conditions that could cause harm?

Certain conditions, actions, and events could expose you to non-ambient conditions.

To determine if you are at risk of being exposed to non-ambient conditions, ask yourself the following critical thinking questions:

- Is pressure involved?
- Is temperature involved
- Are there unusual light conditions?
- Will noise be excessive?
- Will there be hazardous emissions?
- Will there be an oxygen-deficient (or excessive oxygen) atmosphere?
- What type of harm does the non-ambient condition pose?
- What conditions, actions, and events could expose me to non-ambient conditions?
- What can I do to prevent being harmed by non-ambient conditions?

With practice, when you think about the work or see a non-ambient condition in your workplace, you will automatically consider the possibility of being harmed.

Use the *SafeThink* strategy when you complete the learning activity for non-ambient conditions.

Part 5 Non-Ambient Conditions

Does the work involve non-ambient conditions that could cause harm? What conditions, actions, and events could expose me to non-ambient conditions?

This learning activity will help you learn to identify and predict conditions, actions, and events that make non-ambient conditions hazardous to workers.

1. List three tasks that you perform that involve non-ambient conditions. For each task identify the most critical conditions, actions, or events that could place you in danger of being harmed by the non-ambient conditions.

Task	Conditions, Actions, Events
1.	
2.	
3.	

To complete the remainder of this learning activity, break each task into its major steps. For each major step, think about the specific action steps and the associated conditions, actions, and events that could expose you or others to non-ambient conditions.

2. Select one of the tasks from question 1. First, break the task into major steps; then complete questions 2a, 2b, and 2c.

   Task _____

   Major step 1 (before working) _____

   Major step 2 (while working) _____

   Major step 3 (while working) _____

   Major step 4 (while working) _____

   Major step 5 (while working) _____

145

Major step 6 (while working) _____

Major step 7 (after work is complete) _____

2a. Identify conditions, actions, and events involving non-ambient conditions that exist **before** doing the work that could cause harm to you or others. Identify possible controls to reduce the risk of an incident.

_____
_____
_____
_____
_____

2b. Identify conditions, actions, and events involving non-ambient conditions that exist or develop **while** doing the work that could cause harm to you or others. Identify possible controls to reduce the risk of an incident.

_____
_____
_____
_____

2c. Identify conditions, actions, and events involving non-ambient conditions that exist **after** the work has been completed that could cause harm to you or others. Identify possible controls to reduce the risk of an incident.

_____
_____
_____
_____

3. Name a task that involves non-ambient conditions:

_____

3a. Ask *What if...?* questions to identify what can go wrong in relation to non-ambient conditions and fill in the table on the next page. To focus your thinking, consider conditions, actions, and events associated with each PEMEO domain.

What can go wrong with non-ambient conditions?		
Domain	**What if . . . ?** (conditions, actions, and events)	**Immediate effect**
People		
Equipment		
Materials		
Environment		
Organization		

3b. From the table you have completed, select one effect that may create or lead to a hazardous situation and answer the following questions:

Could I or others become ill and/or injured? What would be the consequences?

_____
_____

What should be my first response if an incident occurs?

_____
_____

What can I do to minimize the probability of an incident occurring and/or the severity of consequences?

_____
_____

The SafeThink Strategy

The *SafeThink* strategy to identify and predict hazardous situations caused by one category of hazard is as follows:

1. Identify the task.

2. Break the task into two to nine **general steps**.

3. Break **general step** 1 into **action steps**.

4. For each **action step**, ask the general *SafeThink* question for the specific category of hazard.

5. If you answer **yes** at step **4**, then ask *Are there any conditions, actions, and events that will lead to or create a hazardous situation?*

6. If you answer **yes** at step **5**, then ask the remainder of the follow-up questions and select effective controls.

7. Repeat steps **4**, **5**, and **6** for the remaining **action steps**.

8. Repeat steps **3** to **8** for each of the remaining general steps

Before starting work, apply the *SafeThink* strategy to the entire task (major steps and action steps) to prevent illness and injury. While working, focus on completing one major step at a time. Apply the *SafeThink* strategy before starting a general step and before carrying out each action step. Later in this book you will learn ways to make the thinking process more efficient.

Option

Many participants have found that writing helps them learn and remember the questions. Write the critical thinking questions for non-ambient conditions in the box below. The questions are listed in the Job Aid.

FOOD for THOUGHT

Developing good safety habits

As part of learning good safety habits, you need to learn the *SafeThink* questions well enough that you automatically apply the questions at work and in your personal life. Learning the *SafeThink* questions and strategy takes repetition and practice. With practice, the strategy becomes automatic (second nature). And all of us, young and old, can learn and refine our safety strategies.

When my son and daughter were about thirteen and eleven years old, they learned to be vigilant about pointed objects. At the supper table, I explained to them that it is more difficult to see a pointed object looking at the end than it is from the side. I then turned the handles of the spoons in the bowls to point towards them. Soon they were both turning the handles of the spoons to point at each other. And the conflict was on—to their mother's chagrin! I laughed because their actions were great reinforcements to being vigilant and taking action when there were pointed objects close to them.

When my children were in their early twenties, I wanted to see if they still retained the good safety behavior. My daughter was at the kitchen table just before supper talking to her mother and not facing me. I turned the handle of a spoon towards her. Soon, she noticed the spoon and said, "Dad, you bug me. You taught me about pointed objects a long time ago and now I can't stand pointed objects facing my way." My son was not in the room so I turned one of the handles of the spoons towards his plate. When he went to sit down, he turned the handle away and said, "You know, Dad, the habit about pointed objects has served me well in my trade."

Young and old can learn new safety habits. With age, my balance and coordination have diminished. A few years ago, I stepped on some ice and fell hard. Fortunately, I was not hurt. Over the winter I taught myself a new habit to keep my footing. Whenever I see a slippery surface (ice, wet floor)

I automatically lift my knees and plant my feet squarely (a marching step). I have not slipped once since developing this new safety habit.

There are many good safety habits such as:
- flipping a screw driver so the handle is first and the shaft is pointed towards your arm (i.e., parallel to your wrist) when using the fingers of that hand to make an adjustment to a component. The action prevents the screwdriver shaft from coming in contact with equipment causing damage, getting caught in moving parts, or making an electrical contact.
- maintaining three-point contact when climbing or descending a ladder
- using eye protection at work and at home when there is potential for the eyes to be damaged
- moving cautiously around blind corners and through openings

Think of a safety habit you can develop or refine and work at making it second nature. Share your good habits with others so they can improve.

Some people call good habits *intuition*. When they see an agent of cause (stimulus), they automatically do the right thing to be safe (response). They may not be aware of their safe behavior because they do it automatically (intuition) when the stimulus is present.

Part 6
Electricity

Is current or static electricity a factor in doing the work?

What conditions, actions, and events could cause current or static electricity to harm me?

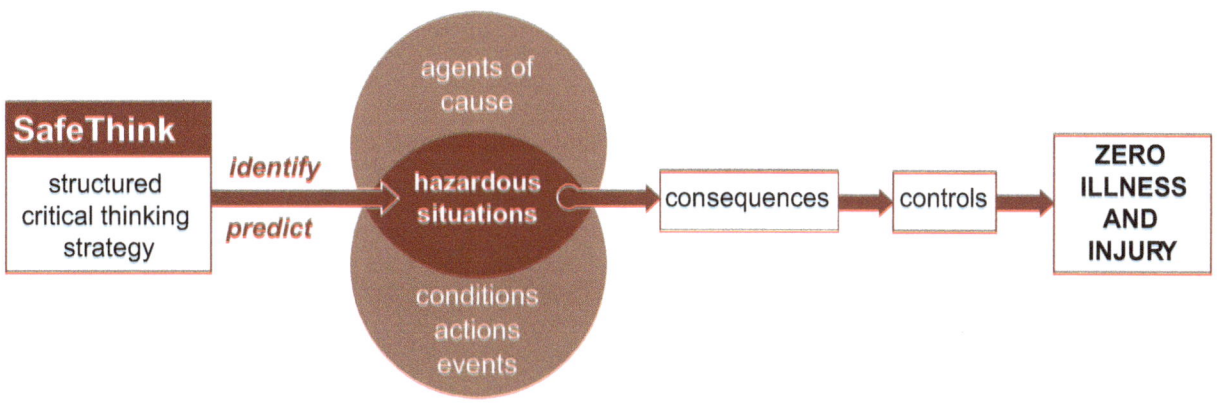

Training Objectives

Upon completion of this part, you will be able to identify and predict conditions, actions, and events that could make current and static electricity hazardous to workers.

- Identify where current electricity is used in your workplace
- Identify the harm the current electricity can cause
- Identify conditions, actions, and events that could cause electrically-driven equipment to start or stop
- Identify conditions, actions, and events that could cause you to come in contact with current electricity
- Identify potential sources of static electricity in your workplace
- Identify the harm the static electricity can cause
- Identify conditions, actions, and events that could create an electrical spark that could cause a fire or explosion
- To prevent being harmed by current or static electricity, identify precautions that could be taken
  - before starting a task
  - during the task
  - after the task is complete

The SafeThink Strategy		
Part	Category of hazard	Critical thinking question
Part 3	Hazardous Materials	Does the work involve hazardous materials?
Part 4	Objects, Motion, Force	Does the work involve objects, motion, or force that could cause harm?
Part 5	Non-Ambient Conditions	Does the work involve non-ambient conditions that could cause harm?
Part 6	**Electricity**	**Is current or static electricity a factor in doing the work?**
Part 7	Radiation	Is radiation present when doing the work?
Part 8	Changes	Could changes lead to or create a hazardous situation?

Part 6   Electricity

A learning activity at the end of Part 6 helps you apply your learning about potential electrical hazards at your workplace. The goal is to identify the conditions, actions, and events which lead to hazardous situations involving electricity.

6   Electricity

Two types of electricity, current and static, are present in most workplaces. Both types can be hazardous:
- **Current electricity** is used in homes and industry to provide light, heat, and to drive electric motors to provide movement. Electric generators are used to produce the electrical energy provided to industry and homes. Current electricity can also be produced by other means such as batteries and solar cells.
- **Static electricity** is the electrical charge that results primarily from friction between two different materials.

6.1   Current Electricity

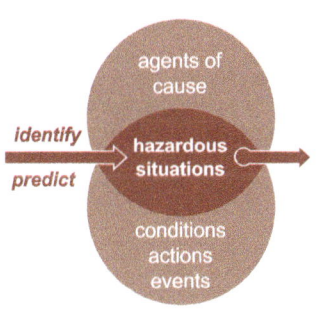

Current electricity can cause immediate injury or death. Examples of conditions, actions, and events creating hazardous situations include:
- workers adjusting and repairing electrically-driven equipment
- electrical equipment, including hand power tools and light fixtures, used in atmospheres containing flammable gases, dusts, or fibers
- electrical equipment with damaged, worn, or loose cords or fittings
- extension cords that are inadequately rated for the job
- extension cords lying in standing water
- equipment (e.g., cranes, backhoes) contacting or cutting overhead or underground electrical lines
- ungrounded power tools, ungrounded outlets

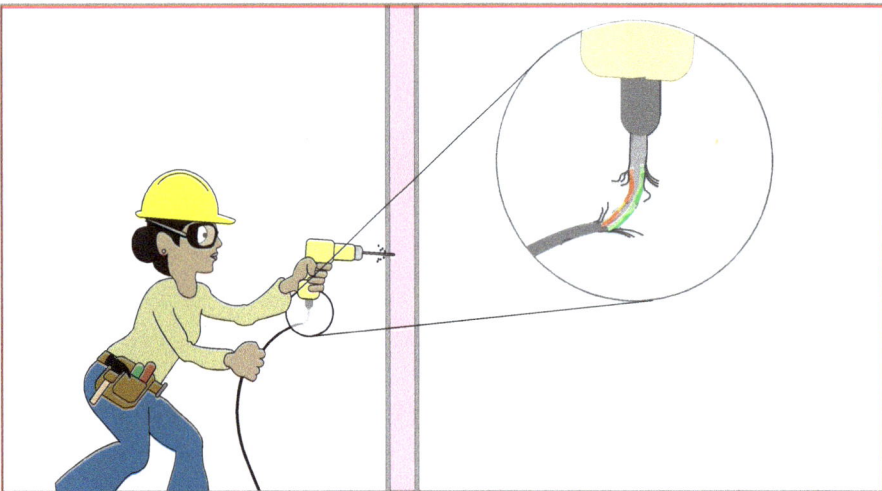

Tanks and piping that are in contact with soil may have an electric current imposed on them to reduce corrosion (cathodic protection). Before maintenance is performed on equipment and piping that has cathodic protection, the electrical circuit for the cathodic protection must be isolated (shut off or disconnected).

Consequences

Potential consequences of being in contact with current electricity include:
- electrical shock
- thermal burns
- electrocution (death) from directly contacting an electrical energy source or a source containing residual electrical energy

Indirect consequences relating to current electricity include:
- physical injury caused by electrical equipment accidentally started during servicing
- accidents and injuries from fires and explosions caused by electrical ignition of flammable gases, dusts, or fibers

Electrical Hazard Ratings

Work areas where flammable gases, liquids, dusts, and fibers may be present are considered hazardous atmospheres. Electrical codes provide rating systems for both hazardous atmospheres and for electrical equipment. The rating for electrical components installed or used in a hazardous atmosphere must match the hazard rating for that atmosphere. The rating system for hazardous atmospheres and electrical equipment varies among countries (e.g., U.S. ratings list class and division or zone; in Europe, ratings list class and zone).

 Government regulations require that only qualified electricians perform specific tasks involving electrical circuits. Before performing these types of tasks, make sure you are qualified to carry out the work.

Electrical components for hazardous atmospheres are designed to prevent electrical sparks from igniting flammable substances.

Several different types of electrical components are available, including:
- explosion-proof components, which are designed to contain any spark or explosion that occurs inside the component housing
- intrinsically-safe circuits, which use low voltages and low currents. Intrinsically-safe circuits do not have enough energy to ignite any flammable substances that may be present.
- dustproof and fiber-proof enclosures, which prevent flammable substances from contacting the electrical components
- safety barriers (plugs) in conduits, which prevent flammable gas and fibers from migrating through the conduit

Equipment and vehicles contacting electrical sources

You may be electrocuted if the equipment or vehicle you are operating comes in contact with a buried electrical line, overhead electrical line, or pad-mounted transformer. Before starting work, if there is a possibility of coming in contact with live electrical lines, the best precaution is to have the utility company de-energize the lines.

When moving high equipment and loads under electrical lines, use a spotter to ensure a safe distance from the lines is maintained. The safe limit of approach to overhead lines

depends on the voltage of the lines. Consult your local electrical or utility company to determine the safe limit of approach to electrical lines.

Weather conditions can affect the safe distance from overhead electrical lines:

- Wind can swing the lines horizontally.
- An increase in temperature causes lines to expand and hang lower, reducing the vertical clearance.
- Ice buildup on lines can also cause lines to hang lower, reducing the vertical clearance.

If your equipment or vehicle comes in contact with an electrical source, try to break the contact, provided you will not cause more damage or pull more electrical lines down on you. Stay in your vehicle until a utility person says it is safe to leave. The risk of electrocution is highest when a person tries to exit the equipment or vehicle. The safest place is inside the equipment or vehicle.

If you touch the vehicle and the ground at the same time, your body will provide a path for the electricity to flow to ground.

You can be electrocuted. Warn others **not** to approach the equipment or vehicle within 10 metres (30 feet). Stay in the equipment or vehicle. If you have a cell phone, call for help or honk the horn. Inside the cab, it is safe to touch everything without being electrocuted.

If you must leave the equipment or vehicle, for example, due to a fire, use the following steps to exit:

1. Locate the electrical source. You must exit the equipment or vehicle as far away from the source as possible.

2. Check the ground at the point where you will be jumping. Ensure that the ground is flat. If possible, pick a dry location (water increases electrical conductivity).

3. Open the door as far as possible and make sure the door stays open.

4. Grasp the top of the door and roof and slowly stand up on the door sill (rocker panel).

5. Place your feet together.

The next step (Step 6) is to jump clear of the equipment or vehicle. This specific method of jumping from the vehicle must be followed to prevent being electrocuted:

- Cross your arms to prevent contacting the door when you jump.
- Do not try to jump too far, you could lose your balance and fall backwards towards the vehicle.
- Land with both feet together to prevent electricity in the ground from flowing from one leg to the other.
- Do not roll.
- After landing, do not try to close the door. You could be electrocuted.

6. Cross your arms, lean forward, jump, and land with both feet together.

7. Keeping your feet together, hop or shuffle at least 10 metres (30 feet) from the vehicle.

Do **not** return to the vehicle until a utility person indicates it is safe to do so. Do **not** let others approach the vehicle.

Controls

Some controls you can use to reduce the risk of harm from current electricity include:

- Unplug electrical power tools before exchanging parts (e.g., blades).
- Lock out electrically-powered equipment before the equipment is serviced, repaired, tested, or adjusted. Refer to Part 9—*Apply Your SafeThink Strategy* for a detailed explanation about lockout and tagout.
- Before starting repairs to electrically-powered equipment:
  - Ensure *all* sources of electrical energy are isolated so that the power cannot be turned on or the equipment started while repairs are taking place. Some equipment has more than one electrical energy source, for example,

Lockout:
the use of locks to ensure that devices which control energy or material remain in a safe position and cannot be operated inadvertently

One Hand Rule

Use only one hand when testing circuits. Put your other hand in your pocket to reduce the possibility of getting an electrical shock.

Grounding Grids:

grids made of conductive materials that are embedded in or installed beneath concrete pads and floors. The grid is connected to a ground and provides connectors for electrically-driven equipment.

a pump motor is powered by one source of energy and the motor controls are powered by a second source of energy. When *all* sources of electrical energy are **not** isolated, two problems may occur: the worker could be electrocuted and the equipment could be started remotely, causing injury.

- Turn the control switch on to ensure the machine does not start, then turn the control switch back off.
- Use a circuit tester to ensure all circuits are deactivated. See the *One Hand Rule* sidebar.

• When using ladders or moving equipment near overhead electrical lines, ensure that there is adequate clearance.
• In hazardous areas, only use electrical equipment that has the applicable electrical hazard rating.
• Make sure ground fault circuit interrupters (GFCIs) are installed on electrical equipment used in damp or wet areas. GFCIs are designed to interrupt the circuit in time to prevent serious injury or death if an electrical short occurs.
• Wear insulated footwear.
• Do **not** stand in water.
• Stay clear of grounded metal fixtures (e.g., plumbing fixtures).
• Ground electrical equipment (including portable generators) to a copper cold water line, grounding grid or plate, or to a copper-clad grounding rod driven into the ground to at least 2.4 m (8 ft.) depth.
• Consult your local electrical and utility regulations to determine the safe limit of approach to overhead electrical lines. Use a spotter when moving high equipment and loads over or under electrical lines to ensure the equipment remains at a safe distance from the lines. The safe limit depends on the voltage of the electrical line: the safe distance from an electrical line increases when the voltage on the line increases.

6.2 Static Electricity

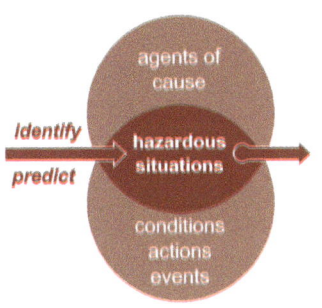

Examples of ways static electricity can be created include:
- a static charge buildup in flowing flammable liquids (e.g., poured or pumped fuel)
- a static charge buildup in flowing grain and feed dust
- a static charge buildup during an electrical storm
- a static charge buildup during paper manufacturing in an atmosphere filled with paper fibers or dust
- static electricity building up on a person. An electric spark is created when reaching to touch tools that are electrically grounded.

Consequences

Potential consequences of static electricity include:
- electrical shock
- electrocution
- fires and explosions caused by the ignition of flammable gases, vapors, dusts, or fibers

Controls

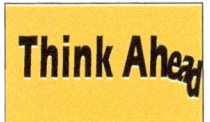

Controls you can use to reduce the risk of harm from static electricity include:
- Before loading, unloading, transferring, or sampling flammable or combustible liquids from transport tankers, ground equipment and pipes containing the liquids.
- In areas where fuels, solvents, or flammable liquids are dispensed into a smaller container, use metal bonding straps to ground tanks, drums, or metal buckets.
- Do **not** dispense hydrocarbon liquids into plastic buckets because the buckets cannot be grounded.

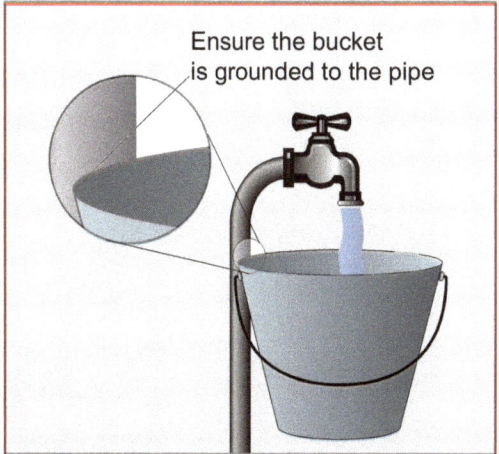

Ensure the bucket is grounded to the pipe

- When fuelling vehicles, take care to prevent fuel vapors from being ignited by a spark from static electricity. If the nozzle has been put in the hands-free operating position, before touching the nozzle, touch the pump housing or other grounded metal to discharge any static electricity that has built up on your body.
- Do **not** fill portable fuel containers in the back of a truck that has a plastic liner. A static charge can build up on the container and cause a spark when you replace the cap.
- When removing valves or blinds from a pipeline, install jumper cables across the gap to prevent the equipment from being isolated from the ground and to prevent the two sections of the pipeline from developing different electrical potentials.
- Before entering a building in which there is a potential for a flammable gas leak, touch a metal handrail or steel door frame to discharge any static electricity that may have built up on your body.
- Use sparkless hand tools (made of brass) in areas where flammable gases, vapors, dusts, or fibers are present.
- Before starting work in a hazardous area
  - obtain a work permit
  - use a gas detector to check combustible gas levels (%LEL) and oxygen concentrations in the atmosphere. Continue to monitor concentrations during the work.

6.3 What Can Go Wrong?

An important strategy to keep you and others from harm is to consider what can go wrong. For electricity, ask *What if... ?* questions about conditions, actions, and events that could occur and cause PEMEO to function poorly, behave abnormally, or fail. If there is a concern, determine the immediate effect.

The following table provides examples of using *What if...?* questions about what can go wrong with current and static electricity. Note that, in the examples, the worker may be performing a specific task or may be in the area that is affected.

What can go wrong with current and static electricity?		
Domain	What if…? *(conditions, actions, and events)*	Immediate effect
People	• What if I open the panel door to adjust the cathodic protection?	• I will be exposed to energized electrical wires.
	• What if a person slides out of the vehicle to remove the pump from the gas tank?	• The person could build up a strong static charge.
	• What if the wrong breakers are locked out?	• The electrical circuit to the equipment that maintenance people will be working on remains energized.
Equipment	• What if a large electric-driven pump tries to start at the same time the electrician is opening the breaker?	• The breaker could fail and continue to arc.
	• What if vibration wears and loosens electrical wires on a portable electric saw?	• The metal housing on the saw could become electrically energized.
	• What if the boom on the truck touches the overhead electrical line?	• The truck could become electrically energized.
Materials	• What if the electrical wire buried between the house and shed is not rated for underground use?	• The wire becomes weak over time and breaks.
	• What if the electrical copper wire lead has a nick?	• The wire could break at the lead and cause a fire.
Environment	• What if an electrical storm develops while gauging a tank?	• The gauger could get struck by lightning.
	• What if the electrical lines get covered with ice?	• The electrical lines could break and fall to the ground.
Organization	• What if the electrical utility company has an emergency shutdown?	• Only emergency power is available at the facility.
	• What if the company providing electrical service has not conducted routine condition checks of the electrical equipment?	• Some electrical switchgear could be overheating.

Having determined the possible immediate effects, you can ask additional questions:
- Could I or others become ill and/or injured?
- What should be my first response if an incident occurs?
- What can I do to minimize the possibility of an incident

occurring and the severity of the consequences should an incident occur?

For many of the incidents identified by the *What if...?* questions, your response will be more effective when you:
- pre-determine the best response
- rehearse your response by imagining responding to the incident. Rehearsing increases the possibility that you will respond immediately and effectively.

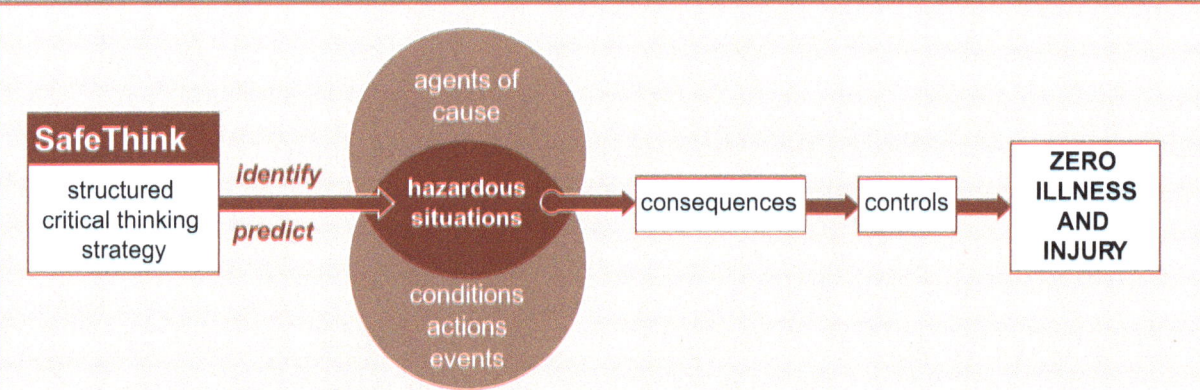

Using the SafeThink strategy

Is current or static electricity a factor in doing the work?

Certain conditions, actions, and events could expose you to electrical hazards. Whenever your work involves electricity, you need to determine whether or not you are at risk.

To determine if you are at risk, ask yourself the following critical thinking questions:
- What conditions, actions, and events could cause electrically-driven equipment to automatically start and harm me?
- What conditions, actions, and events could cause me to come in contact with current electricity?
- What conditions, actions, and events could create an electrical spark that could cause a fire or explosion?
- What can I do to prevent being harmed by current and static electricity?

With practice, when you think about the work or see electrical components and wiring or a potential source of static electricity in your workplace, you will automatically consider these questions. Answers to these questions help you determine if a hazardous situation exists or can be created.

Use the *SafeThink* strategy when you complete the learning activity for electricity.

Is current or static electricity a factor in doing the work? What conditions, actions, and events could cause current or static electricity to harm me?

This learning activity will help you learn to identify and predict conditions, actions, and events that make electricity hazardous to workers.

1. List two tasks that you perform in which current electricity may be encountered. For each task, identify the critical conditions, actions, or events that could result in:
   - electrically-driven equipment automatically starting and putting you at risk of being injured by moving parts
   - you receiving an electrical shock

Task	Conditions, Actions, Events
1.	
2.	

2. List two tasks that you perform in which static electricity may be encountered. For each task, identify the critical conditions, actions, or events that could result in static electricity causing a fire or explosion.

Task	Conditions, Actions, Events
1.	
2.	

To complete the remainder of this learning activity, break each task into its major steps. For each major step, think about the specific action steps and the associated conditions, actions, and events that could expose you or others to harm as a result of the presence of electricity.

# SafeThink

3. Select one of the tasks from questions 1 or 2. First, break the task into major steps; then complete questions 3a, 3b, and 3c.

Task _____

Major step 1 (before working) _____

Major step 2 (while working) _____

Major step 3 (while working) _____

Major step 4 (while working) _____

Major step 5 (while working) _____

Major step 6 (while working) _____

Major step 7 (after work is complete) _____

3a. Identify conditions, actions, and events involving current or static electricity that exist **before** doing the work that could cause harm to you or others. Identify possible controls to reduce the risk of an incident.

_____
_____
_____
_____

3b. Identify conditions, actions, and events involving current or static electricity that exist or develop **while** doing the work that could cause harm to you or others. Identify possible controls to reduce the risk of an incident.

_____
_____
_____
_____

3c. Identify conditions, actions, and events involving current or static electricity that exist **after** the work has been completed that could cause harm to you or _____

Part 6   Electricity

others. Identify possible controls to reduce the risk of an incident.

_____
_____
_____
_____

4. Select a task that involves current or static electricity:

   Task _____

4a. Ask *What if…?* questions to identify what can go wrong in relation to current or static electricity and fill in the table below. To focus your thinking, consider conditions, actions, and events associated with each PEMEO domain.

What can go wrong with current and static electricity?		
Domain	**What if…?** *(conditions, actions, and events)*	**Immediate Effect**
People		
Equipment		
Materials		
Environment		
Organization		

4b. From the table you have completed, select one effect that may create or lead to a hazardous situation and answer the following questions:

Could I or others become ill and/or injured? What would be the consequences?

_____
_____

What should be my first response if an incident occurs?

_____
_____
_____

What can I do to minimize the probability of an incident occurring and/or the severity of consequences?

_____
_____

The SafeThink Strategy

The *SafeThink* strategy to identify and predict hazardous situations caused by one category of hazard is as follows:

1. Identify the task.

2. Break the task into two to nine **general steps**.

3. Break **general step** 1 into **action steps**.

4. For each **action step**, ask the general *SafeThink* question for the specific category of hazard.

5. If you answer **yes** at step **4**, then ask *Are there any conditions, actions, and events that will lead to or create a hazardous situation?*

6. If you answer **yes** at step **5**, then ask the remainder of the follow-up questions and select effective controls.

7. Repeat steps **4**, **5**, and **6** for the remaining **action steps**.

8. Repeat steps **3** to **8** for each of the remaining general steps

Before starting work, apply the *SafeThink* strategy to the entire task (major steps and action steps) to prevent illness and injury. While working, focus on completing one major step at a time. Apply the *SafeThink* strategy before starting a general step and before carrying out each action step. Later in this book you will learn ways to make the thinking process more efficient.

Option

Many participants have found that writing helps them learn and remember the questions. Write the critical thinking questions for electricity in the box below. The questions are listed in the Job Aid.

FOOD for THOUGHT

■ The one-hand rule

The one-hand rule is useful for many hazardous situations besides working with electricity, for example, when working near hot surfaces, sharp or protruding objects, or moving parts. While you focus on the task, you may not be aware of what your free hand is doing—it could come in contact with an agent of cause. Under these conditions, sticking your free hand in your pocket prevents you from moving your free hand into the hazard zone.

■ The downside of intuition

Developing good habits is important for preventing illness and injury. When good habits become so automatic that you are not aware of the actions, the habit may not always serve you well:
- When performing pre-job hazard assessments and you rely on intuition, you may not be able to recall the potentially hazardous situation and explain the concern to others (i.e., if the behavior is subconscious, you may be unaware of what you know or do).
- When mentoring others, you may not be aware of your automatic safety actions and overlook telling the apprentices. The apprentices are then put in a position of learning by trial and error.
- If you have not applied the good habit for a long time, you could forget and be at risk of being harmed.

To maintain your safety habits and communication skills, you must become more aware of your good habits. When performing work, pay attention to how you carry out each action step so that you can identify and become aware of your subconscious safety behaviors.

■ **Person states**

Good safety habits or intuition can sometimes keep you out of harm's way at times when you are:
- experiencing strong emotions
- overconfident
- complacent
- rushed
- fatigued
- distracted

Under these personal states, your thinking can be impaired. If there are unexpected changes as well, the risk of illness or injury is even greater. Although good safety habits are helpful, do not assume they will always keep you out of harm's way.

Strong emotions such as joy, anger, and worry can prevent us from concentrating on the task at hand and from predicting hazardous situations. When you feel strong emotions, make it a warning to yourself to be even more vigilant in applying the *SafeThink* strategy to reduce the risk of injury. Before engaging in the work, try to calm down. Concentrate on the work, which will have a calming effect. If you feel you will putting be yourself and others at risk if you engage in the work, do not start working until you are in a more normal emotional state.

When people are overconfident, complacent, or bored they do not worry about potential dangers. They lose respect for the equipment and possibly that slight sense of fear they may have had when first performing the tasks. Their attention to the task at hand may diminish because an incident has not happened in the past. Unsafe behavior is even more serious. People who have gotten away with unsafe behaviors in the past without consequences believe they will be able to get away with it in the future too. A change in conditions or a lack of attention to the task can result in unfortunate consequences. Overconfidence can also result in incidents. When people are overconfident, they may not consider that conditions can change and may let their

attention wander. Correcting overconfidence and complacency can be difficult. Some people believe that a person must have an incident before there is a change in attitude. Corrective measures include:

- reinforcing the dangers associated with the equipment and tasks
- discussing safety incidents to heighten awareness of consequences. Be careful not to be overdramatic because some people may then deny that it can happen to them (a psychological defensive mechanism). The result will be no change in behavior.
- encouraging the use of *What if...?* questions
- encouraging the use of the *SafeThink* strategy
- having the person demonstrate the task and explain the hazardous situations and controls associated with the equipment and actions steps
- providing negative consequences when unsafe acts are performed
- providing positive consequences for a job well done

Being rushed can increase the potential for a safety incident. Rushing can cause incidents due to:

- not thinking each step through and making mistakes
- missing steps
- applying larger forces to get the work done faster, requiring better footing and strength (which may be lacking)
- applying larger forces which can cause tools and materials to fail
- failing coordination when moving faster than usual
- a tendency, when moving hands and body quickly, to go directly to the location and not circumvent objects in the way such as corners

Ways to reduce the risk of an incident when rushing include:

- reminding yourself that, when rushed, mistakes are more likely to happen and you increase the potential of putting yourself and others at risk of injury
- consciously slowing down
- concentrating on each step
- applying the *SafeThink* strategy

Fatigue can be caused by many factors including:
- long hours of work
- shift work
- strenuous work
- inadequate rest breaks
- lack of sleep
- monotonous or repetitive work
- information overload
- medications that act as sedatives
- poor health

When people are fatigued, the likelihood of injury increases due to a lack of attention, impaired judgment, or loss of strength and coordination. Rest periods and taking naps (especially if driving) can reduce fatigue. Caffeine and other stimulants are only short-term solutions. If you are fatigued and cannot adjust your work to compensate, you should discuss your concerns with others so that they can be more vigilant in watching out for you. Doing low risk tasks when fatigued may be a viable option. If fatigue is ongoing in the workplace, dialogue between workers and management is required to find ways to reduce the risk of incidents.

When distracted, you are not paying attention to the work at hand nor are you thinking about the work and potentially hazardous situations. Distractors include:
- sudden, loud noises
- movement of equipment and materials
- attention on what others are doing rather than on what you are doing
- talking to others while you are working
- talking on a cell phone
- thinking about personal issues or planned personal activities

The first line of defense is to be aware that you are being distracted and could get hurt. Only then can you take action to minimize the influence of the distractor. Using methods to remain vigilant and mentally engaged minimizes the effect that distractors can have on you.

 SafeThink™

■ Ways to remain vigilant and mentally engaged

Often people are told to be aware of their surroundings, think about safety, and focus on the work. However, people are often not told, shown, and given strategies to think about safety, be aware of their surroundings, and focus on their work. Using *SafeThink* and asking *What if...?* questions can help you to remain vigilant and to continually identify and predict hazardous situations. There are other strategies to remain mentally engaged. My three favorite strategies are:

- pretend demonstrating the task. When working alone, to maintain focus on the work, I pretend that I am showing someone how to do the task effectively, efficiently, and safely. The act of demonstrating requires focusing on critical issues affecting PEMEO—resulting in being mentally engaged and thinking ahead.
- practice. When I am doing routine activities, especially when driving, I practice to maintain my skills. I focus on the skill of handling the vehicle, following regulations, being courteous, and anticipating what others might do. Practicing keeps me mentally engaged and focused on my driving.
- friendly competition. When Elaine, my wife, and I take out-of-town trips, we compete as to who is driving the best. Comparison criteria include: holding the vehicle in the center of the lane on the straight of way and around corners; going around curves with the minimal correction to the steering to give the passenger the most comfort; and predicting what other drivers might do. The competition focuses on self-assessment so the feedback from the other person is friendly. A little modest bragging adds interest.

Part 7
Radiation

Is radiation present when doing the work?

What conditions, actions, and events could expose me to excessive radiation?

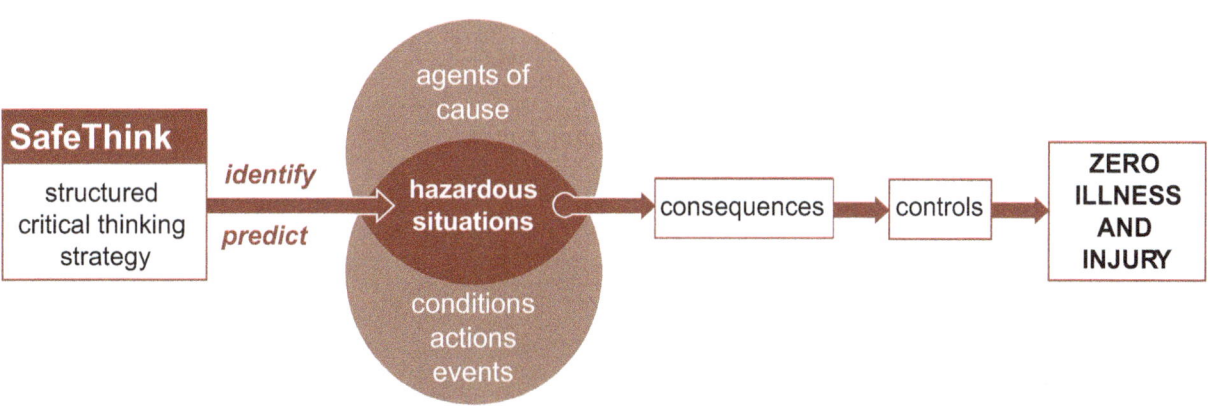

Training Objectives

Upon completion of this part, you will be able to identify and predict conditions, actions, and events that could make radiation hazardous to workers.

- Identify ionizing radiation in your workplace
- Identify the harm the ionizing radiation can cause
- Identify non-ionizing radiation in your workplace
- Identify the harm the non-ionizing radiation can cause
- Identify the harm ultrasound can cause
- Identify the conditions, actions, and events in your workplace that could cause you to be exposed to excessive radiation
- To prevent being exposed to excessive radiation, identify precautions that could be taken:
  - before starting a task
  - during the task
  - after the task is complete

The SafeThink Strategy		
Part	Category of hazard	Critical thinking question
Part 3	Hazardous Materials	Does the work involve hazardous materials?
Part 4	Objects, Motion, Force	Does the work involve objects, motion, or force that could cause harm?
Part 5	Non-Ambient Conditions	Does the work involve non-ambient conditions that could cause harm?
Part 6	Electricity	Is current or static electricity a factor in doing the work?
Part 7	**Radiation**	**Is radiation present when doing the work?**
Part 8	Changes	Could changes lead to or create a hazardous situation?

A learning activity at the end of Part 7 helps you apply your learning about radiation to your work and workplace. The goal is to identify the conditions, actions, and events which lead to hazardous situations involving radiation.

7 Radiation

Workers can be exposed to:
- ionizing radiation
- non-ionizing radiation

The following illustration shows the types of radiation in the electromagnetic spectrum.

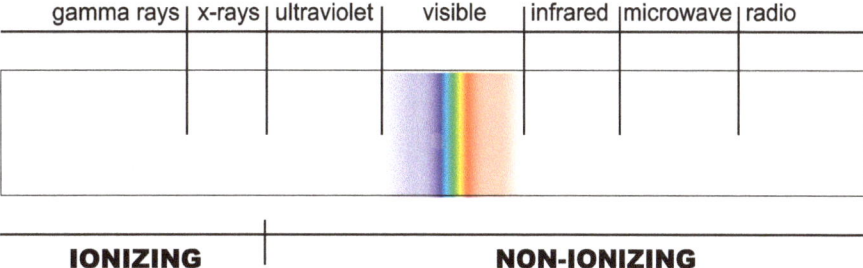

7.1 Ionizing Radiation

Ionizing radiation (e.g., X-rays) is very high-frequency energy that travels through space. Ionizing radiation is present:
- at workplaces where radioactive ores are handled
- at industrial workplaces that use radiation equipment

Ionizing radiation causes atoms and molecules in the human body to give up electrons to form ions. The ions are chemically reactive and can disrupt the natural chemical processes within cells and potentially damage DNA. A radiation symbol must be displayed wherever an ionizing radiation source is present. If any device at your workplace has this symbol, ask your supervisor to explain the safety precautions you should take.

You cannot see, hear, taste, smell, or feel ionizing radiation, and the effects of overexposure may not be obvious right away. The effect of ionizing radiation on your health depends on the type of radiation you receive. Five types of ionizing radiation are gamma, X-rays, neutron, alpha, and beta.

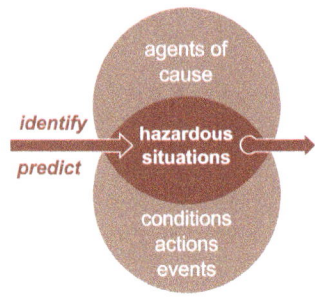

Gamma radiation

Gamma rays are used:
- in cancer treatment
- for brain and body scans
- to sterilize medical equipment
- in non-destructive testing and inspection of pipeline welds, metal tubulars (e.g., drill pipe), metal castings, and concrete
- to measure soil density and moisture
- to gauge the thickness of metals
- to measure and control the flow of liquids in industrial processes
- to ensure the proper fill level for packages of food, drugs and other products

Gamma radiation can penetrate your body, but as long as your exposure is within the safe limit, the radiation is unlikely to cause damage to internal organs and tissues. Excessive exposure can cause hair loss, genetic mutations to cells, cancer growth, and immune system suppression.

X-rays

X-rays are very similar to gamma rays and are used in many of the same applications. X-rays can penetrate your body but, as long as your exposure is within the safe limit, are unlikely to cause damage to internal organs and tissues. Excessive exposure can cause hair loss, genetic mutations to cells, cancer growth, and immune system suppression.

Neutrons

Neutrons, which are part of an atom's nucleus, become unstable under certain conditions and emit beta particles as they disintegrate. Measurement devices which contain a neutron source are used to measure the density and moisture content of soils. If you ingest neutrons, they can damage your internal organs.

Alpha particles

Alpha particles are emitted from radioactive sources and consist of two protons and two neutrons (the same as the nucleus of a helium atom).

Alpha particles are used:
- to treat cancer
- to eliminate static electricity in paper mills and other industries
- in smoke detectors

Alpha particles travel only a few centimeters (inches) through the air and cannot penetrate very thin shields (e.g., a piece of paper). Alpha particles do not pose a radiation hazard unless they enter your eyes or open wounds or you ingest or inhale them.

Internal exposure to alpha particles is not likely to cause immediate health effects. Excessive exposure over a prolonged period may damage internal tissues (including DNA), bone marrow, and the immune system. The risk of cancer also increases.

Beta particles

Beta particles are sub-atomic particles that are emitted from the nucleus during decay of radioactive materials. They are about the size of an electron and can have either a positive or negative charge.

Beta particles are used in:
- the treatment of thyroid disorders
- molecular biology and genetics research
- medical and agricultural studies
- luminous signs, dials, gauges, and wrist watches
- industrial thickness gauges

Beta particles can travel slightly farther than alpha particles but a thin shield (e.g., a sheet of aluminum or a layer of skin) can effectively stop beta particles. If you are exposed to excessive beta radiation, you may sustain burns to your skin or damage to your eyes or open wounds. Tissue damage can result from ingestion or inhalation of beta particles.

Potential effects of internal exposure to beta particles over time include damage to internal tissues (including DNA), bone marrow, and the immune system. The risk of cancer also increases.

Naturally Occurring Radioactive Material (NORM)

Radioactive sources such as uranium, thorium, potassium, radium, and radon occur naturally in nearly all rocks, soils, and water. The processing of raw materials can cause NORM to become concentrated in the scale formed:
- inside pipes
- in sludge that collects at the bottom of vessels
- in pipeline pig traps

NORM is also present at workplaces where phosphate is processed to make fertilizer. The radioactivity level of NORM varies depending on the geology and the industrial activity. Generally, NORM radioactivity levels are very low. For example, the radioactivity level in a nuclear gauge may be a billion times greater than the radioactivity level of NORM.

When NORM is suspected, samples must be taken for testing to a laboratory with highly sensitive equipment. If NORM is a concern at a facility, the company establishes site-specific policies for material handling, storage, and disposal. The goal is to keep workers' exposure to radiation as low as reasonably achievable (ALARA).

To protect against excessive exposure to NORM:
- wear protective clothing including gloves, boots, and safety eyewear
- use an air purifying respirator rated for radioactive particulates
- ventilate the area if excessive concentrations of radon gas may be present; if ventilation is not possible, use a supplied air respirator

Controls for ionizing radiation hazards

Workplaces that use ionizing radiation sources are regulated and inspected by government agencies. Workers who use radiation equipment wear film badges, pocket dosimeters, or other devices to monitor their exposure. Other controls depend on the source of the radioactive material and the application.

Ionizing radiation hazard controls fall into three categories:
- *time* controls—minimizing the exposure time. The dose of

radiation received is directly related to exposure time. For example, reducing the exposure time by half will cut the dose received in half.
- *distance* controls—maintaining a safe distance from the radioactive source. For example, when possible, facilities are designed so that operations involving radioactive materials are carried out in a separate wing of the main building or in a separate building on the site.
- *shielding* controls—placing a dense material such as lead between the radiation source and the worker. For example:
  – X-ray equipment has shutters and shielding to ensure that radiation emissions are within specified limits when the machine is not being used
  – X-ray rooms have lead shields inside the walls; the X-ray technician goes outside the shielded room before turning on the X-ray machine
  – a lead blanket is placed on the patient before dental X-rays are taken to minimize patient exposure

If you work with materials or equipment that emits ionizing radiation, you must receive specialized training in radiation safety. Controls you can routinely use to prevent excessive exposure include:
- Do not use or store food, beverages, cigarettes, or cosmetics in the area.
- Wear the protective clothing and footwear provided.
- Wear your dosimeter.
- Plan all procedures for handling radioactive materials carefully.
- If you handle radioactive liquids:
  – do **not** pipette radioactive solutions by mouth
  – cover workbench surfaces with an absorbent material and change it often
  – use a spill tray when transferring large volumes of liquids between containers
- Label radioactive materials and wastes and use designated containers to dispose of radioactive wastes.
- On farms, where portable X-ray equipment is being used, keep pregnant women and children away from the X-ray area.

- Do not take apart or let pets play with used smoke detectors.
- Follow your company's procedures for decontaminating your hands, clothing, and work area when the work is complete and/or your shift is finished.

7.2 Non-Ionizing Radiation

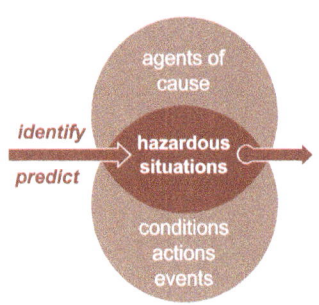

Non-ionizing radiation includes:
- ultraviolet radiation
- infrared radiation
- microwaves
- radio waves
- extremely low frequency radiation

Ultraviolet radiation

Ultraviolet (UV) radiation sources include:
- direct sunlight
- fluorescent lights
- germicidal lamps
- electric welding arcs
- black lights. Black lights are used in blueprinting, laundry mark identification, instrument panel lighting, crime detection, photoengraving, and for air, food, and water supply sterilization.
- fixed gas and flame detection systems. Some systems use ultraviolet light sources for detection.

Safety and health effects from exposure to intense or ongoing doses of UV radiation sources include:
- eye damage (e.g., during welding, from looking at the arc and from flashes off nearby walls)
- sunburn and skin damage, including skin cancer. Note that workers can become more sensitive to UV radiation (photosensitivity) when certain:
  - prescription drugs are used (e.g., drugs that control blood pressure)
  - chemical vapors are present (e.g., coal tars, creosote)
  - plant materials are handled (e.g., celery)
- occupants of a vehicle can get sunburned if the sun is shining intensely through side windows or the back

window. Provide shading or rotate the position of the occupants to prevent excessive exposure.
- phosgene gas exposure. Phosgene gas is a poisonous gas produced when UV radiation contacts chlorinated hydrocarbon vapors. Phosgene gas may be present in shops where cleaning and degreasing solvents are used near welding operations.

Phosgene gas

Phosgene gas (CCl_2O) and hydrochloric acid (HCl) can form when chlorinated hydrocarbons are exposed to intense ultraviolet light from welding arcs, bright sunlight, and molten metals. Examples of chlorinated hydrocarbons include solvents such as carbon tetrachloride, trichloroethane, methylene chloride, and perchloro-ethylene (PERC). Some washing solvents, degreasers, adhesives, metal coatings, and paints may contain chlorinated hydrocarbons.

Phosgene is very toxic (8 Hour Exposure Limit is 0.1 ppm). The gas tends to settle in low areas/breathing zone because it is 3.4 times heavier than air. Effects are often delayed for five or six hours. In the lungs, phosgene gas reacts with moisture to form hydrochloric acid. Symptoms of exposure include dizziness, coughing, cramps, and vomiting. Exposure to phosgene gas can cause permanent eye and lung damage and death.

Controls used to prevent exposure to phosgene gas include:
- Remove chlorinated hydrocarbon vapors from tanks and piping before welding. Removal methods include purging, flushing, steam cleaning, and washing.
- Do not weld within 65 metres (200 feet) of parts washers and tanks containing chlorinated hydrocarbons.
- Use local ventilation instead of general ventilation. General ventilation such as opening doors and windows may cause the gas to spread through the area.
- Use shielding to minimize the UV field.
- Provide PPE for the welder and others working in the area.

Controls to prevent exposure to UV radiation in the vicinity of welding operations include:
- Provide welding goggles/helmets with UV filters rated for the type of work being done.
- Screen welding operations (use either permanent or portable screens) to protect the eyes of nearby workers.

Controls you can use to protect your eyes and skin from UV radiation emitted by the sun and artificial light sources include:
- If you work outside, protect your skin from excessive sun exposure (wear a hat and protective clothing and use sunscreen on exposed skin) and wear sunglasses with UV-blocking filters to protect your eyes.
- If you use prescription lenses (e.g., for distance, reading, computer work), ask your optometrist to provide lenses with UV-blocking filters.

Infrared radiation

Infrared (IR) radiation can be created by heating metals and glass to high temperatures. IR radiation is used in industrial applications such as:
- drying and baking paints, lacquers, inks, coatings, adhesives
- heating metal parts for shrink fit assembly, forging, thermal aging, brazing, and surface conditioning
- dehydrating textiles, paper, leather, meat, and vegetables
- drying clay and sand products and molds
- space heaters
- fixed gas and fire detection systems. Some systems use infrared sources for detection.

Infrared radiation heats the surfaces it contacts but does not heat the surrounding air. Depending on the wavelength, dose, and duration, excessive exposure to infrared radiation can damage or burn your skin and eyes.

Controls you can use if your work involves IR sources include the following:
- Use the recommended PPE (eyewear, face shields, and skin protection).

- Stay a safe distance away from the IR source and do not stare directly at the IR source (refer to the manufacturer's recommendations).
- Keep combustible materials and clothing a safe distance away from IR space heaters.

Radio Waves (including microwaves)

Radio waves are used for communications (e.g., radios, television, cellular phones, and radar), and for industrial heating applications such as:
- hardening cutting tools and bearing surfaces
- soldering and brazing
- sterilizing containers
- molding plastics
- curing and vulcanizing rubber
- thermosealing
- cooking

Microwaves are used for communication and in medical applications, food processing, freeze-drying and wood gluing. If human tissues are exposed to excessive doses of microwave energy, they become very hot and can be irreversibly damaged.

All microwave and radio equipment must be equipped with protective shielding/seals. The device should be checked periodically to make sure the shielding/seals are effective.

Legislation sets exposure limits for workers exposed to microwave or radio frequency waves. If you work with equipment that emits microwaves or radio waves, follow your site safe work procedures to prevent excessive exposure.

Lasers

Lasers have many applications, including communications, modifying materials, controlling processes, aligning components, surveying, and medical procedures. Lasers produce extremely high-intensity light beams that can cause irreversible eye injuries and severe skin burns. Secondary hazards of lasers include electrical shock, toxins produced when target materials are vaporized, and (in gas lasers) buildup of high pressures. The low-temperature gases,

solvents, and flammable materials used with some lasers are also hazardous.

If you work with or near laser equipment, you should receive specialized training in laser safety and your company should have written safe work procedures. Follow your company's safe work procedures and take these precautions:

- Use protective eyewear that is appropriate for the intensity of the beam.
- Do not look directly at the beam.
- Minimize your exposure (e.g., turn off the laser when it is not being used).
- Make sure that hazard warnings are posted in the vicinity of the laser equipment.
- Communicate with your co-workers to make sure they know when the laser equipment is operating.
- Have regular medical examinations (including eye exams).
- Shield combustible solvents from the laser beam.

Strong magnetic fields

Strong magnetic fields have a variety of industrial and medical applications such as:

- transfer of rail containers
- separation and transport of scrap metal
- removal of metal fragments from feedstock (e.g., wood chips)
- internal inspection of pipelines for corrosion and anomalies
- analysis of oil and gas well formations
- diagnosis of human body conditions (magnetic resonance imaging)

Potential hazards associated with strong magnetic fields include:

- interference with bioelectronic devices such as pacemakers
- movement of metallic implants in the human body (e.g., wires, pins, screws, clips, and plates) and metal fragments (e.g., in the eye). Movement of metal implants and fragments can rupture blood vessels and damage tissues.
- interference with electronic equipment such as digital watches and gas detectors

- destruction of coded information on magnetic storage devices, security cards, and credit cards
- strong attraction of loose metal objects (e.g., tools, bolts, and steel cuttings), causing the objects to "fly" and strike people or equipment in their path
- if a direct current magnetic field suddenly collapses (a quench), strong electrical currents (eddy currents) are produced in electrically conducted materials. The heat from the eddy currents can destroy the insulation on electrical wires. The exposed electrical wires, including lead wires, can short out causing sparks or fire and expose unprotected personnel to electrically energized circuits.

Controls you can use if you work in the vicinity of strong magnetic fields include:
- Post warning signs restricting access to the magnetic hazard area.
- Do not enter the magnetic hazard area if you:
  - have bioelectronic devices or metal implants in your body
  - possibly have metal fragments in your eyes or skin
- Keep electronic equipment, magnetic storage devices, and magnetic cards away from the magnetic hazard area.
- Keep loose metal tools and parts away from the magnetic hazard area.
- If metal tools and parts must be used in the magnetic hazard area, keep the tools and parts between you and the magnet (i.e., stay out of the *fly path*).
- If a quench occurs, follow your company's emergency response procedures.

7.3 Ultrasound

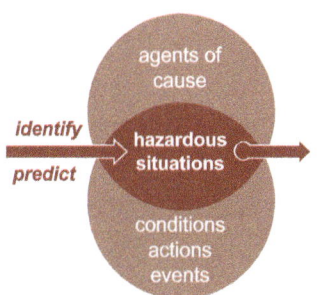

Sound is not part of the electromagnetic spectrum but is classified under radiation by occupational health and safety. Ultrasound includes frequencies above 20,000 Hertz. These frequencies are higher than the hearing range of humans.

Ultrasound is used in medical, dental, and industrial applications, including:
- diagnostic imaging (e.g., to check for fetal abnormalities during pregnancy, to check integrity of welded metals)

- therapeutic and medical procedures (to relieve muscle pain, break up kidney stones)
- cleaning and degreasing instruments, electronic equipment, parts and components, jewelry, and optical lenses
- bonding plastics
- brazing, soldering, and welding metals
- machining (abrasive grinding, drilling)
- mixing and homogenizing liquids, slurries, and creams
- atomizing (e.g., for humidification, to improve fuel combustion efficiency)
- defoaming and degassing liquids and slurries
- electroplating
- drying heat-sensitive materials (e.g., pharmaceuticals)
- measuring flow and level of liquids and slurries

Potential hazards associated with high levels of ultrasound include:
- contact hazard: immersing your hand in the bath of an operating ultrasonic humidifier can cause immediate pain, likely due to overheating of finger bones
- airborne hazard: exposure to excessive ultrasound can damage your hearing; some people experience headaches, dizziness, and nausea when working in the vicinity of ultrasonic equipment for prolonged periods.

To prevent being harmed by excessive exposure to ultrasound:
- Post hazard warnings in the vicinity of ultrasonic equipment, and ensure workers are aware of the potential hazards.
- Restrict access to areas where ultrasonic equipment is operating. Keep children away, because children are more noise-sensitive than adults. If you experience adverse effects from ultrasound, minimize your exposure.
- Develop safe work procedures for operating ultrasonic equipment, particularly if there is potential for contact exposure.
- Wear hearing protection in the vicinity of high-level ultrasonic equipment; although you cannot hear the

sound, excessive exposure can contribute to hearing loss. Include ultrasonic equipment in your company's hearing conservation program and monitor ultrasound levels to ensure worker exposure is within the recommended Occupational Exposure Limits.
- Use only the recommended gels and cleaning agents (e.g., never use hydrocarbon-based solvents in ultrasonic parts washers, because the resulting vapors can ignite. Use the recommended water-based solvent.)

7.4 What Can Go Wrong?

An important strategy to keep you and others from harm is to consider what can go wrong. For radiation, ask *What if... ?* questions about conditions, actions, and events that could occur and cause PEMEO to function poorly, behave abnormally, or fail. If there is a concern, determine the immediate effect.

The following table provides examples of using *What if... ?* questions about what can go wrong with radiation. Note that in the examples, the worker may be performing a specific task or may be in the area that is affected.

What can go wrong with radiation?		
Domain	What if…? *(conditions, actions, and events)*	Immediate effect
People	• What if I reach under an infrared heater that is being used to bake paint?	• My clothing and skin will become hot.
	• What if I help the welder?	• Exposed skin on my neck will get burned from the ultraviolet light.
	• What if I get in the path of the laser light used to measure distances?	• My eyes could be exposed to the laser light.

(continued)

What can go wrong with radiation?		
Domain	What if…? *(conditions, actions, and events)*	Immediate effect
Equipment	• What if the radioactive source is larger than expected?	• The radiation dose will be higher.
	• What if the toluene drum leaks and vapors migrate to the welding area?	• Toxic phosgene gas may be produced.
	• What if the forklift hits a gauge that contains a radioactive source?	• The housing for the radioactive source could get damaged.
Materials	• What if the material I work with is combustible and I am working close to an infrared heater?	• The material could catch fire.
	• What if I am working beside a shiny metal wall exposed to the sun?	• My eyes could get injured from the glare.
Environment	• What if the sludge from the pipe contains NORM?	• Radiation would be present in the immediate area.
Organization	• What if a crew is examining the equipment in my area with X-rays?	• X-rays could be present in the immediate area.
	• What if a crew is using a special pipe inspection tool that has a strong magnet to examine the condition of the piping?	• Loose metal objects could be drawn towards the magnet.

Having determined the possible immediate effects, you can ask additional questions:
- Could I or others become ill and/or injured?
- What should be my first response if an incident occurs?
- What can I do to minimize the possibility of an incident occurring and the severity of the consequences should an incident occur?

For many of the incidents identified by the *What if… ?* questions, your response will be more effective when you:
- pre-determine the best response
- rehearse your response by imagining responding to the incident. Rehearsing increases the possibility that you will respond immediately and effectively.

Part 7 Radiation

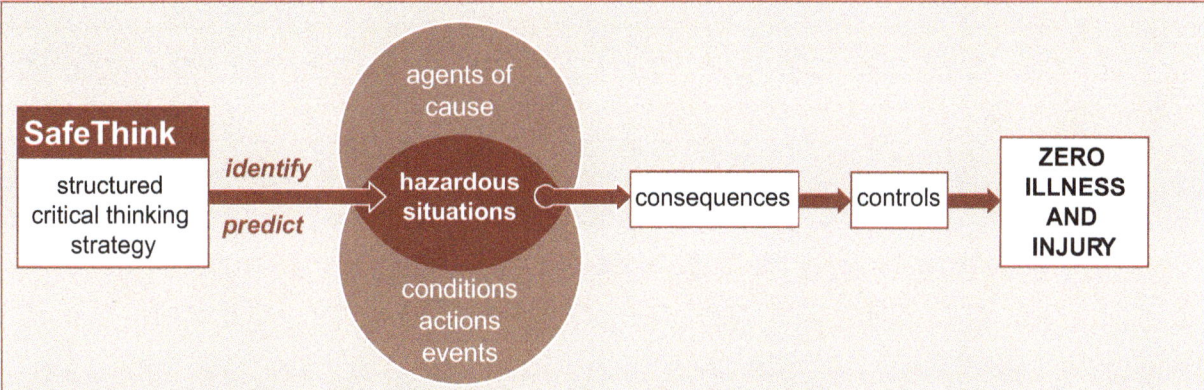

Using the SafeThink strategy

Is radiation present when doing the work?

Whenever your work involves radiation, you need to determine whether or not you are at risk.

To determine if you are at risk, ask yourself the following critical thinking questions:
- What type of radiation is involved?
- What type of harm does the radiation pose?
- What conditions, actions, and events could expose me to excessive radiation?
- What can I do to prevent being exposed to excessive radiation?

With practice, when you think about the work or see sources of ionizing or non-ionizing radiation in your workplace, you will automatically consider these questions to determine if a hazardous situation exists or can be created.

Use the *SafeThink* strategy when you complete the learning activity.

Is radiation present when doing the work? What conditions, actions, and events could expose me to excessive radiation?

This learning activity will help you learn to identify and predict conditions, actions, and events that make radiation hazardous to workers.

1. On the next page, identify the types of ionizing radiation in your workplace. Describe some precautions you can take to prevent excessive exposure to ionizing radiation.

_____
_____
_____
_____
_____

2. List two tasks or activities that you perform that could expose you to ionizing radiation. For each task or activity, identify the most critical conditions, actions, or events that could place you in danger of being harmed by the radiation.

Task	Conditions, Actions, Events
1.	
2.	

To complete question 3, break each task into its major steps. For each major step, think about the specific action steps and the associated conditions, actions, and events that could expose you or others to excessive amounts of ionizing radiation.

3. Select a task that could expose you or others to ionizing radiation. First, break the task into major steps; then complete questions 3a, 3b, and 3c.

   Task _____

   Major step 1 (before working) _____

   Major step 2 (while working) _____

   Major step 3 (while working) _____

   Major step 4 (while working) _____

   Major step 5 (while working) _____

   Major step 6 (while working) _____

   Major step 7 (after work is complete) _____

3a. Identify conditions, actions, and events involving ionizing radiation that exist **before** doing the work that could cause harm to you or others. Identify possible controls to prevent exposure. Note that, for some tasks, radiation is not present before doing the task and exposure to radiation only occurs while doing the task. Before doing the task, your most important activities are to predict hazardous situations that will occur while performing the task and to select controls that will prevent you and others from being exposed to excessive radiation.

_____
_____
_____
_____
_____

3b. Identify conditions, actions, and events involving ionizing radiation that exist or develop **while** doing the work that could cause harm to you or others. Identify possible controls to prevent exposure.

_____
_____
_____
_____
_____

3c. Identify conditions, actions, and events involving ionizing radiation that exist **after** the work has been completed that could cause harm to you or others. Identify possible controls to prevent exposure.

_____
_____
_____
_____

4. Identify the types of non-ionizing radiation in your workplace. Describe the precautions you can take to prevent excessive exposure to each type of non-ionizing radiation you identified.

_____
_____
_____
_____
_____

To complete question 5, break each task into its major steps. For each major step, think about the specific action steps and the associated conditions, actions, and events that could expose you or others to harm as a result of the presence of non-ionizing radiation.

5. Select a task that could expose you or others to non-ionizing radiation. First, break the task into major steps; then complete questions 5a, 5b, and 5c.

   Task _____

   Major step 1 (before working) _____

   Major step 2 (while working) _____

   Major step 3 (while working) _____

   Major step 4 (while working) _____

   Major step 5 (while working) _____

   Major step 6 (while working) _____

   Major step 7 (after work is complete) _____

5a. Identify conditions, actions, and events involving non-ionizing radiation that exist **before** doing the work that could cause harm to you or others. Identify possible controls to prevent exposure. Note that, for some tasks, radiation is not present before doing the task and exposure to radiation only occurs while doing the task. Before doing the task, your most important activity is to predict hazardous situations that will occur while performing the task and to select controls that will prevent you and others from being exposed to excessive radiation.

_____
_____
_____
_____
_____

5b. Identify conditions, actions, and events involving non-ionizing radiation that exist or develop **while** doing the work that could cause harm to you or others. Identify possible controls to prevent exposure.

_____
_____
_____
_____

5c. Identify conditions, actions, and events involving non-ionizing radiation that exist **after** the work has been completed that could cause harm to you or others. Identify possible controls to prevent exposure.

_____
_____
_____
_____
_____

6. Name a task that involves radiation: _____

6a. On the next page, ask *What if... ?* questions to identify what can go wrong in relation to radiation and fill in the table below. To focus your thinking, consider conditions, actions, and events associated with each PEMEO domain.

What can go wrong with radiation?		
Domain	What if . . . ? (conditions, actions, and events)	Immediate effect
People		
Equipment		
Materials		
Environment		
Organization		

6b. From the table you have completed, select one effect that may create or lead to a hazardous situation and answer the following questions:

Could I or others become ill and/or injured? What would be the consequences?

_____
_____

What should be my first response if an incident occurs?

_____
_____

What can I do to minimize the probability of an incident occurring and/or the severity of consequences?

_____
_____

Part 7 Radiation

Option

Many participants have found that writing helps them learn and remember the questions. Write the critical thinking questions for radiation in the box below. The questions are listed in the Job Aid.

FOOD for THOUGHT

■ Harmful effects from electrical devices

There is controversy about the harmful effects of electro-magnetic fields generated by electrical devices such as:
- cell phones
- microwave ovens
- heating blankets
- high voltage electrical lines

If you have any concerns about the potential of hazardous effects from these devices, investigate the research so that you can make an informed judgment. If you use the internet to gather information, make sure that the sources are credible.

■ Mentoring others on the use of generalities

Generalities are powerful in keeping people out of harm's way. It is no longer acceptable for workers to learn generalities through experience. If you are mentoring others, you can reduce their risk of illness and injury by coaching them about generalities before they engage in the work or personal activities. Here are some suggestions for mentoring about generalities:

- Explain that a safety strategy called *SafeThink* is a practical way for people to prevent illness and injury. Emphasize that the strategy focuses on thinking and not on memorizing a great amount of information.
- Explain that a generality is a principle or concept that holds true for many different situations. Provide one or two examples of generalities (e.g., all hot objects can potentially burn, sharp objects can cause cuts). Explain that people often create generalities through experience or as a result of learning large amounts of information (e.g., while taking a course).
- Emphasize that using generalities makes identifying hazardous situations effective and efficient and can be used at work, at home, while driving, or at play.

- Identify the six categories of hazard as generalities of agents of cause. The six categories provide a framework for learning specific health and safety information efficiently. Providing a framework at the beginning of a learning process can improve long-term retention by as much as 25%.
- Identify any generalities about agents of cause that may be specific to the discipline or trade and make a point of identifying them before the person engages in the work. For each generality, provide lots of work and non-work examples. By doing so, you help that person improve his or her comprehension and give meaning to the generality.
- Point out the importance of framing the six categories of hazard as questions because asking questions of oneself helps you to remain mentally engaged in the work. Asking yourself questions tends to beg answers, answers that can prevent illness or injury.
- Explain that conditions, actions, and events in the workplace and personal environments can interact with agents of cause to create a hazardous situation. Show the two overlapping circles (agents of cause; conditions, actions, and events). Provide examples.
- Describe the basic *SafeThink* strategy (ask the six general questions about agents of cause and the three generic questions to identify a hazardous situation and the consequences, and select practical controls).
- Encourage the person you are mentoring to learn and practice using the six general questions and three generic questions.
- Encourage the person to ask questions if he or she has any doubt about doing work safely and effectively. You do not want that person to learn by trial and error—the consequences can be unfortunate and preventable.

Part 8
Changes

Could changes lead to or create a hazardous situation?

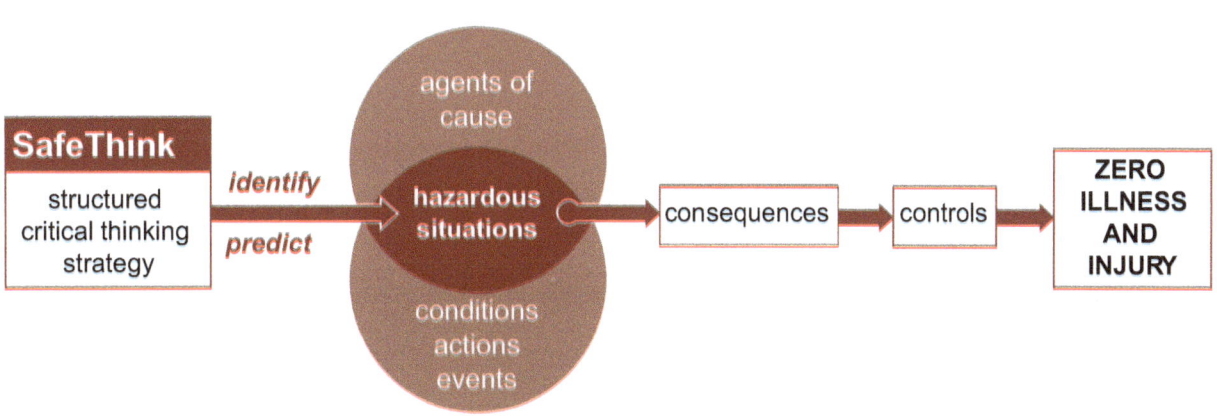

Training Objectives	Upon completion of this part, you will be able to identify and predict changes in conditions, actions, and events that could lead to or create a hazardous situation.

- Identify changes in your workplace that could cause hazardous situations that are initiated by:
  - workers (e.g., operators and maintenance)
  - technology
  - external sources
- Identify potential consequences of hazardous situations created by changes in the workplace
- To prevent changes in conditions, actions, and events that could lead to or create a hazardous situation, identify precautions that could be taken:
  - before starting a task
  - during the task
  - after the task is complete

The SafeThink Strategy		
Part	**Category of hazard**	**Critical thinking question**
Part 3	Hazardous Materials	Does the work involve hazardous materials?
Part 4	Objects, Motion, Force	Does the work involve objects, motion, or force that could cause harm?
Part 5	Non-Ambient Conditions	Does the work involve non-ambient conditions that could cause harm?
Part 6	Electricity	Is current or static electricity a factor in doing the work?
Part 7	Radiation	Is radiation present when doing the work?
Part 8	**Changes**	**Could changes lead to or create a hazardous situation?**

A learning activity at the end of Part 8 helps you apply your learning about changes that can lead to or create a hazardous situation in your workplace. The goal is to identify the conditions, actions, and events which lead to hazardous situations involving changes.

8 Changes

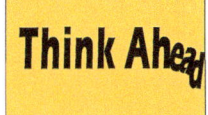

With proper controls, specific categories of hazards may not be hazardous. However, a change in conditions, workers' actions, or events can lead to or create a situation that is hazardous. Often, a hazardous situation is caused by a combination of conditions, actions, and events. To be safe, you must be vigilant of your work environment to identify hazardous situations. It is also important for your safety (and others) that you can predict changes and determine if the changes could lead to or create hazardous situations.

There are two types of changes: predictable and unpredictable. Changes, especially events, are often predictable because:
- they are planned as part of carrying out a work assignment (e.g., a crane will be used to lift an air conditioning unit onto the roof of a building; once a month, the production train is shut down for two hours for routine maintenance)
- historical evidence that the event has occurred before suggests that the event may occur again (e.g., records show that one out of ten shipments of raw feed stock to a mill contains undesirable foreign materials; every 500 hours filter F3 becomes plugged)

A change, especially an event, is often not predicted because:
- no one had thought about it
- the likelihood of the event occurring was considered very low (e.g., lightning causes a fire in a manufacturing facility; an arsonist starts a fire in a log pile)
- the equipment is normally very reliable
- workers who will be affected by a planned event are not informed that the event will take place. For these workers, the event is unpredicted.

Changes in the workplace, especially planned changes, may not be inherently hazardous. However, a combination of planned and unplanned conditions, actions, and events could lead to or create a hazardous situation. An example in Part 2 (see page 19) identified an event—a plumber using a torch to make repairs. The work is probably not very hazardous.

However, when the container of flammable materials was spilled close to the open flame, a hazardous situation was created.

To be safe in a changing work environment, you must do three things:

1. You must identify changes:
   - watch for changes
   - predict changes

2. You must determine if the changes could lead to or create a hazardous situation.

3. You must take action to either:
   - reduce or eliminate the probability of the hazardous situation occurring
   - minimize or eliminate the severity of consequences (e.g., wear protective equipment)

Part 9 of this book provides suggestions about planning work to prevent and control potentially hazardous situations.

Changes that lead to or create hazardous situations can be initiated by:
- workers
- technology
- external sources

8.1 Worker-Initiated Changes

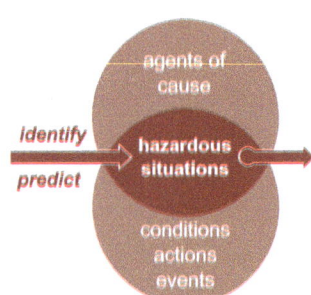

At many workplaces, two groups of workers initiate many of the changes:
- operators who monitor and control equipment
- maintenance workers who monitor, maintain, and repair the equipment

When facilities are being modified, upgraded, or shut down for inspection and maintenance (turnarounds), operators and maintenance workers may have extra responsibilities for ensuring that work activities are carried out safely. During turnarounds, the number of work activities and the number of workers at a site can increase dramatically. The increased level of activity increases the likelihood of hazardous situations developing. The increased number of workers from outside the company (e.g., contracted workers) on site can also increase the likelihood of a hazardous situation developing. Contracted workers who are not familiar with the facility layout, technology, operations, work activities, and safety procedures may make poor decisions and take actions that create hazardous situations. Careful planning, coordination of activities, supervision, good communication, and ongoing hazard identification and control are critical to workplace safety.

8.1.1 Operator-Initiated Changes

Operator-initiated changes include:
- performing pre-start equipment checks in which specific equipment or components in a system are temporarily started or operated to ensure proper functioning
- starting equipment and systems
- starting tasks that involve equipment operation or movement of materials
- adjusting equipment for rate and quality requirements
- switching, stopping, or starting equipment in response to changes in production rates, abnormal equipment operation, or external sources
- shutting down equipment and systems
- conducting routine equipment maintenance

Whenever equipment is started, adjusted, or stopped, there is a possibility that someone (the operator or another worker) could be exposed to energized equipment (e.g., rotating and reciprocating components, moving materials, and electrically-energized circuits). The risk of exposure to energized equipment is highest when the operator is located remotely from the equipment or out of the line of sight of other workers.

Controls

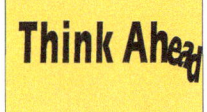

The most important controls for preventing injury from operator-initiated changes are planning and communication. For example:
- Before starting, adjusting, switching, or stopping equipment:
  - Make sure that your actions will not affect other workers or the process operation. At some workplaces, starting, stopping, or adjusting equipment affects upstream or downstream operations.
  - Inform all workers who will be affected by the change in equipment status so they can prepare for the change.
- When working with electrical equipment, make sure the equipment is electrically locked out. Test the effectiveness of the lockout before you work on the equipment.
- When operating mobile equipment such as a forklift:
  - Block off the work area and put up warning signs.
  - Make eye contact with bystanders and keep track of where they are. If you cannot see them, you may have to stop the equipment and check.
  - Maintain a safe distance from structures, overhead wires, and protruding equipment.

8.1.2 Maintenance-Initiated Changes

The nature of maintenance work and associated hazards changes throughout the work cycle. To effectively predict and identify potentially hazardous situations and provide appropriate controls, you must consider each phase of the maintenance work cycle, one at a time:
- before starting the work
- while performing the work
- after completing the work

Before starting the work

When equipment is shut down for repair, very hazardous (and sometimes unexpected) conditions can still exist. For example, after a motor and pump are shut down for repair:
- A remote command could be given to start the motor and pump.
- The pump could still start automatically.
- The equipment is hotter than expected.
- The piping to the pump has been depressurized but the pump still contains pressurized fluid (which may be hot, toxic, or corrosive).
- The equipment and pad are covered with ice from freezing rain.

While performing the work

Often repair work requires performing tasks or using equipment that may create hazardous situations (e.g., working on scaffolding or raised platforms, using special jacks and cranes). Controls must be provided to protect both maintenance workers and others nearby.

Sometimes diagnostic and repair work must be done on energized and/or operating equipment, exposing maintenance workers to hazards that are normally controlled. For example, workers may have to remove machine guards to observe rotating components.

While working, adjacent equipment and structures could get damaged, creating a hazardous situation. Promptly report all damage.

When working in areas where asbestos insulation is used, take care not to disturb the asbestos. If the asbestos is disturbed, immediately leave the area and report the incident.

NOTE Organizations with facilities containing asbestos insulation have site-specific policies and procedures for handling, storage, and disposal of the insulation.

During maintenance work, components hidden from view can be damaged inadvertently, creating new hazards and disrupting service. Utilities such as electrical and communication circuits hidden in walls, floors, or ceilings may be damaged during drilling and cutting. Pipes and vessels containing flammable liquids may be located behind the wall on which the work is being performed. Welding or cutting walls could overheat or damage hidden pipes and vessels containing flammable or pressurized substances.

Digging trenches and boring holes in the ground can damage buried utilities and pipelines. Telephone books for most cities and districts list a *dial before you dig* or *one call* number for requesting that buried utilities be marked before you dig.

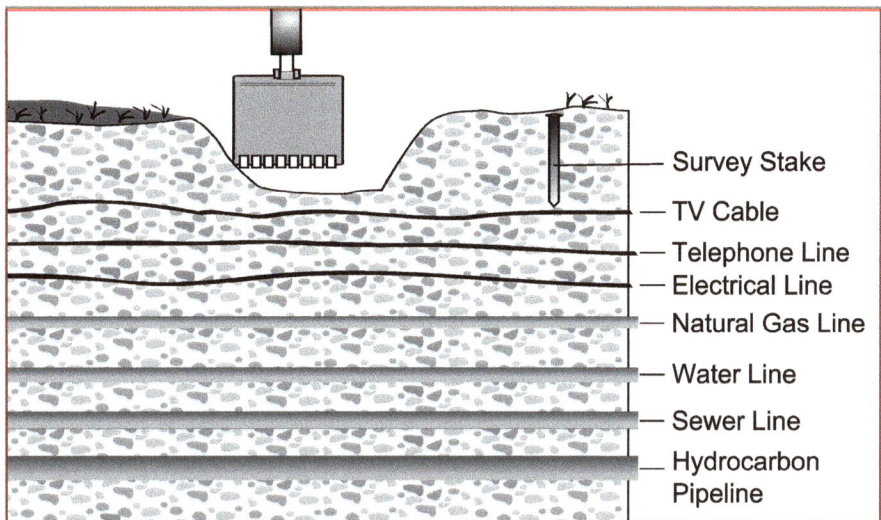

The sequence of different maintenance and repair operations must be planned carefully to prevent new or unfamiliar hazards from being created during the work. Carrying out two or more projects at the same time may be dangerous. For example, a structure is being welded and at the same time maintenance personnel are removing a valve from a large gas line located in the vicinity. Combustible gas escaping from the piping could migrate to the welding area and be ignited.

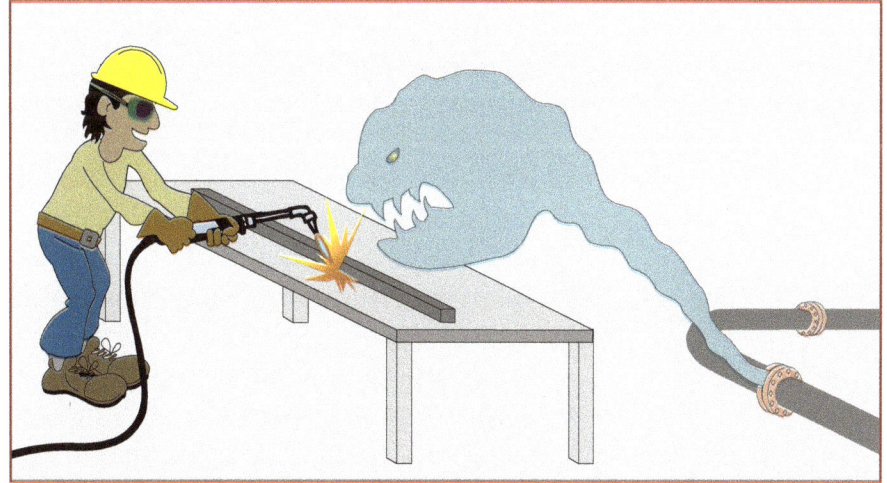

After completing the work

At the completion of a maintenance project, hazardous situations may exist as a result of maintenance activities or the condition of the equipment or workplace. For example:
- A vessel that processes a flammable gas has been opened for repair. After the repairs are complete, the vessel

contains air. When the flammable gas is re-introduced into the vessel, the air gas mixture could ignite or explode. The vessel must be purged before flammable gas is re-introduced.
- A pump that transfers a toxic liquid has been opened for repair. After repairs, the pump needs to be purged and primed, tasks that could expose workers to toxic substances and physical hazards.
- High-speed cutters have been replaced on a machine. Upon startup, a cutter, if not tightened properly, could fly loose. Stay clear of the line of fire when starting the machine.
- Hydraulic oil is spilled on the floor when a forklift hose is replaced. If the oil is not cleaned up promptly, someone may slip and fall.

Before leaving your work area (whether the work is complete or not), determine if others entering the area could be at risk of being harmed. Controls may be needed to prevent others from being exposed to the hazards, for example:
- Restrict access by erecting barriers or taping off the area.
- Clear the area of tools, materials, and waste.
- Inform others of the status of the equipment and condition of the work area.
- Post hazard warnings.

After repairs are complete, several methods can be used to prevent or control hazardous situations, including:
- planning the startup
- testing repaired equipment before starting up
- ensuring equipment safeguards are back in place before starting up
- removing lockouts and informing workers that the equipment is being returned to normal operation
- informing workers in the vicinity that equipment is about to be started
- starting up equipment cautiously
- after startup, periodically checking equipment function and condition

8.2 Technology-Initiated Changes

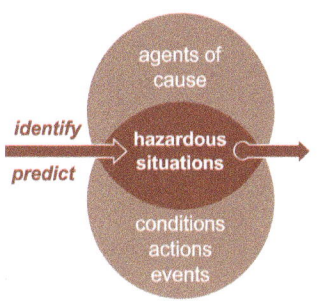

Technology-initiated changes include:
- equipment automatically making adjustments to stay within operating limits (e.g., fans and augers automatically starting or stopping; valves automatically closing or opening; pumps automatically starting or stopping)
- energy temporarily being supplied in response to manufacturing cycles (e.g., rotating and reciprocating equipment starting and stopping; high electrical voltages or intense light temporarily present)
- equipment operating abnormally or failing (e.g., an internal combustion engine operating at reduced power or producing excessive carbon monoxide; failure of moving and stationary components)

When equipment function decreases or the equipment fails, correcting the problem may create new hazards at the equipment or at other locations. For example:
- Some equipment deficiencies can only be corrected by shutting down production. Shutting down production may cause hazardous conditions or events at other locations in the process.
- Temporary repairs may have to be made to maintain production until the scheduled time for maintenance. Adjustments to equipment operation, system operation, and procedures may be required to compensate for abnormal equipment operation. For example, a valve, which is normally open when a piece of equipment is not in use, may be closed temporarily to stop a slow leak in the line. If the valve remains closed when the equipment is started, the equipment could fail to start, the equipment could be damaged if left operating, or the line could become over-pressured.

Some components are known to wear or fail over a specific period of time. These types of components are often repaired or replaced on a regular basis. As the component wears, the component functions differently, requiring operators to make adjustments to equipment or procedures to compensate for the changes. When the worn component

is replaced by a new one, adjustments to equipment and procedures must be returned to normal. Failure to make the necessary changes to the equipment and procedures could create a hazardous situation.

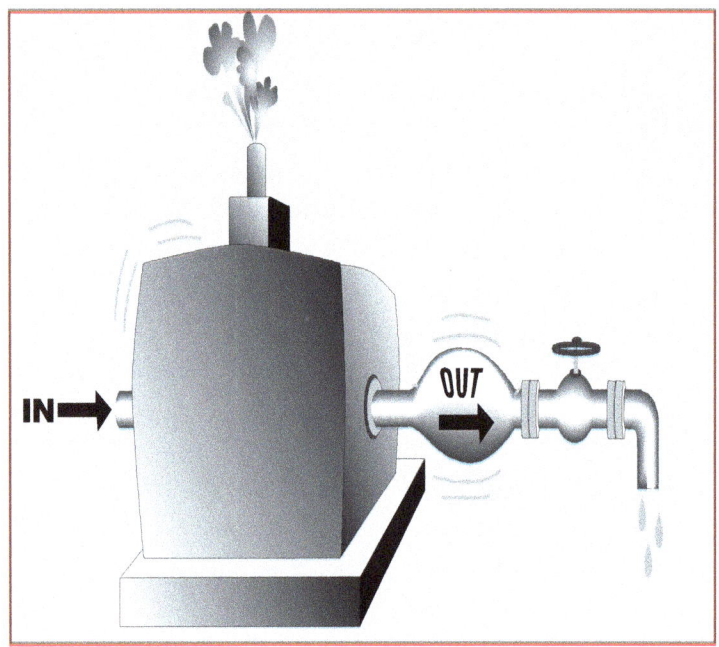

Controls

If you are an operator or maintenance person in a process or production facility, ways to prevent or control hazardous situations include:

- Learn which equipment is automated and/or operated remotely in your area. Understand how the equipment responds to control commands.
- Identify who operates the equipment and the communication requirements between workers.
- Routinely communicate with the other workers before, during, and after making changes (e.g., starting and stopping equipment, adjusting settings, making temporary repairs, or bypassing equipment). Good communication is especially important when other workers are out of the line of sight.
- Routinely document all operations and maintenance activities.

Part 8   Changes

- Take part in shift change meetings so that you receive/pass on information about conditions, actions, or events that may lead to or create hazardous situations.

8.3 Externally-Initiated Changes

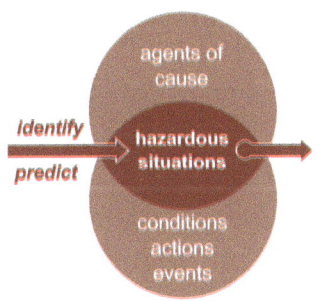

Externally-initiated changes that could create hazardous situations include:
- changes in raw material specifications that could:
  - impact the technology (e.g., straw being mechanically mulched contains rocks causing the mulcher blades to break and be discharged from the chute)
  - introduce a hazardous substance (e.g., a hydrocarbon liquid containing hydrogen sulfide—a highly toxic substance—is supplied by mistake. Workers in a plant may experience immediate toxic effects that could include loss of consciousness or death.)
  - inflict physical injuries (e.g., paper waste that is being sorted for recycling contains broken glass)
- a sudden increase in the supply of raw materials which exceeds the capacity of the equipment
- electrical power failure which results in equipment stoppage. As the equipment slows down, the equipment functions differently, potentially causing a hazardous situation (as milling equipment slows down, the cutting

characteristics change and can cause materials to jam). In some situations, extended periods of power failure can result in process changes that pose a hazard. A power failure can cause an untimely stoppage of equipment.
- inclement weather such as rain, sleet, or snow, which can create a hazardous situation. Surfaces become slippery and visibility may be reduced, putting workers at risk of injury and making controlling vehicles more difficult. The risk of lightning strikes can also increase.
- changes in supplier or customer requirements (quality, quantity, and type of product or service), which affect production and work processes

Controls

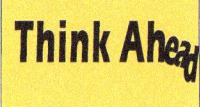

Some externally-initiated changes may be planned and you may be informed about them. However, some externally-initiated changes may not be planned and you may not know that they have occurred or will occur. For your own safety, try to anticipate externally-initiated changes that could occur and determine if the changes could lead to or create a hazardous situation.

Plan the actions you would take to prevent or control hazardous situations that could develop as a result of different types of externally-initiated changes. Ask yourself questions such as:
- Do I know what externally-initiated changes are planned?
- What would happen if:
  - the electrical power failed?
  - raw product specifications changed?
  - the weather suddenly changed?
- How would the externally-initiated changes, in combination with workplace conditions, actions, or other events, create a hazardous situation?
- How would I prevent the hazardous situation from occurring?
- If a hazardous situation occurs, what would I do to control the hazards and keep from being injured?

8.4 Predicting Changes, Determining Consequences, and Using Controls

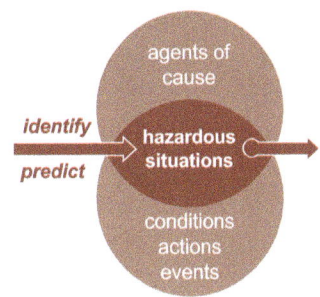

The importance of identifying and predicting changes is to determine if a hazardous situation could be created. And if there is a possibility of a hazardous situation being created, take action to:
- reduce the probability of the hazardous situation occurring
- minimize the severity of potential consequences

Identify and predict hazardous situations

To identify potentially hazardous situations caused by changes:
- identify changes that are planned or will probably occur
- determine if the condition, action, or event in itself is hazardous
- determine if the condition, action, or event in combination with other conditions, actions, and events can lead to or cause a hazardous situation
- determine if one change can cause a chain reaction, creating other changes
- for unexpected changes, determine the effects and possible consequences on health and safety. For unexpected changes, ask yourself *What if...?* questions about what can go wrong regarding PEMEO.

NOTE Care must be taken to ensure deliberate changes to work and to technical processes do **not** have a negative impact on equipment, technical systems, and other work processes. Changing a process operation without concern for the total operation can lead to unpredicted changes to variables such as pressure and temperature. Equipment components may be subject to excessive stress or be exposed to extreme environments that degrade components over time or cause immediate failure. Before changes are made, vendors and engineers may have to be consulted to ensure that the changes do not lead to losses. Some companies have a formal management of change process.

Reduce the probability of hazardous situations occurring

Depending on the circumstances, different control methods may be required to reduce the probability of a hazardous situation being created. For example you may decide to:
- cancel, postpone, or reschedule the work (e.g., wait until the electrical storm is over before gauging a tank)
- change the location of the work (e.g., to prevent the dust hazard from sandblasting your workplace equipment, send equipment to an off-site sandblasting facility)
- change the sequence of the work (e.g., postpone cleaning parts with flammable solvent until the welder working nearby is finished)
- modify the work environment to reduce the likelihood of injuries (e.g., put up barriers)
- change the materials used for the work (e.g., use solvents that are not flammable)

Reduce the severity of consequences

To reduce the severity of consequences if a hazardous situation may develop during the work:
- plan your response in advance (e.g., hold a pre-job meeting, review the emergency procedures)
- adjust or be prepared to adjust equipment and work processes before, during, and after the work is complete
- follow company safe work practices (e.g., assign a fire watch)
- use personal protective equipment

8.5 What Can Go Wrong?

An important strategy to keep you and others from harm is to consider what can go wrong. For change, ask *What if...?* questions about what can go wrong regarding PEMEO. For each domain of PEMEO, you need to consider conditions, actions, and events that could occur and cause PEMEO to function poorly, behave abnormally, or fail. If there is a concern that involves any of the six categories of hazard, determine the immediate effect.

The following table provides examples of using *What if...?* questions about what can go wrong with both planned and unplanned changes. Note that, in the examples, the worker may be performing a specific task or may be in the area that is affected.

\multicolumn{3}{c}{What can go wrong with changes?}		
Domain	**What if...?** *conditions, actions, and events involving:* • *hazardous materials* • *objects, motion, force* • *non-ambient conditions* • *electricity* • *radiation*	**Immediate effect**
People	• What if the operator tries to start the gravel crusher that is mechanically locked out?	• The crusher will not start.
	• What if the mechanic suffers fatigue because of working long hours to complete a shutdown?	• The mechanic's ability to think through the work and to concentrate is diminished.
	• What if the operator responds to an increase in equipment temperature by turning on building fans?	• An air draft will be set up inside the building.
Equipment	• What if the bearing fails?	• The equipment will be very hot and noisy.
	• What if during a turnaround it is discovered that the interior of a vessel is badly corroded?	• Major adjustments to the turnaround schedule will have to be made.
	• What if the equipment is put on computer control?	• Equipment will start and stop without warning.
Materials	• What if plywood is replaced with a medium density fiber board (MDF)?	• Machined edges will be much sharper and the material will be heavier to handle.
	• What if the concentration of H_2S (a toxic product) in processed oil suddenly increases due to a process upset?	• H_2S will vent from the top of the tank when the gauging hatch is opened.
	• What if high-grade sockets are replaced with low-grade sockets?	• The sockets could break when the usual force is applied.

(continued)

What can go wrong with changes?		
Domain	**What if...?** *conditions, actions, and events involving:* • *hazardous materials* • *objects, motion, force* • *non-ambient conditions* • *electricity* • *radiation*	Immediate effect
Environment	• What if there is a downpour that lasts all day?	• The containment dikes around the tanks will be flooded.
	• What if there is a 600% increase in the number of workers on site during a shutdown?	• The variety and dynamics of work activities on site will increase dramatically.
	• What if a forest fire starts upwind of the plant?	• The plant will be at risk of burning down.
Organization	• What if the crew is short staffed?	• Coordination and completion of the job activities will be difficult.
	• What if the department makes major changes to work processes?	• Individuals and groups will have to learn to do their jobs differently.
	• What if a customer wants the product to be built to a different standard than required by other customers?	• Work and technical processes will have to be changed to meet the customer's expectations.

Having determined the possible immediate effects, you can ask additional questions:
- Could I or others become ill and/or injured?
- What should be my first response if an incident occurs?
- What can I do to minimize the possibility of an incident occurring and the severity of the consequences should an incident occur?

For many of the incidents identified by the *What if...?* questions, your response will be more effective when you:
- pre-determine the response you would make
- rehearse your response by imagining responding to the incident. Rehearsing increases the possibility that you will respond immediately and effectively.

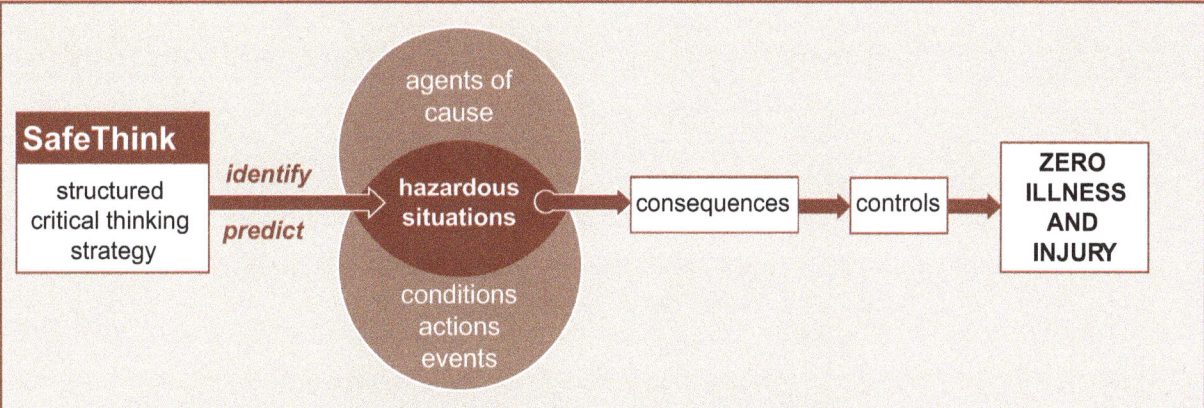

Using the SafeThink strategy

Could a change lead to or create a hazardous situation?

At any time before, during, and after your work is complete, you need to determine whether or not changes can put you at risk.

To determine if you are at risk, ask yourself the following critical thinking questions. If questions 1, 2, or 3 identify a change, go to question 4.

1. What worker-initiated changes will occur?
   - What equipment will be started, operated, adjusted, switched, or stopped?
   - What maintenance activities are or will be taking place?
2. What technology-initiated changes will occur?
   - What equipment will be automatically started, adjusted, switched, or stopped?
   - What could go wrong with the equipment and materials?
3. What externally-initiated changes could occur?
   - Could there be off-site changes that affect the workplace?
   - Will inclement weather create a hazardous situation or power failure?
4. Could these changes create or lead to a hazardous situation?
   - What are the possible consequences of the hazardous situation?
   - What can I do to prevent or minimize the hazardous situation?
   - How can I prevent being harmed?

With practice, when you think about your work, you will automatically consider these questions about changes to determine if a hazardous situation could develop.

Use the *SafeThink* strategy when you complete the learning activity.

| LEARNING ACTIVITY | 8 |

Could changes lead to or create a hazardous situation?

This learning activity will help you learn to identify and predict changes in conditions, actions, and events that create hazardous situations. The focus of the learning activity is on health and safety issues caused by:

- changes that are initiated by *others* and affect you
- changes that are initiated by *you* and affect others
- changes that are initiated by *technology* and affect you and others
- changes that are initiated by *external events* and affect you and others

1. List three tasks that you perform in which potential changes may occur that could lead to or create a hazardous situation. For each task, identify the change that creates the hazardous situation. Describe the precautions you can take to prevent you or others being harmed.

Task	Change	Precautions
1.		
2.		
3.		

218

Part 8 Changes

To complete the remainder of this learning activity, break each task into its major steps. For each major step, think about the specific action steps and the associated conditions, actions, and events that could expose you or others to harm as a result of changes.

2. Select a task that could expose you or others to changes initiated by **operators** (not you). First break the task into major steps, then complete questions 2a, 2b, and 2c.

   Task _____

   Major step 1 (before working) _____

   Major step 2 (while working) _____

   Major step 3 (while working) _____

   Major step 4 (while working) _____

   Major step 5 (while working) _____

   Major step 6 (while working) _____

   Major step 7 (after work is complete) _____

2a. Identify conditions, actions, and events involving operator-initiated changes that exist **before** doing the work that could cause harm to you or others. Identify possible controls to reduce the risk of an incident.

   Changes:_____

   _____

   _____

   Controls: _____

   _____

   _____

2b. Identify conditions, actions, and events involving operator-initiated changes that exist or develop **while** doing the work that could cause harm to you or others. Identify possible controls to reduce the risk of an incident.

   Changes:_____

   Controls: _____

   _____

   _____

2c. Identify conditions, actions, and events involving operator-initiated changes that exist **after** the work has been completed that could cause harm to you or others. Identify possible controls to reduce the risk of an incident.

   Changes:_____

   _____

   _____

   Controls: _____

   _____

   _____

3. Select a task that could expose you or others to changes initiated by **maintenance** (not you). First break the task into major steps, then complete questions 3a, 3b, and 3c.

   Task _____

   Major step 1 (before working) _____

   Major step 2 (while working) _____

   Major step 3 (while working) _____

   Major step 4 (while working) _____

   Major step 5 (while working) _____

   Major step 6 (while working) _____

   Major step 7 (after work is complete) _____

3a. Identify conditions, actions, and events involving maintenance-initiated changes that exist **before** doing the work that could cause harm to you or others. Identify possible controls to reduce the risk of an incident.

Changes: _____

_____

_____

Controls: _____

_____

_____

3b. Identify conditions, actions, and events involving maintenance-initiated changes that exist or develop **while** doing the work that could cause harm to you or others. Identify possible controls to reduce the risk of an incident.

Changes: _____

_____

_____

Controls: _____

_____

_____

3c. Identify conditions, actions, and events involving maintenance-initiated changes that exist **after** the work has been completed that could cause harm to you or others. Identify possible controls to reduce the risk of an incident.

Changes: _____

_____

_____

Controls: _____

_____

_____

4. Select a task that could expose you or others to changes initiated by **technology**. First break the task into major steps, then complete questions 4a, 4b, and 4c.

Task _____

Major step 1 (before working) _____

Major step 2 (while working) _____

Major step 3 (while working) _____

Major step 4 (while working) _____

Major step 5 (while working) _____

Major step 6 (while working) _____

Major step 7 (after work is complete) _____

4a. Identify conditions, actions, and events involving technology-initiated changes that exist **before** doing the work that could cause harm to you or others. Identify possible controls to reduce the risk of an incident.

Changes:_____

_____

_____

Controls: _____

_____

_____

4b. Identify conditions, actions, and events involving technology-initiated changes that exist or develop **while** doing the work that could cause harm to you or others. Identify possible controls to reduce the risk of an incident.

Changes:_____

_____

_____

Controls: _____

_____

_____

4c. Identify conditions, actions, and events involving technology-initiated changes that exist **after** the work

Part 8   Changes

has been completed that could cause harm to you or others. Identify possible controls to reduce the risk of an incident.

Changes: _____

_____

_____

Controls: _____

_____

_____

5. Select a task that could expose you or others to **externally-initiated changes**. First break the task into major steps, then complete questions 5a, 5b, and 5c.

Task _____

Major step 1 (before working) _____

Major step 2 (while working) _____

Major step 3 (while working) _____

Major step 4 (while working) _____

Major step 5 (while working) _____

Major step 6 (while working) _____

Major step 7 (after work is complete) _____

5a. Identify conditions, actions, and events involving externally-initiated changes that exist **before** doing the work that could cause harm to you or others. Identify possible controls to reduce the risk of an incident.

Changes: _____

_____

Controls: _____

_____

_____

5b. Identify conditions, actions, and events involving externally-initiated changes that exist or develop **while** doing the work that could cause harm to you or others. Identify possible controls to reduce the risk of an incident.

Changes:_____

_____

_____

Controls: _____

_____

_____

5c. Identify conditions, actions, and events involving externally-initiated changes that exist **after** the work has been completed that could cause harm to you or others. Identify possible controls to reduce the risk of an incident.

Changes:_____

_____

Controls: _____

_____

6. Name a **task** that could involve change: _____

6a. Ask *What if...?* questions to identify what can go wrong in relation to planned and unplanned changes and fill in the following table. For each domain of PEMEO, consider conditions, actions, and events that could occur, function poorly, behave abnormally, or fail. If there is a concern about a change that could impact or involve any of the six categories of hazard, determine the immediate effect.

Part 8 Changes

What can go wrong with changes?		
Domain	**What if…?** *conditions, actions, and events involving:* • *hazardous materials* • *objects, motion, force* • *non-ambient conditions* • *electricity* • *radiation*	**Immediate effect**
People		
Equipment		
Materials		
Environment		
Organization		

6b. From the table you have completed, select one effect that may create or lead to a hazardous situation and answer the following questions:

Could I or others become ill and/or injured? What would be the consequences?

_____

_____

What should be my first response if an incident occurs?

_____

_____

What can I do to minimize the probability of an incident occurring and/or the severity of consequences?

_____

Option

Many participants have found that writing helps them learn and remember the questions. Write the critical thinking questions for changes in the box below. The questions are listed in the Job Aid.

FOOD for THOUGHT

Risk of loss

A critical task must be performed well to prevent illness or injury. Some tasks are more critical than others. The criticalness of a task is often measured in terms of the risk of loss. Having an understanding about risk of loss can be of value to you. You can:
- assess the seriousness of the hazardous situation and the effectiveness of a control
- use the information as part of a strategy to convince others to take action to reduce a hazardous situation

Risk of loss is a function of the:
- **probability** of an incident occurring, and the
- **severity** of the consequences

If the probability of an incident is very low and the severity of the consequences very high, the risk of loss is low. An absurd example must be used to explain this extreme in probability and severity. The probability that you are sitting on an ancient, buried volcano and that it will erupt in the next ten minutes is very low but the consequences would be catastrophic! In this example, the risk of loss is extremely low because the event will not happen. One way of calculating risk of loss is to multiply probability and severity to achieve a risk of loss number.

0 probability x catastrophic consequences = 0 risk of loss

If the probability of an incident is high but the severity of consequences is very low, the risk of loss is extremely low. For example, the probability of getting a minor paper cut stuffing thousands of envelopes is high, but the severity of the consequences is very low.

100% probability x 0 consequences = 0 risk of loss

When both the probability of an incident and the severity of the consequences are very high, the risk of loss is extreme. For example, in wartime, the probability that an ammunition depot will be bombed is very high and the consequences will be disastrous.

100% probability x disastrous consequences = extreme risk of loss

Risk of loss can be illustrated using a risk matrix as shown below.

CRITICAL TASK RISK MATRIX		Probability (increasing →)		
		A low	B moderate	C high
Severity (increasing ↓)	A – minor	1	2	3
	B – serious	2	4	6
	C – major	3	6	9

- 1 = very low risk of loss
- 2 = some risk of loss
- 3 & 4 = high risk of loss
- 6 = very high risk of loss
- 9 = extreme risk of loss

In the above matrix, when either the probability or the severity increases, the risk of loss increases. When both the probability and severity increase, the rate at which the risk of loss increases is the greatest.

Risk of loss matrices can have four or five columns and rows.

CRITICAL TASK RISK MATRIX		Probability			
		rare	occasional	frequent	continuing
Severity	minimal	low	low	moderate	high
	significant	low	moderate	high	very high
	extensive	moderate	high	very high	extreme
	disastrous	high	very high	extreme	extreme

The levels of probability and severity can also be specified. For example:
- probability (one occurrence every 10 years, one occurrence every three years, one in ten thousand, etc.)
- severity (minor injury, loss time injury, permanent injury, fatality)

Other, more precise criteria can be used but it is beyond the scope of this book to elaborate.

The ratings for risk of loss can be used to make decisions about carrying out the work. For example:

Low: acceptable, proceed with caution, identify ways to further reduce the risk of loss

Moderate: get permission from supervisor to proceed, follow written procedure, identify ways to further reduce the risk of loss

High: get permission from supervisor to proceed, specialist must supervise task, identify ways to further reduce the risk of loss

Very High: task must not proceed, specialists plan procedure, implement very rigorous controls

Extreme: cancel task, major rethink required to find better ways to resolve problem or achieve desired results

IMPORTANT
On the job, when a hazardous situation is identified, often the worker decides at the time what criteria should be used for assessing the level of probability and severity and the degree of risk of loss. The decisions made by different workers can vary. For example a person who has a very low risk threshold (low tolerance for risk) may use different criteria than a person who has a very high risk threshold (e.g., someone who is involved in extreme sports). A worker may also be a poor judge of the probability of an incident occurring and the severity of the consequences.

The concept of risk of loss can also be applied to all PEMEO domains to determine the total loss to an operation.

NOTE Part 9—*Apply Your SafeThink Strategy* uses both risk threshold and total loss to the operation as part of considering how to convince others to reduce the risk of loss.

SafeThink is **not** about rating tasks for their levels of risk of loss—it's about identifying and controlling hazardous situations. If you identify a hazardous situation, do something, if possible, to eliminate the hazardous situation. If you cannot eliminate a hazardous situation, at the least, you will be aware of the potential for illness or injury (e.g., getting a paper cut, bumping into stored material, receiving a burn from the cooking grill).

With the *SafeThink* strategy, the concepts of risk of loss are useful in selecting controls that are effective. Controls reduce the probability of an incident occurring and/or the severity of consequences. For example, lockouts/tagouts prevent incidents, fire extinguishers and fire retardant clothing reduce the severity of consequences.

When selecting controls, select controls that will be effective:
- reducing or eliminating the probability of an incident is the preferred choice of control
- reducing the level of hazard (i.e., severity) is the next preferred choice (e.g., replacing a very toxic solvent with a less toxic solvent)
- using personal protective equipment as a barrier to reduce the severity of the consequences is the least preferred choice of control

Reasons for safe and unsafe behaviors

Why do some people always use seatbelts and others only occasionally use them?

Why do some people always wear eye protection at home when there is the potential of receiving an eye injury while others only wear eye protection at work?

What motivates some people to act or behave safely and others to act or behave unsafely?

■ Reasons

To encourage others to improve their safety behavior, you must first understand the reasons for their unsafe behavior. The following table lists some of the common reasons given by workers for safe and unsafe acts/behaviors.

Reasons for Safe and Unsafe Acts/Behaviors		
Why safe acts/behaviors	**Why unsafe acts/behaviors**	
• company rule • reduce the potential for an injury • fear of a fine (law) • fear of reprimand • fear of being fired • personal experience with past incident • feel responsible to significant others • to stop warning alarms • company pays for safety gear • company pays to take the time to be safe • gear readily available and convenient • gear easy to use • receive praise • set an example for others • concern for others (an injury can upset others) • would feel foolish if performed unsafe act/behavior and got injured	• gear hot • gear cumbersome • gear doesn't fit well • gear causes discomfort • gear hard to adjust • gear a nuisance • gear takes too much time to put on or use • gear reduces mobility • gear hard to use • gear could contribute to illness or injury • gear grubby, worn, torn • gear looks ugly • gear dangerous if covered with flammable product • don't believe lab tests prove it is safe • don't believe I'm acting unsafely • it's inconvenient • safety gear not readily available • not enough devices (e.g., seatbelts for number of passengers)	• it makes it awkward to carry out action • unaware of hazardous situation • didn't know better • forgot • in a hurry, rushed • have got away with it in the past; it won't happen to me • I'm safe enough already • don't think it matters • peer pressure • get laughed at for safe behavior • thrill of taking risk • showing off • supervisors don't need to • just visiting • it's overkill • I'm an expert, more careful than others • misjudged the risk

> **NOTE** Maintaining and improving safe behaviors is an ongoing challenge because there are many more reasons for unsafe behavior than for safe behavior.

■ Motivation

Reasons provide explanations for behaviors but may not explain the motivation for the behavior. On closer examination of the worker's reasons, the outcomes created by the reasons are either positive or negative. For example:

- *The gear is uncomfortable.* Perhaps the gear causes mild pain. It may be hot to wear. These outcomes are negative consequences—motives for not wearing the safety gear.
- *Reduce the potential for an injury.* The motive for wearing the safety gear is to reduce the fear and potential of being injured—a positive consequence.
- *Receive praise.* Most people like to receive praise. The motive to act safely is to feel good about the safe behavior—a positive consequence.

The consequences of safe or unsafe behavior are either positive or negative. So, consequences are the motivators (incentives or disincentives) for both safe and unsafe behavior.

In the previous table, many of the reasons for safe and unsafe behavior can be explained in terms of positive or negative consequences. Workers can view consequences as being negative or positive, rewarding or punishing. People usually seek rewards and avoid punishment.

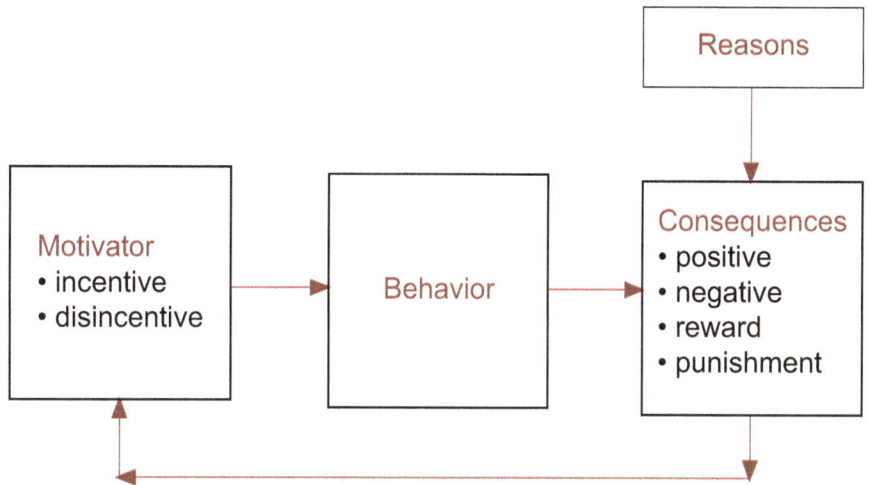

Unfortunately, the process of deciding to act safely or unsafely can be complex. People can often be torn between several conflicting consequences when deciding on their actions. For example, a family wants their neighbors to ride with them to a local event. There is one person too many for the number of seatbelts. The driver may be torn between:

- having the neighbors ride along with them which is a pleasant social event (positive consequence)
- not having the neighbors ride along with them (negative consequence)
- doing someone a favor (positive consequence)
- not doing someone a favor (negative consequence)
- believing that safety is very important (positive consequence)
- knowing that a passenger not wearing a seatbelt is unsafe (negative consequence)
- having a commitment to keeping within the law (positive consequence)
- breaking the law (negative consequence)

In the decision-making process to act safely or unsafely, other factors may also come into play. For example, the person's threshold for risk of loss could be an important factor for decision-making.

■ Changing behavior

When trying to convince another person not to perform a specific unsafe act, you need to understand *how that person perceives* reward or punishment. You then can take measures to change the rewards and punishments to encourage safe behavior and discourage unsafe behavior.

The most effective way to achieve long-term safe behaviors is through positive consequences and positive reinforcement such as praising and rewarding safe behaviors. Provide reinforcements that the person perceives as being positive. Workers who perform a safe behavior repeatedly and feel rewarded will gradually develop the belief that the safe behavior is desirable. These workers are more likely to act safely in other situations, on and off the job.

Provide negative reinforcements such as reprimands when necessary but limit your use of negative reinforcements. Workers may act safely when you're supervising but, when you are not around, they may try to get away with the unsafe behavior.

Sometimes negative reinforcements may be necessary when the worker is:
- not responding to the positive reinforcements and continues to perform the unsafe behavior.
- in imminent danger. Immediate intervention and negative reinforcement may be required.

As a general rule:
- positive reinforcements encourage long-term behavior.
- negative reinforcements only work in changing behavior when that person is being supervised.

Maintaining and improving safe behaviors is an ongoing challenge because there are many more reasons for unsafe behavior than for safe behavior. To encourage safe behavior, a conscious effort must be made to provide more positive and stronger reasons (reinforcements) for safe behavior than there are reasons for unsafe behavior.

Lead by example. Demonstrate your commitment to behaving and working in a safe manner. Be consistent: walk the talk.

■ Jerry-rigging

Jerry-rigging is using a temporary measure to keep equipment operating or to prevent injury. Jerry-rigging is a quick fix to make do. For example:
- A leg of a wooden ladder is beginning to split. The crack is fastened with wire to reduce further splitting.
- A hole in a walkway causes people to stumble. The hole is filled with sand.

The problem with jerry-rigging is that the temporary fix is not as reliable as fixing the problem properly—risk of loss increases. Sometimes a jerry-rigged solution becomes a permanent solution.

Some people may use a jerry-rig that is not reliable for reasons identified in the previous table. They may also have a high threshold of risk.

Do not jerry-rig if possible. If a jerry-rigged solution is chosen, make sure to test the reliability of the fix. Make sure that others who could be affected are informed. Have the problem corrected properly as soon as possible.

■ Management of change

Sometimes a change to make work more efficient and less strenuous in one work area can cause safety issues for other work areas or, over the longer term, reduce the life of equipment (e.g., increase corrosion). In some organizations, especially in manufacturing and process industries, a formal management of change process may be used. The management of change process requires that a thorough analysis be conducted to identify any risk issue before a change is implemented. People from different disciplines, such as operators, maintenance personnel, safety and environment advisors, engineers, and vendors, are involved in the analysis process.

If there is a formal management of change process in your workplace, as a minimum, you should seek answers to the following questions:
- *How does the management of change process work?*
- *What types of change require using the formal change process?*
- *Who is involved in the analysis process?*
- *Who makes the changes?*
- *How are others informed of changes?*
- *What are your personal roles and responsibilities regarding change?*

Part 9
Apply Your Safethink Strategy

- **Apply your SafeThink strategy to identify and predict hazardous situations**

- **Select controls to reduce or eliminate:**
  - **the probability of an incident occuring**
  - **the severity of the consequences**

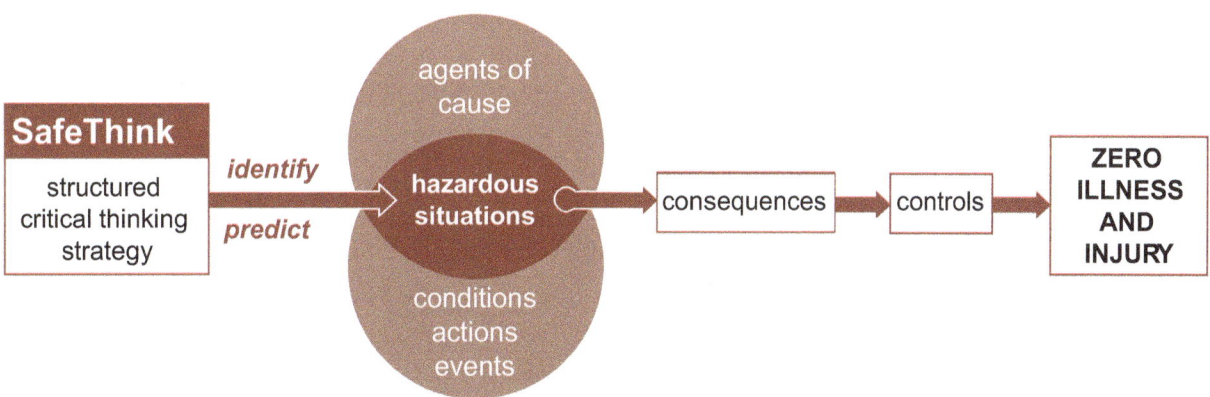

Training Objectives

Upon completion of this part, you will be able to apply the structured critical thinking strategy to identify and predict hazardous situations before working, while working, and after work is completed.

- Apply the *SafeThink* strategy to your workplace
- Determine possible controls to eliminate or reduce the hazardous situations

	The SafeThink Strategy	
Part	**Category of hazard**	**Critical thinking question**
Part 3	Hazardous Materials	Does the work involve hazardous materials?
Part 4	Objects, Motion, Force	Does the work involve objects, motion, or force that could cause harm?
Part 5	Non-Ambient Conditions	Does the work involve non-ambient conditions that could cause harm?
Part 6	Electricity	Is current or static electricity a factor in doing the work?
Part 7	Radiation	Is radiation present when doing the work?
Part 8	Changes	Could changes lead to or create a hazardous situation?

A learning activity at the end of Part 9 helps you apply the entire *SafeThink* strategy to your work and workplace.

9 Apply Your SafeThink Strategy

Parts 3 to 8 presented the six questions, one question at a time. To use the *SafeThink* strategy effectively, you must apply all six questions to every work situation before working, while working, and after your work is complete. The goal of Part 9 is to help you apply all six questions as a strategy continually throughout your workday. Part 9:

- identifies controls used to protect workers before you begin a task, while you are performing the task, and after you have completed the task
- helps you apply the six questions at the same time to develop your own *personal protective strategy*

9.1 Controls Used to Protect People

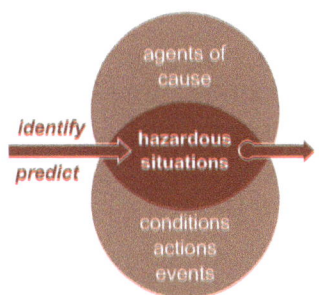

In an industrial workplace, the risk of harm to people (and losses to equipment, materials, the environment, and the entire organization) is always present. You are responsible for carrying out your work in a thoughtful manner, using critical thinking strategies before doing work, while working, and after the work is complete to identify hazardous situations. You must use appropriate methods to prevent an incident from occurring.

Occupational health and safety regulations specify control requirements for some types of hazards (e.g., safeguards for rotating equipment; guardrails for raised platforms). For other types of hazards, equally-effective types of controls may be available. In these circumstances, the employer is permitted to select the controls that are most suited for the workplace and most readily accepted by the workers.

When selecting controls, consideration must be given to:
- the effectiveness of the controls to reduce the *probability* of an incident occurring and/or the *severity* of the consequences
- delays in starting work caused by the time it takes to implement the controls (e.g., the need to purchase or rent equipment)
- cost of implementing the controls

- potential for the controls to create other hazards (e.g., use of self-contained breathing apparatus can restrict vision and ease of movement)

The following table provides examples of controls that site management and workers can often implement as part of doing work. Note that these are **not** engineering controls that would take a long time to implement.

Controls Frequently Used to Protect Workers		
Before task	**During task**	**After task**

• Prepare work plan
• Hold safety meeting
• Obtain work permit
• Depressure
• Purge
• Blind or block and bleed
• Perform mechanical lockout
• Perform electrical lockout
• Perform system lockout
• Vent vessels
• Steam
• Erect hazard warning signs
• Erect and check scaffolding
• Erect guard rails or barriers
• Ventilate area
• Test for combustible and toxic gas and oxygen concentrations
• Notify designated personnel
• Provide emergency equipment
• Plan escape routes/procedures
	• Use personal protective equipment
	  – hard hat
	  – safety glasses
	  – flame-resistant clothing
	  – safety footwear
	  – hearing protection
	• Use specialized safety equipment
	  – face shields
	  – welding goggles
	  – specialty gloves
	  – specialized protective clothing
	  – respiratory protection
	  – fall protection and safety lines
	• Ensure equipment guards are in place
	• Use a safety watch
	• Keep work area clean
	• Notify proper personnel
	• Monitor atmosphere
	• Apply forces in a safe direction
		• Perform quality check
		• Remove tags and lockouts
		• Remove blinds
		• Dispose of wastes
		• Clean up area
		• Notify proper personnel
		• Perform cautious startup
		• Inspect equipment after startup
		• Maintain records and compile reports

In some cases, one control can apply to several hazardous situations. For example, barriers to a work area can prevent people from falling objects and exposure to hazardous materials.

Part 9 Apply Your SafeThink Strategy

 When selecting controls, consider how the controls might create other hazards. For example, using ventilation equipment to remove dust-laden air from a sandblasting area may affect workers downwind of the exhaust vent.

Using double barriers

Workers often use *double barriers* to further protect themselves. Double barriers are two independent, unrelated controls that are used at the same time such as:

- locking out equipment electrically *plus* using electrically insulated tools
- installing guard rails around a tank roof *plus* using fall protection equipment
- using a fume hood *plus* wearing a respirator while working with infectious materials

Work permits

At many worksites, a safe work permit must be issued before work can begin. The work permit system is a formal process to keep track of work being performed in the facility and to ensure that all potential hazards are identified and appropriate controls are implemented before work begins. Issuing safe work permits provides a formal means of assessing the workplace for potential hazards. Your *SafeThink* strategy provides you with an informal means of continually assessing the work and workplace to identify and predict hazardous situations.

9.2 Lockout and Tagout

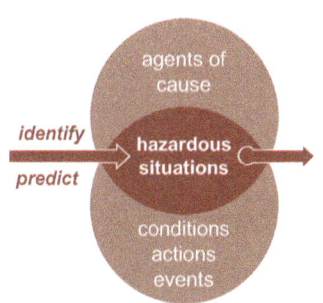 Before workers adjust, test, service, repair, or maintain equipment, the equipment must be in a safe condition:
- Hazardous materials inside equipment, vessels, and piping must be removed by methods such as venting, draining, purging, and steaming.
- At the equipment being worked on, all energy sources must be isolated and brought to a zero energy state. Energy sources include:
  - electrical
  - mechanical

- pneumatic
- hydraulic
- steam
- thermal
- potential (stored energy)
- bio-hazard

• Components, materials, and tools that have potential energy due to gravity must be adequately secured to prevent falling.

• An unexpected startup of the equipment or the sudden release of energy must be prevented by locking out and tagging the devices that isolate the energy sources.

NOTE

Lockout means to physically lock devices that control hazardous energy in the *safe* or *off* position. *Tagout* means to install a warning tag prohibiting anyone from either removing the lock or from activating the starting device.

When it is not possible to lock out a machine or piece of equipment, another equally effective method must be used to prevent workers from being injured.

Many different methods are used to lock out equipment. Pins, bars, blocks, and chains prevent mechanical components from moving, even when someone tries to start the equipment. Isolation valves on pneumatic, hydraulic, and process lines can be chained to prevent them from being operated. Locks prevent unauthorized removal of the lockout devices or the inadvertent starting of the equipment.

Electrical lockout involves shutting off breakers to de-energize *all* electrical circuits associated with the equipment (including control circuits) and putting locks on the breakers.

Along with the lock, a tag is also placed on the isolation device to provide critical information, such as:
• date the lock was attached
• name and signature of the person who attached the lock
• name of the person who requested the lockout

To electrically isolate equipment that can be operated both remotely and locally, such as a motor-operated valve:
- The breakers to the motor and control circuits for the valve are placed in the "open" position, locked out, and tagged.
- At the valve, the local control device is set to the "closed" position and a tag is attached to warn others not to manually operate the valve.

 Each person working on a piece of equipment (e.g., operator, electrician, millwright) must install his or her personal locks and tags on the isolation devices. As one means of ensuring locked out equipment is safe for restarting, only the person who installs the lock is authorized to remove that lock.

The equipment must be tested after the locks are installed to ensure the equipment cannot be started.

The keys to the locks are stored on a lockout board or in a lockable box. Only authorized personnel (e.g., supervisor) hold the key(s) to unlock the box. On isolation devices that cannot hold all the locks, a group lock box is used.

Lockout/tagout procedures are used in every industry, from baking to shipbuilding to manufacturing. Companies often have written generalized lockout and tagout procedures as well as very specific procedures for locking out specific pieces of equipment.

 Lockout and tagout requirements vary from one government jurisdiction to the next and from one company to the next. Follow your company's specific procedures.

As a minimum, lockout and tagout procedures address the following requirements:

Before work begins
- Notify other workers of the impending machine/equipment shutdown.
- Prepare to safely shut down the machine/equipment.
- Shut down the equipment.

 SafeThink™

- Lock a safety device onto each separate energy source to immobilize the source in the safe or off position.
- Place personal tags on energy sources and equipment controls to notify everyone of the lockout and to prohibit removal of tags and locks and starting of equipment.
- Verify that all energy sources are safely locked out.
- Make a list of locked out devices and post the list near the equipment.

During the work
- Periodically verify that energy sources are still safely locked out.
- Periodically verify that stored energy is not accumulating during servicing (e.g., a valve can have a slow leak, causing downstream piping to pressurize; ice can build up on a roof, exceeding the load capacity). If accumulation of energy does occur, the energy must be periodically released in a controlled and safe manner to prevent injuries from a sudden, unexpected release.

After the work
- Notify all workers in the vicinity that the lockout will be removed.
- Inspect the equipment to ensure it is operable and that non-essential tools, parts, and supplies are removed.
- Ensure everyone is safely clear of the equipment.
- Remove the locks and tags (each person who worked on the equipment removes his or her personal locks and tags).
- After verifying that it is safe to do so, restore the hazardous energy source to the "energized" or "on" position.
- Perform a cautious startup of the equipment and resume normal operations.

 Always follow your company's site-specific lockout/tagout procedures.

244

 Moving parts that get jammed can accumulate a great deal of energy. If parts suddenly come unjammed, components can accelerate rapidly and with a great deal of force (e.g., a conveyor belt driven by a gear-reduced driver).

When you need to solve a problem quickly (e.g., freeing a jammed log on a conveyor belt), do not take shortcuts. **Always** lock out the equipment. Locking out is your best protective strategy to prevent being injured from a sudden startup or release of hazardous energy.

9.3 Thinking and Planning Ahead

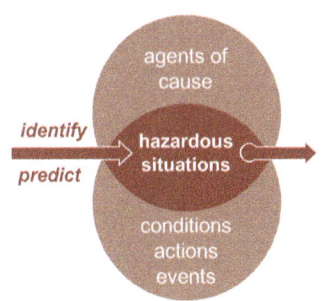

One of the most important things you can do to protect yourself and others from hazards is to take the time to consider consequences before taking action. There are many opportunities to think and plan ahead:
- on a moment-to-moment basis
- during natural breaks in the work process
- at pre-job meetings

Thinking ahead moment to moment

While you are working, think about the next step of the task or the next action you are going to take and ask yourself the **six SafeThink questions**:
- Does the work involve hazardous material?
- Does the work involve objects, motion, or force that could cause harm?
- Does the work involve non-ambient conditions that could cause harm?
- Is current or static electricity a factor in doing the work?
- Is radiation present when doing the work?
- Could changes lead to or create a hazardous situation?

If you answer "yes" to any of these questions, ask yourself, "Are there any conditions, actions, or events that can lead to a hazardous situation?" If there is potential for a hazardous situation, ask yourself, "What are the potential consequences and possible controls?"

For each category of hazard, also ask yourself *What if...?* questions about what can go wrong:
- Could I or others become ill or injured?
- What can I do to prevent illness or injury?
- If something goes wrong, what should I do about it?

Planning ahead during natural breaks in the work process

Work assignments often consist of several major activities or steps. After a major activity has been completed, work often stops temporarily, for example:
- when the first of many rooms has been painted; when equipment has been isolated and locked out
- after the floor has been prepared for tiling

At the completion of an activity, there is often an opportunity to pause and think about the next activity:
- What has to be done?
- Who is going to do it?
- Who needs to be informed about the work that is going to take place?
- What specific tools, equipment, and materials are going to be used?
- What other activities at the worksite will affect the work?
- What other activities at the worksite will be affected by the work?
- What conditions, actions, or events can create a hazardous situation?
- How can I prevent being injured?
- What should I do if something goes wrong?

While you think about the work to be done, ask yourself the six *SafeThink* questions. These questions can help you identify agents of cause. After identifying the agents of cause, identify the specific conditions, actions, and events that could put you and others at risk of being injured.

Planning ahead at pre-job meetings

Many different terms are used to describe pre-job meetings, including:
- pre-job meeting
- tailgate meeting

- work plan meeting
- job safety meeting
- toolbox talk
- field-based assessment
- hazard identification meeting

Some of these meetings are informal and occur whenever someone thinks there is a need to think things through and plan ahead. Some of the meetings are formal, planned, and scheduled. At formal meetings, notes are taken to provide a record about the discussions, decisions, and assigned roles and responsibilities.

All of these meetings have a strong emphasis on identifying hazards. Less emphasis may be placed on identifying the conditions, actions, and events that could cause a hazardous situation. Controls are identified to prevent incidents. Sometimes, structured risk assessment and hazard analysis methods are used at the meetings to identify potential hazards. Using the *SafeThink* strategy to identify and predict potentially hazardous situations is also useful. Other important parts of these meetings are to coordinate work and to ensure that everyone understands his/her role and responsibilities.

9.4 SafeThink Thinking Processes

The illustration shows two thinking processes you can use to apply your *SafeThink* strategy.

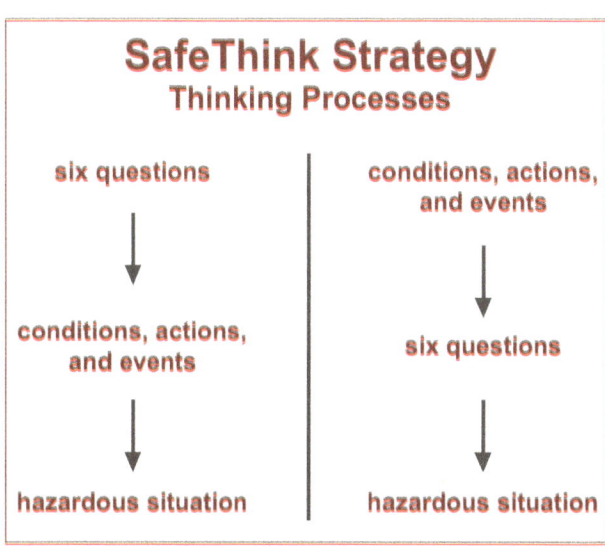

At times, especially in unfamiliar situations, you will find it beneficial to consciously ask yourself the six questions to determine if the workplace could potentially be hazardous. With practice, you will find yourself reversing the thinking process to identify potentially hazardous situations. You will ask yourself, *Could conditions, actions, and events concerning one or more categories of hazard lead to or create a hazardous situation?*

9.5 Strategies for Working Safely, Effectively, and Efficiently

The following table identifies some strategies (and controls) that workers can take to ensure tasks are performed safely, effectively, and efficiently.

Strategies for Working Safely, Effectively, and Efficiently
• Identify hazardous situations and controls before starting the task.
• Gather all the items needed to do the work before starting the task.
• Ensure tools and equipment are in "good" condition.
• Set up equipment and materials to minimize moving of materials and to provide an escape route.
• Before starting the task, ensure the site is safe for carrying out the specific type of work.
• Identify hazardous situation and controls needed before carrying out each step of the task.
• Identify the correct type and size of tools and materials for each step of the task.
• Identify conditions that can change while carrying out a step of the task, and identify appropriate actions to take in response to the conditions (e.g., engine stalls).
• Identify methods or procedures that must not be used when performing the task or task step.
• Plan and sequence task steps to be compatible with physical layout, to promote efficiency, and minimize physical effort.
• Adjust lighting and ventilation to meet requirements for optimizing task steps.
• For specific steps, shield equipment and materials from dust, vapor, mist, chemical, heat, and physical damage.
• Specify the standards of performance for each step. Specify operating limits and what to do if the limits are exceeded.

(continued)

Part 9 Apply Your SafeThink Strategy

Strategies for Working Safely, Effectively, and Efficiently
• Specify indicators that the step was performed successfully/unsuccessfully.
• Identify strategies that make carrying out a step more effective.
• Identify strategies that make carrying out a step more efficient or easier.
• Use appropriate equipment to lift and move materials.
• Identify methods for carrying out a step that will cause the least stress or damage to equipment or materials.
• Identify strategies to use the least amount of materials and products such as solvents, degreasers, and lubricants (e.g., on-site filtering or recycling systems).
• Keep the work area clean while performing the task.
• Keep others informed in advance about conditions, actions, and events that will affect them and the coordination of work.
• Do a quality check when a major task step has been completed.
• Clean up the area after the task has been completed and return tools and equipment to designated storage areas.
• Complete and file documentation about the work, equipment, and site conditions.

9.6 Reporting

In keeping with regulatory requirements and company policies, you are required to immediately report:
- work-related injuries and illness
- health, safety, and environmental hazards
- near-misses (near-hits), which could result in injuries or other losses
- hazardous conditions, actions, or events
- safety violations by employees or contracted workers

When any of the above reports are received, the supervisor or safety officer works with site personnel to:
- investigate the reported incident or hazard.
- recommend appropriate controls to prevent future incidents.
- ensure the controls are implemented promptly.
- learn your company's reporting policies and procedures.

Make sure you know how to report an incident, near-miss, or safety violation (e.g., when to report, who to report to, and how to report). If you see another worker jeopardizing his or her safety or the safety of others, you have a responsibility to point out the violation to the worker. If that fails to change the situation, talk with your supervisor or safety officer about the safety violation. The goal of reporting near-misses and violations is to determine the causes and identify ways and means of preventing similar incidents from occurring in the future.

9.7 Continuous Improvement

The goal of company reporting policies is to continually improve safety. As part of a company's commitment to continually improve safety, safety inspections and safety audits to identify safety deficiencies may be conducted regularly. Inspection checklists and assessment and audit reports are reviewed. Appropriate controls are selected and implemented as necessary. Types of changes that could be made include:
- modifications to the equipment and processes
- improvements to fixed monitoring systems (e.g., gas detection)
- uses of additional or improved personal protective equipment changes to work practices and procedures
- changes in the requirements for communicating and documenting

A major concern to companies is ensuring that all workers are promptly informed of the changes that affect them. In some cases, a memo stating the changes is sufficient; in other cases (e.g., changes to procedures) workers require additional training. You also have a responsibility to ensure that you:
- are aware of any changes to the workplace that affect your work
- have received the required training before performing the tasks that are affected by the changes
- are properly fitted if the new controls include personal protective equipment and/or respiratory protective equipment

Newly-implemented controls must be closely monitored to ensure that they are:
- effective
- do not create new or different hazards
- do not have hazardous or negative impacts at other locations in the facility or process

Consideration must also be given to ensure control equipment (e.g., respirators, fume hoods) is properly maintained.

9.8 What Can Go Wrong?

An important strategy to keep you and others from harm is to consider what can go wrong. Ask *What if...?* questions about what can go wrong regarding PEMEO. For each domain of PEMEO you need to consider conditions, actions, and events that could occur and cause PEMEO to function poorly, behave abnormally, or fail. If there is a concern that involves any of the six categories of hazards, determine the immediate effect.

Having determined the possible immediate effects, you can ask additional questions:
- Could I or others become ill and/or injured?
- What should be my first response if an incident occurs? What can I do to minimize the possibility of an incident occurring and the severity of the consequences should an incident occur?

For many of the incidents identified by the *What if...?* questions, your response will be more effective when you:
- pre-determine the response you would make.
- rehearse your response by imagining responding to the incident. Rehearsing increases the possibility that you will respond immediately and effectively.

LEARNING ACTIVITY 9

Apply your SafeThink strategy and select controls to eliminate or reduce the hazard.

In Parts 3 to 8 of this book, you learned about each of the six categories of hazard, one at a time. For each category of hazard, you identified specific conditions, actions, or events in your workplace that can lead to or create a hazardous situation. Part 9 combines all six questions as a thinking strategy to identify and predict hazardous situations. Learning Activity 9 gives you the opportunity to practice using all six questions at once to identify and predict hazardous situations in your workplace and job. In the learning activity, you will apply all six questions before, during, and after work is completed.

1. Select one task that you perform that has the potential to cause harm to you or others, and list the major steps.

    Task _____

    Major step 1 (before working) _____

    Major step 2 (while working) _____

    Major step 3 (while working) _____

    Major step 4 (while working) _____

    Major step 5 (while working) _____

    Major step 6 (while working) _____

    Major step 7 (after work is complete) _____

2. Use the task you selected in question 1 and complete the table on pages 254 and 255. This learning activity gives you the opportunity to identify conditions, actions, and events involving each of the six categories of hazard that exist before, while, and after working that could lead to or create a hazardous situation. Below is a general description of applying the *SafeThink* strategy to a task. For each major step, think of each action step, and:
    - ask yourself the six *SafeThink* questions, one for each category of hazard
    - if you answer *no* to a question, go to the next question
    - if you answer *yes* to a question, you need to ask, *Are*

there any conditions, actions, or events that can lead to or create a hazardous situation?

- if you cannot identify any conditions, actions, and events, proceed to the next question

After identifying all the hazardous situations, select controls that you can use to protect yourself and other workers. You may have to implement the controls several steps earlier or before starting the task (e.g., lockout and tagout).

The SafeThink Strategy (detailed description)

The *SafeThink* strategy to identify and predict hazardous situations caused by all six categories of hazard is as follows:

1. Identify the task.
2. Break the task into two to nine **major steps**.
3. Break **major step** 1 into **action steps**.

For the first **action step**:

4. Ask the first general *SafeThink* question about hazardous materials.
5. If you answer:
   - *no* at step **4**, go to step **7**
   - *yes* at step **4**, then ask *Are there any conditions, actions, and events that will lead to or create a hazardous situation?*
6. **If you a**nswer:
   - *no*, at step **5** about hazardous situations, go to step **7**
   - *yes* at step **5** about hazardous situations, then ask the remainder of the related follow-up questions and select effective controls
7. **Ask the next general** *SafeThink* **question.**
8. **Repeat steps 5 to 7** for the remaining general questions.

For the remainder of the **action steps** (**major step** 1):

9. repeat steps **3** to **8**.

For each of the remaining major steps:

10. repeat steps **3** to **9**.

To make the *SafeThink* strategy more efficient, eliminate those hazard categories that do not apply to the task. For example, if you know a task does not involve hazardous materials or electricity, you can eliminate the major questions for these categories. You then have only three major questions to apply to the task. You can also use elimination for each of the major steps.

Category of Hazard	Major step 1 *(before)*	Major step 2 *(while)*	Major step 3 *(while)*
hazardous materials			
objects, motion, force			
non-ambient conditions			
current and static electricity			
radiation			
changes			
controls			

Major step 4 *(while)*	Major step 5 *(while)*	Major step 6 *(while)*	Major step 7 *(after)*

3. Select a **major step**: _____

3a. Ask *What if...?* questions to identify what can go wrong and fill in the table below. For each domain of PEMEO, you need to consider conditions, actions, and events that could occur and cause PEMEO to function poorly, behave abnormally, or fail. If there is a concern regarding any of the six categories of hazard, determine the immediate effect.

What can go wrong with changes?		
Domain	**What if...?** *conditions, actions, and events involving:* • *hazardous materials* • *objects, motion, force* • *non-ambient conditions* • *electricity* • *radiation*	**Immediate effect**
People		
Equipment		
Materials		
Environment		
Organization		

3b. From the table you have completed, select one effect that may create or lead to a hazardous situation and answer the following questions:

Could I or others become ill and/or injured? What would be the consequences?

_____

_____

Part 9   Apply Your SafeThink Strategy

What would be the consequences for other PEMEO domains?

_____

_____

What should be my first response if an incident occurs?

_____

_____

What can I do to minimize the probability of an incident occurring and/or the severity of consequences?

_____

_____

_____

4. Another useful strategy for identifying and controlling hazards is to apply the "zero-energy" concept. Select a task involving energy sources that is different from the task used in questions 2 and 3. In the table below, place an "X" in the boxes where the energy source exists.

Task _____

Energy	Before	While	After
electrical			
mechanical			
pneumatic			
hydraulic			
steam			
thermal			
potential			
bio-hazard			

 SafeThink™

Opportunities to Practice

Use *SafeThink* at work, at home, and at play. Incorporate the strategy in your daily life to reduce the possibilities of personal injury.

At work, practice the strategy continually, before, during, and after completing a task. Use the strategy during safety meetings, pre-work meetings, and post-work meetings. With time, applying the strategy will become routine.

With practice, for familiar tasks, you will react automatically to any condition, action, or event that could cause harm. However, in a new situation, you may not recognize potentially hazardous conditions, actions, or events. During new work situations, you may have to consciously think about each question, one at a time.

■ FOOD for THOUGHT

■ Using SafeThink efficiently

The *SafeThink* strategy requires you to continually ask all six general questions before working, while working, and after work is complete. You can make the thinking process even more efficient if you know that one or more categories of hazard are not present when performing the task. You only need to ask the questions that apply to the agents of cause that are present or will be created. You still need to be cautious. You must be certain that the category of hazard doesn't apply.

You can also make the *SafeThink* strategy efficient when performing a specific action step of the task. Often only one or two categories of hazard apply to the step.

■ Using controls to identify agents of cause

The *SafeThink* strategy requires that you ask yourself questions to identify the agents of cause and the conditions, actions, and events that can lead to or create a hazardous situation. When a hazardous situation is identified, controls are selected to reduce or eliminate the hazardous situation. Refer to Appendix 4 for a list of practical controls.

Some people think of controls first to identify the agents of cause and the conditions, actions, and events that can create a hazardous situation. This approach is useful provided you are aware of the limitations. Controls routinely used in the workplace may not protect you from all hazardous situations associated with a specific task.

■ Critical task analysis

SafeThink is an informal form of a critical task analysis to identify hazards and select controls. There are differences in how a critical task analysis can be conducted, however, the processes are similar. Here is a general description of a formal critical task analysis.

- a group consisting of specialists such as operators, maintenance, health and safety advisors, and engineers is formed
- a task is selected
- a critical task analysis form consisting of three columns is filled out

Major Steps (or specific action steps)	Hazards	Controls

- the major steps or action steps are listed in the left column
- for each step, hazards are identified and controls selected

The form is an excellent aid in developing procedures. The form should never be used on the job as a reference for carrying out the task. Controls identified for any given step may have to be implemented several steps earlier or before starting the task.

In some ways, the *SafeThink* strategy is more rigorous than a traditional critical task analysis. *Agents of cause create a broader category than hazards. SafeThink* places *a stronger emphasis on conditions, actions, and events* that can lead to or create a hazardous situation.

When using *SafeThink* as part of pre-job hazard assessments, work is thought through more thoroughly. Not only is the work done safely, it is often done more efficiently and effectively. That is one of the benefits of *SafeThink*—work can be more efficient, effective, and safer.

■ Negotiating to convince others to improve safety

There may be times when you identify serious safety deficiencies but do not have the responsibility to correct the deficiencies; someone else has the responsibility. You may have talked to that person before, only to have your concerns dismissed or postponed. One way to increase your success in convincing others to correct safety deficiencies is by negotiating a win-win solution without causing conflict. The following suggestions may help you present your case more strongly. A brief explanation of each suggestion follows.

1. Clearly specify your safety concerns
2. Determine the risk of loss for workers
3. Determine the risk of loss for the entire operation or business
4. Identify the root cause(s) for the hazardous situation
5. Identify alternatives to correct the deficiency
6. Determine the effectiveness of each option to prevent injury
7. Determine the costs, effort, and time to implement each option
8. Do a cost-benefit analysis
9. Select viable options for correcting the deficiency
10. Determine reasons for correcting the deficiency
11. Determine reasons for not correcting the deficiency
12. Plan to present your case
13. Present your case for correcting the deficiency

1. **Clearly specify your safety concerns**
   - What is the hazardous situation?
   - What are the potential consequences if an incident occurs?
   - Determine if an incident has occurred in the past and, if so, what the consequences were. Was the incident a near miss, a minor injury, or a serious injury?
   - Is the current situation a breach of health and safety regulations?

2. **Determine the risk of loss for workers**
   - Determine the probability of an incident occurring. You may want to use general terms such as *quite high, high,* and *very high* probability of an occurrence.
   - Determine the potential consequences for the person that could be injured.
   - Determine the risk of loss using one of the risk of loss matrices identified in Part 8.

3. **Determine the risk of loss for the entire operation or business**

   Ask yourself *What if...?* questions about each PEMEO domain to determine the immediate effect on each domain and the consequences for the operation. Here are some consequences to consider:
   - damage to equipment, materials, buildings, and other structures
   - costs to clean up the environment
   - loss of morale when a person is injured
   - emotional stress when a person is injured
   - lost time responding to the incident
   - lost income if a family member is injured
   - additional stress on others to provide care
   - stress on others to take over that person's work while he or she recovers
   - cost of hiring a replacement and training time
   - continuing loss of productivity and costs if the injuries are permanent
   - costs for medical care, travel, and accommodations
   - loss of reputation

4. **Identify the root cause(s) for the hazardous situation**

   The root cause(s) must be corrected to achieve a long-term solution. Often there is a combination of factors creating the hazardous situation. For example, to adjust a component in a feed mill, a worker's hand and arm must come very close to moving parts. To make the situation worse, the equipment location makes it awkward to reach the component.

5. **Identify alternatives to correct the deficiency**

   Consider a broad range of options, some of which you will probably reject with further investigation. Using the feed mill as an example, consider:
   - modify the task (if possible)
   - repair equipment (if a solution)
   - redesign the equipment (e.g., mount customized guards)
   - reposition equipment for easy access to components that need adjusting
   - move the wall or other restrictions limiting access to the components
   - replace the old equipment with new equipment that is safer
   - hire a company to do the milling
   - purchase a different feed (e.g., pellets)
   - abandon that part of the operation

6. **Determine the effectiveness of each option to prevent injury**

   Use a risk matrix to determine the effectiveness of each option. Delete any option that is not effective in preventing injury.

7. **Determine the costs, effort, and time to implement each option**

   In addition to the costs associated with purchases and possibly hiring a contractor to implement the solution, calculate the cost for the time you and others will spend implementing the solution.

   There may also be continuing costs. For example, it may take more time to carry out the task. Make an estimate of the continuing costs of the solution. If the work will be more efficient, note the efficiency when listing the benefits of correcting the deficiency.

8. **Do a cost-benefit analysis**

   Compare the cost to correct the deficiency to the loss should an incident occur. Financially, some options may cost more to implement than the potential loss. However, when also considering breach of regulation, ethics, emotional stress, loss of morale, and loss of reputation, the corrective action may be warranted.

9. **Select viable options for correcting the deficiency**

   When making a selection, consider the cost to correct the deficiency and the effectiveness of the solution. There may be one obvious solution or there may be two or more solutions that seem viable. To increase the credibility of your position you may want to get an expert's opinion.

   When presenting your argument to correct the deficiency, present your best solution first and be prepared to present a second solution if the first one is rejected.

10. **Determine reasons for correcting the safety deficiency**

    For your job and the business, you need to identify reasons that would have value to the decision maker. Example of reasons include:
    - prevent potential losses
    - reduce the risk of losses
    - good risk management
    - demonstrates caring for the wellbeing of others
    - improves morale
    - others do it (provide one or more specific examples to be credible)
    - meets legislation
    - increases job satisfaction
    - some refuse to do the task because they think it's too dangerous
    - your reputation and the reputation of your operation is at stake if you don't act
    - others do not want to work here because of the risks

11. Determine reasons for not correcting the deficiency

Do not assume you know the reasons for inaction. You will need to explore with the decision-maker why the deficiency has not been corrected. Consider these possibilities:

- The decision-maker was not aware of the safety deficiency.
- The decision-maker is unethical and does not care about protecting others from harm. In industrialized countries, the belief is that supervisors and managers care for the welfare of employees and co-workers. However, the level of caring can vary somewhat from one supervisor to the next. Assuming that the decision-maker is ethical, there must be other reasons for not correcting the deficiency.
- The decision-maker has a high threshold of risk.
- The decision-maker has only considered the probability of an incident occurring and has not put much thought into the potential consequences of a serious incident. You may have to discuss risk of loss (versus risk/probability). You might consider describing an incident where a person regretted their decision. For example, a person was speeding to get to an appointment on time. He hit a pedestrian. After the accident, he realized that getting to the appointment on time was not that important compared with seriously hurting someone. For the rest of his life, he has to live with the knowledge that he made a poor decision and injured someone.
- Make sure you explain the potential consequences if the deficiency is not corrected. State that, *You (the decision-maker) would regret not correcting the deficiency if there was an incident—wouldn't you?* You are trying to get the decision-maker to acknowledge that the potential consequences are serious.
- Only minor incidents have occurred in the past so we can get away with not correcting the deficiency.
- The decision-maker may not be aware of the total loss to the operation if there was a serious incident.
- It costs too much to correct.
- We don't have time to fix it.
- The decision-maker has only considered one very costly solution to correcting the deficiency and not thought of any other options

12. Plan to present your case

Safety concerns are often discussed in person. But, for some decision-makers, a written case may work better. Consider how, where, and when to discuss the case.

- What is your working relationship with the decision-maker? Cordial or confrontational?
- Maybe someone other than you should present the case.
- Would it add credibility if you and another person presented the case together?
- Are there regular safety meetings where the case can be presented?
- Identify the topics and the sequence of your presentation. Do not provide a lot of detail on each topic; select key points to continue focusing on the issue and build your case.
- Build in opportunities to ask the decision-maker questions so he or she participates in the discussion. You also gain a better understanding about his or her thinking regarding the safety deficiency.
- Appeal to both his or her intellect and emotions.
- Does the decision-maker tend to make decisions to avoid problems or to achieve goals? You may want to put a stronger emphasis on goals or on avoiding problems.
- Determine how you are going to initiate the discussion. Consider starting the negotiating by getting agreement that safety is important.

13. Present your case for correcting the deficiency

- Be prepared to adjust your presentation.
- Do not present your case as a lecture (you talk and decision-maker listens).
- Be prepared to listen to the decision-maker and encourage him or her to explain his or her thinking. You could ask, *What do you think?*
- One way to keep the decision-maker involved and move forward with the negotiation is to end your key statements with a question to get agreement. Here are some examples:
  - *Isn't it?*
  - *Wouldn't it?*
  - *Couldn't it?*
  - *Shouldn't it?*

- *Wouldn't you?*
- *Don't you?*

For example:
- *Safety is important, isn't it?*
- *If a worker got injured, you would feel really bad, wouldn't you?*

- If the decision-maker appears unwilling to listen to you, you may want to consider showing that you have done your homework. Indicate that, if he or she listens to you, you will prove that it's a benefit to him or her to take corrective action.
- If the meeting begins to be confrontational, try to maintain a level voice. You may want to suggest that the discussion is getting confrontational and, for the benefit of both of you, take a break.
- You could suggest putting your case in writing for the decision-maker to review and meet with you at a designated time.
- At the end of the meeting, give the person time to think about taking corrective action.
- If there is a decision to take action, get a commitment as to when the deficiency will be corrected.

Internalizing SafeThink

The goal of the *SafeThink* program is for people to learn the strategy so well that they internalize it—they personalize the strategy. When the strategy is internalized, *SafeThink* becomes part of how they think about work, plan work, do work, and follow up on work. When people internalize the strategy, they also use it in their personal lives. For example, those who use safety glasses at work will also use them at home when doing tasks that could damage their eyes.

■ Sustaining the use of SafeThink in the workplace and personal lives

Learning to *SafeThink* is an important first step. Organizations get the most benefit from the strategy when they take initiatives to integrate the strategy into day-to-day routines and take action to reinforce the use of the strategy. The *SafeThink* Coach-the-Coach program provides many suggestions for integrating and sustaining the use of *SafeThink* in the workplace.

In recent years, governments have placed a greater emphasis on prevention of illness and injury to reduce health care costs. Other organizations are also promoting prevention because it makes good business sense. Prevention of illness and injury is most successful within a culture of safety—a culture in which everyone, young and old, takes measures to prevent illness and injury. *SafeThink* is a powerful intervention for promoting a culture of safety. It not only gives people the tools to remain vigilant and prevent illness and injury, it also promotes positive safety attitudes. When people see value in using *SafeThink* to prevent incidents, they are intrinsically motivated to use the strategy. Intrinsically motivated people usually encourage others to learn and apply the strategy. When a group learns to *SafeThink*, a common identity with key concepts is developed which, in turn, influences attitudes of individuals. Collectively, when a group identifies with *SafeThink*, they can shift individual safety attitudes significantly.

Appendices

Appendix 1—Learning Concepts and Generalizations

Appendix 2—Safety Models

Appendix 3—Safethink: Philosophy and Concepts

Appendix 4—Hazard and Control Tables

Appendix 1—Learning Concepts and Generalizations

People's thinking skills and preferred learning styles differ. Some people are abstract thinkers, others require concrete examples. People also have personal learning styles; for example, some people prefer to learn from the general to the specific, others prefer to learn from the specific to the general. The *SafeThink* book requires a shift away from the type of thinking and approach to learning that has often been part of traditional health and safety books.

Traditionally, health and safety books tend to focus on memorizing information. *SafeThink*, however, focuses on learning concepts (and generalizations) and applying them to the job. The goal is for people to think for themselves about:
- agents of cause and the conditions, actions, and events that can lead to or create a hazardous situation
- selecting controls and assessing their effectiveness to prevent illness and injury

Workers need to understand that the *SafeThink* approach to learning concepts and their applications is different from learning facts.

Concepts and generalizations are learned by observing something in common among several different situations. For example:
- touching a hot stove burns the skin
- touching a hot frying pan burns the skin
- touching a hot clothes iron burns the skin

The concept from these observations is that touching anything hot burns the skin, regardless of the type of object that is hot (i.e., a hot object is an agent of cause). In this example, knowing the concept that hot objects burn the skin (a generalization) can be useful for examining a variety of other situations. The goal is to determine if there is a hot object and to assess whether or not there is a possibility that conditions, actions, and events can result in being burned.

Appendix 1 Learning Concepts and Generalizations

The *SafeThink* strategy described in this book presents concepts about six categories of hazards (e.g., hazardous material, electricity). Each category of hazard has the potential of causing harm, given *certain* conditions, actions, or events. For each category of hazard, the book identifies agents of cause that are common to many workplaces.

For people to learn concepts and generalizations about workplace health and safety on their own, they have to be exposed to a variety of situations, some of which may have negative consequences. Learning through trial and error is risky and inefficient.

A more effective way to help people learn a concept or generalization is to give them the concept and provide many different concrete examples of the concept being applied in the workplace and home. Providing examples of applying the concept is especially important if people have had little exposure to that concept—the examples give meaning to the concept.

The next level of learning is to apply the concept effectively in the workplace. At the application level, a person thinking about or observing a condition, action, or event for which the concept applies learns to automatically recognize a situation that could potentially cause harm. Practice, encouragement, reinforcement of the concept, and recognizing the need to apply the concept in the workplace help people learn.

After learning to apply the six categories of hazards, one at a time, the next step is to learn to apply all six categories at the same time. The six categories are applied continually before doing work, while working, and after the work has been completed. Applying the six categories of hazards to identify agents of cause and the conditions, actions, and events that can lead to or create hazardous situations is the most critical part of the *SafeThink* strategy. The second part of the strategy is to make sure that controls are being used to prevent a safety incident and to have a personal action plan in mind in case something goes wrong.

The best way to learn to use the *SafeThink* strategy is to practice on the job and in your personal life. On the job, there are many opportunities to practice the strategy, for example:
- continually, **before** doing work, **while** working, and **after** the work has been completed
- during safety meetings
- when holding formal meetings to plan work
- when two or more workers have on-the-spot meetings before, during, and after the work is complete

With practice, you will automatically identify agents of cause and the conditions, actions, and events that could potentially cause harm throughout your work shift. You will know that you are applying the *SafeThink* strategy when you realize that you constantly think about and look for hazardous situations that could harm you and/or others.

Appendix 2—Safety Models

Many psychology concepts apply equally to education and safety and can be grouped into three safety models.
- behavior-based safety
- person-based safety
- cognitive-based safety

The illustration on the following page shows the relationships between the three models.

The behavior-based safety model places a strong emphasis on reinforcing safe behavior. Critical task analyses are carried out on high risk tasks. Specific action steps are identified where safe performance is critical to prevent injury. Workers are then observed to ensure they perform the steps safely. Constructive feedback and positive reinforcements are given. Management encourages workers to behave (perform) in a safe manner. The belief is that, if workers perform the safe behaviors often enough, they will develop the belief that safety is important (i.e., person-based safety).

The person-based safety model places a strong emphasis on developing positive beliefs and attitudes that safety is important. The thinking is that, if workers believe safety is important, they will perform their work safely. Management must walk the talk. Safety is Number One. Policies and practices are developed that support day-to-day safety. For example, every morning, a pre-job safety meeting is held. Everyone, management and workers, is encouraged to stop work if there is a safety concern. Posters and other visuals can be used to remind people that the work cannot proceed unless it can be done safely. The goal is to develop a culture of safety where everyone believes that safety is most important. Safety is **not** a priority, it is a commitment. Priorities can change. Commitment to safety is when you don't compromise on safety measures for yourself and others regardless of the demands and challenges of the day. Commitment is when you continually take action to improve

safety. Evidence that workers believe safety is important is when they are conscious of safety and act safely not only on but also off the job.

The cognitive-based safety model places a strong emphasis on thinking strategies (knowledge, analysis, and decision-making). Psychological concepts are applied to make the thinking strategy effective and efficient. The belief is that workers doing the work in a dynamic workplace are in the best position to identify, predict, and control hazardous situations throughout the workday. Generally, when workers are given the tools to perform effectively, they are more likely to use the tools. *SafeThink* provides the means (the tools) for workers to rigorously think through their work to identify and predict hazardous situations, be it a few seconds ahead of carrying out an action to many hours ahead to put in effective controls.

SafeThink relates to and supports both **person-based** and **behavior-based** safety models. Ideally, integrating all three safety models provides the most comprehensive initiative to prevent illness and injury.

SafeThink **and the person-based safety model**—The belief is that when workers internalize and personalize the thinking strategy to their work and workplaces, they take ownership of the strategy. They are more motivated to use the strategy and encourage others to use the strategy as well. They develop a strong belief that safety is important and they can contribute to a safe workplace. (In the *SafeThink* course, group dynamics are used to promote positive safety attitudes and beliefs.)

SafeThink **and the behavior-based safety model**—In the *SafeThink* course, positive reinforcements are provided to encourage participants to act safely. The importance of providing positive reinforcements to encourage safe behavior on the job is also addressed in the course. In the workplace, with *SafeThink*, workers are more effective at observing themselves and others perform their work (safely or unsafely) and providing reinforcements to work safely.

Appendix 2 Safety Models

Safety Models

SafeThink™
Zero Illness and Injury

A structured critical thinking strategy

Cognitive
- Cognitive skill
- Apply knowledge
- Analyzing work
- Making safety decisions

Person
- Beliefs · Values

Behavior
- Actions

SafeThink is a cognitive-based safety model. SafeThink supports and enhances both behavior-based and person-based models.

HDC Human Development Consultants Ltd.

To be most effective, *SafeThink* is integrated into work routines. Workers are encouraged to apply the strategy throughout the day to prevent illness and injury. Positive reinforcements are used by supervisors and co-workers to promote the use of the strategy on and off the job. Applying the *SafeThink* strategy, showing concern, and taking action to prevent others from being harmed encourages the development of positive safety attitudes in the workplace.

Appendix 3—SafeThink: Philosophy and Concepts

> **The vision is zero illness and injury—the strategy is SafeThink**
>
> Health and wellness are values promoted by industrial societies. Large portions of government budgets are spent to maintain excellent health care systems. As health care budgets continue to escalate, greater emphasis is being placed on prevention to reduce health care costs. Product standards, government regulations and enforcement, education, and the promotion of healthier lifestyles are primary preventive methods. Prevention of illness and injury will be most successful within a culture of safety—a culture in which everyone, young and old, takes measures to prevent illness and injury. In a culture of safety, people are vigilant and mentally engaged—throughout the day—in identifying and predicting hazardous situations to prevent illness and injury. And that's how *SafeThink* makes its important contribution: *SafeThink* develops a culture of safety.

SafeThink—Creating a Commitment to Safety

SafeThink is a structured critical thinking strategy to identify and predict hazardous situations. People can *SafeThink on the fly* at work, while driving, at home, at play, and on vacation. When the strategy is internalized, people are intrinsically motivated to use it to keep out of harm's way. Because the internalized strategy is instantly available, it becomes part of how they think about, plan, do, and follow up on work and personal activities to prevent being harmed.

SafeThink—Preventing Illness and Injury

SafeThink places an emphasis on predicting hazardous situations, be it a few seconds or several hours before engaging in work or other activities. The *SafeThink* strategy also emphasizes controls that can be used to remain safe. What's powerful about *SafeThink* is that people apply a mental strategy to rigorously think through their work and personal activities and to act safely.

SafeThink—Contributing to a Safe Environment

Organizations are responsible for ensuring a safe workplace but cannot do it without the help of their employees. Employees are responsible for working safely—*SafeThink* helps keep them out of harm's way all day. With *SafeThink*, employees take a personal initiative to think through the work. When everyone continually looks for and predicts hazardous situations, the risk of illness and injury decreases immensely. The strategy gives employees the tools they need to remain vigilant and focused on their work. With *SafeThink*, employees are rigorous in assessing their environments and actions to identify and predict hazardous situations.

SafeThink—Creating a Culture of Safety

Because participants of *SafeThink* workshops believe that the strategy has personal value, they have an interest in encouraging others to use it. Promoting a culture of safety is more likely to be successful when people have a personal interest in doing so. 90% of workshop participants say that they would feel significantly safer or a major degree safer if their co-workers and peers used the strategy. *SafeThink* is a cognitive mental strategy. It gives people a reason to make the effort to prevent incidents thereby reinforcing positive safety attitudes. Collectively, groups of employees easily identify with *SafeThink*, contributing to a culture of safety.

SafeThink—The Power of Structured Thinking

SafeThink has several powerful features that make it useful and effective:

- *SafeThink* provides a framework to make it easier for people to deal with the complexities of health and safety and to be more structured at identifying and predicting hazardous situations.
- In addition, agents of cause common to a broad range of industries are identified as a set of generalities (concepts), reducing the number of unique agents of cause. Generalities give people more flexibility in identifying agents of cause in unfamiliar workplaces and environments. Together, the framework and generalities

- *SafeThink* requires that people ask themselves a series of hierarchical questions to identify and predict hazardous situations. When people ask themselves a question, it tends to beg an answer, contributing to thorough analysis of the task and work environment. Self-questioning also helps people to remain mentally engaged in identifying and predicting hazardous situations.
- *What if... ?* questions can be very useful for determining *What can go wrong? SafeThink* provides a structured way for people to use a set of *What if... ?* questions so that they are more effective at dealing with potential changes in the workplace.
- Several other critical health and safety issues are also addressed in the *SafeThink* course, including:
  - developing good safety habits
  - ways to remain vigilant
  - reasons and causes for safe and unsafe behaviors
- how people's actions can impact others

SafeThink—Personalizing the Strategy

More experienced workers have often learned the agents of cause and created their own generalities through trial and error. And their learning may be incomplete—they likely haven't been exposed to a broad set of situations.

It is no longer acceptable for workers to learn by trial and error about hazardous situations and create their own generalities. *SafeThink* has identified these generalities. *SafeThink* training ensures that workers know the generalities for agents of cause and the conditions, actions, and events that create hazardous situations. Through a series of learning activities, workers apply the *SafeThink* strategy to their tasks, workplaces, and personal environments to give meaning to the generalities—they personalize the generalities and internalize the structured thinking strategy.

SafeThink—Integrating SafeThink into the Workplace

SafeThink is cognitive-based. It supports the behavior-based safety model by providing the means to make more comprehensive behavior-based observations. *SafeThink* also relates to the person-based model in two ways. Firstly, when people are given a rigorous thinking strategy, they become more effective at meeting their responsibilities for working safely. Secondly, when people internalize *SafeThink*, they are intrinsically motivated to use the strategy on and off the job.

The *SafeThink* course is a powerful intervention that contributes to developing positive safety attitudes. Collectively, when a group identifies with *SafeThink*, they can shift individual worker attitudes significantly. (IEEE Transactions on Professional Communication, Sept. 2007, Vol. 50, Num. 3, P 232-248)

The biggest payback for employers comes after *SafeThink* is integrated into daily routines and the organization makes efforts to reinforce the use of *SafeThink* each and every day.

The culture of safety is enhanced when everyone, young and old, uses *SafeThink* throughout the day, at work and in their personal lives, to prevent illness and injury.

> **The vision is zero illness and injury—the strategy is *SafeThink*.**

Appendix 4—Hazard and Control Tables

Table 1: Types of Hazards Present at Industrial Workplaces	
Type of hazard	**Examples**
Hazardous Materials (Note: classification of materials varies with jurisdiction)	• Compressed gases • Flammable and combustible material • Oxidizing material • Poisonous and infectious material • Corrosive material • Dangerously reactive material

Objects, Motion, Force	• Stationary objects
	• Motion
	• mobile equipment
	   − moving parts
	   − object moving towards body
	   − body moving towards object
	   − vibration
	• Force
	   − elevated objects
	   − pressurized equipment
	   − applied towards body
	   − body applied on tools, equipment, materials

Non-Ambient Conditions (conditions that differ from surrounding workplace conditions)	• Pressure • Temperature • Light • Noise • Vibration • Hazardous emissions • Oxygen-deficient/excessive atmospheres
Electricity	• Current electricity • Static electricity
Radiation	• Gamma radiation and X-rays • Alpha and beta particles, neutrons • Ultraviolet radiation • Infrared radiation • Microwaves and radio waves • Laser radiation
Changes	• Operator-initiated changes • Maintenance-initiated changes • Technology-initiated changes • Externally-initiated changes

Table 2: Types of Workplace Toxic Gas Exposure Limits	
Type	**Concept**
Time-Weighted Average (TWA)	• Maximum time-weighted average concentration of a toxic gas that most workers may be exposed to during an 8-hour work shift, 40-hour work week for a working lifetime (40 years) without incurring adverse health effects. • When the work shift is longer, the exposure limit must be lowered to prevent workers from excessive exposure. • A small percentage of workers may experience adverse effects *at* or *below* the TWA exposure limit.
Short-Term Exposure Limit (STEL)	• Maximum concentration of a toxic gas that a worker may be exposed to for short periods within the work shift without incurring adverse health effects. • The number of exposures and the period of time must be specified (e.g., four 15-minute STEL exposures per shift). • A small percentage of workers may experience adverse effects *at* or *below* the 15-minute STEL exposure limit.
Ceiling Limit	• Maximum concentration of the toxic gas that a worker may be exposed to at *any time*. Most workers will be harmed by any exposure *above* the Ceiling Limit. • Ceiling Limits are usually provided for gases that cause rapid, severe health effects (e.g., immediate unconsciousness). • A time limit is provided for some substances (e.g., Ceiling-5 minutes); for other substances exposure for any amount of time is considered unsafe. • A small percentage of workers may experience adverse effects *at* or *below* the Ceiling Limit.
Peak Exposure Limit *(Discont'd)*	• Formerly described as a brief allowable exposure that exceeds the Ceiling Limit. *This limit is no longer used.*
Skin Notation	• Notation added to the exposure limit to indicate that the toxic gas can damage (or be absorbed through) the skin, mucous membranes, or eyes. • For some toxic gases two different exposure limits may be available: a skin exposure limit and an inhalation exposure limit. To prevent harmful effects, worker exposure must **not** exceed *either* limit. • For some toxic gases, the skin exposure limit is lower than the inhalation limit.
Immediately Dangerous to Life and Health (IDLH) Concentration	• Concentration at which exposure is likely to cause death, rapid, severe health effects that prevent exposed workers from escaping to a safe environment, or permanent adverse health effects (immediate or delayed). • A small percentage of workers may experience adverse effects *at* or *below* the IDLH concentration. • IDLH concentrations include life-threatening environments other than toxic gas environments (e.g., oxygen-deficient/excessive atmospheres, explosive atmospheres).

Exposure limits for hazardous materials are listed on the Material Safety Data Sheets.

Table 3: Stationary Objects That May be Hazardous

Stationary objects that may be hazardous	Workplace examples
Obstructions	Low-hanging pipes, barriers, fences, pillars, posts, ceilings, doorways
Large equipment or installations	Kilns, furnaces, compressors, vessels, hoists, waste bins
Tripping hazards	Electrical cords, carpet edges, misplaced objects, ropes, hoses, concealed piping
Sharp-edged objects	Saw blades, knives, cutting tools, broken tools, sharp-edged objects, metal banding
Brittle objects with sharp edges	Glass, clay, brick, ceramics, concrete
Pointed objects (or objects that can puncture)	Screwdrivers, awls, nails, screws, hooks, pointed sticks or posts, rebar, wire, glass
Suspended objects/equipment	Swing stages, forklift cages, crane hooks and cables, wires, hoses, lights, light fixtures
Excavations, shafts, and tunnels	Trenches, pits, basements, mineshafts, utility tunnels
Holes, openings, and chutes	Construction site chimney holes, openings, materials chutes
Confined spaces	Vessels, lube pits, sheds, sewers, reservoirs, cisterns, cellars, coolers, refrigerators
Water bodies/liquid storage facilities	Sloughs, lakes, sewage lagoons, tailings ponds, reservoirs, cisterns, dugouts, sumps
Splintered or abrasive objects/surfaces	Rough plywood, weathered or rusted metal, surfaces with peeling paint, gravel, rough concrete, brick, shingles
Slippery surfaces	Wet, ice-coated, highly polished or very smooth surfaces; surfaces with spilled liquids (oil, glycol), particulates (e.g., grain, filings)
Uneven surfaces	Flagstone, brick, or broken pavement, misaligned floors or loading docks, vegetated or rocky areas, hidden ditches or holes
Elevated or sloping surfaces	Roofs, girders, ladders, loading docks, platforms, decks, staircases, mezzanines, scaffolds, ledges, utility poles, loading ramps, gangplanks

Table 4: Moving Objects That May be Hazardous	
Moving objects that may be hazardous	**Workplace examples**
Rotating equipment and components (including high-speed rotating equipment)	Power saws, augers, grinders, disc sanders, drills, routers, polishing wheels, milling machines, lathes, rotary pumps, mowers
Belts and conveyors	Conveyors, rotating equipment belts (e.g., fan belts, sanding belts)
Reciprocating parts	Reciprocating pumps, presses, cutoff saws
Abrasive equipment	Sanders, grinders, sandblasters
Loose objects	Objects stored on shelves (e.g. tubular objects), small parts, tools on sloping surfaces, inadequately tightened equipment components
Shrapnel	Metal shrapnel from broken tools or ruptured containers, wood chips, broken glass
Bulk materials	Stockpiled soil, sand, gravel, snow, ore, mine spoil, wastes
Stacked materials	Pallets, lumber, tubular or rolled metal, scrap metal, newspapers, poles, furniture or fixtures
Materials being carried	Long materials, large sheets of material
Components that are loosened or removed and could fall	Elevated valves, light fixtures, ventilation fans, components of overhead heaters
Non-motorized rolling equipment	Hand trolley or carts, office chairs and stools, lab and bakery carts, wheelchairs, wagons
Mobile equipment and vehicles	Trucks, forklifts, front-end loaders, riding mowers, all-terrain vehicles, heavy equipment
Lifting or hoisting equipment	Pulley systems, hoists, jib cranes, overhead cranes, winches, hospital lifts
Moving surfaces	Turntables, escalators, elevators, dumbwaiters, swing stages, boats, moving trailers or ramps
Elevated surfaces	Portable ladders, scaffolds, vehicle hoists, forklift cages, scissor lifts, cherry pickers
Falling objects	Falling trees, windblown objects, tools, materials
Strobe lights	Strobe light used to measure the rpm of a rotating fan

Table 5: Forces That May be Hazardous

Forces that may be hazardous	Workplace examples
Force applied to levers, bolts, and objects	• Worker using a wrench in a tight area; wrench slips and worker's knuckles slam into the wall.
Force applied to sharp or pointed tools	• Worker rests hand on top of paint can, uses a screwdriver to pry off lid; screwdriver slips and punctures hand.
Chains, cables, straps, and ropes	• Crane cable snaps, dropping the load onto the person below. • Worker is tangled in a fishing net that is being winched in.
Sudden failure or shifting of materials	• Stack of plywood shifts, crushing forklift operator.
Excessive physical exertion during manual lifting or awkward positions	• Worker sustains back injury while loading tools onto a truck.
Latent forces	• Buildup of pressure due to rising temperature of a container; recoil potential; paint sprayers, hydraulic hoses, process piping, gravity. • electrical capacitor accumulates energy.
Excessive load	• A shelving unit collapses, spilling contents onto worker. • Overloaded forklift tips.

Table 6: Cryogenic (extremely cold) Liquids—Hazards and Controls

Hazard	Description/examples	Recommended controls
Extreme cold	• Thermal burns to the skin • Eye damage • Lung damage	• PPE (protective clothing, insulated gloves, eye protection, face shield, respiratory protection) • Ventilation
Asphyxiation	• Small amounts of liquid produce large quantities of gas • Gas from cryogenic liquids may accumulate near the floor, displace air/oxygen	• Ventilation • PPE (respiratory protection) • For confined spaces, use safety harness and lines, safety watch
Toxic Effects	• Specific health effects, for example, carbon monoxide gas causes immediate death. Refer to MSDS.	• Use PPE and other preventive measures described in MSDS
Flammability	• Hydrogen, methane, liquefied natural gas, and carbon monoxide are highly flammable and may ignite and/or explode when mixed with air • Clothing contaminated by liquid oxygen is highly flammable for several hours • When liquid oxygen is released, non-combustible materials such as cast iron can burn; organic and combustible materials burn more intensely.	• Remove ignition sources • Use non-sparking tools and intrinsically-safe instruments • Use combustible gas monitor • Ventilate • Place clothing or rags contaminated with liquid oxygen in covered metal containers
Boiling liquid expanding vapor explosion (BLEVE)	• If temperature rises or internal pressure increases (e.g., when relief valve malfunctions, container insulation is damaged, or fire in facility) container will explode.	• Install pressure relief backup device (e.g., bursting disc) • Control ignition hazards • Handle containers carefully to avoid damaging insulation • Locate fire extinguishers near vicinity of hazard

Appendix 4 Hazard and Control Tables

Table 7: Controls Frequently Used to Protect People		
Before task	During task	After task
<ul><li>Prepare a work plan</li><li>Hold safety meeting</li><li>Obtain work permit</li><li>Depressure</li><li>Purge</li><li>Blind or block and bleed</li><li>Perform mechanical lockout</li><li>Perform electrical lockout</li><li>Perform system lockout</li><li>Vent vessels</li><li>Steam</li><li>Erect hazard warning signs</li><li>Erect and check scaffolding</li><li>Erect guard rails or barriers</li><li>Ventilate area</li><li>Test for combustible and toxic gas and oxygen concentrations</li><li>Notify designated personnel</li><li>Provide emergency equipment</li><li>Plan escape routes/ procedures</li><li>Communicate with others</li></ul>	<ul><li>Use personal protective equipment<ul><li>hard hat</li><li>eye protection</li><li>flame-resistant clothing</li><li>safety footwear</li><li>hearing protection</li></ul></li><li>Use specialized safety equipment<ul><li>face shields</li><li>welding goggles</li><li>specialty gloves</li><li>specialized protective clothing</li><li>respiratory protection</li><li>fall protection and safety lines</li></ul></li><li>Ensure equipment guards are in place</li><li>Use a safety watch</li><li>Keep work area clean</li><li>Notify proper personnel</li><li>Monitor atmosphere</li><li>Apply forces in safe direction</li></ul>	<ul><li>Perform quality check</li><li>Remove tags and lockouts</li><li>Remove blinds</li><li>Dispose of wastes</li><li>Clean up area</li><li>Notify proper personnel</li><li>Perform cautious startup</li><li>Inspect equipment after startup</li><li>Maintain records and compile reports</li></ul>

Table 8: Controls to Implement Before Work Begins	
Control measure	Job application example
Safe work permit	Hot and cold work permits for designated area.
Locate and mark concealed utilities and installations	Before drilling boreholes in a storage yard, locate and mark subsurface electrical and gas lines; review historical information such as aerial photos to locate underground storage tanks that may be present but unmarked.
Notify/communicate	Field operator notifies control room operator that the high level tank alarm is about to be tested.
Shutdown plan	Prepare a detailed shutdown plan before annual maintenance turnaround in a pulp mill. Stress safety, efficient and effective coordination, supervision, and monitoring of operations, maintenance, and contractor personnel and activities.
Emergency response plan/training	Prepare a detailed emergency evacuation plan before annual maintenance turnaround in a pulp mill. Designate responsibilities and muster points. Conduct an emergency evacuation drill.
Secure and clear area	Assign personnel to keep non-essential personnel out of portion of storage yard where a mobile crane is hoisting a roof-mounted air supply unit into place.
Barriers	Erect barriers to prevent vehicles and mobile equipment from operating near area where light fixtures are being replaced. Use welding screen to prevent eye damage.
Double barrier	Electrical lockout *plus* electrically-insulated tools. Fume hood *plus* respirator. Guard rail *plus* safety line.
Check for hazardous gases	Use portable gas detectors to determine whether there are hazardous gases in the work area. Provide personal gas monitors to notify workers of hazardous gas levels.
Provide PPE	Provide self-contained breathing apparatus and safety lines to workers entering a vessel.
Depressure	Depressure and purge a butane storage tank to prepare for vessel entry.
Purge	Direct nitrogen gas to flow through an underground flare knockout tank to remove hydrocarbon and acid gases before entering the vessel.
Flush	Flush a pulp transfer chute with water to remove hot pulp slurry before opening the chute.
Block and bleed	Close a water supply pump's suction and discharge block valves and open the bleed valve to drain the pump before opening the casing to do an internal pump inspection.
Blind	Install blind plates at a pump flange before servicing a section of pipe.

(continued)

Appendix 4 Hazard and Control Tables

Table 8: Controls to Implement Before Work Begins	
Control measure	**Job application example**
Mechanical equipment lockout	Lock hydraulic pressure relief valves in the open position to relieve system pressure before servicing hydraulic equipment.
Electrical equipment lockout	Lock out a conveyor belt driver to prevent unintentional startup during bearing/roller servicing.
System lockout	Lock out a tipple conveyor before replacing the belt.
Steam	Steam clean a tank to remove all residual hydrogen sulfide gas.
Ventilate	Ventilate the service pit around a stationary machine before servicing the machine to remove accumulated methane gas from the pit area.
Hazard warnings	Post signs to indicate noise levels and type of hearing protection required.
Tag out	Install tags on locked-out electrical equipment indicating that the equipment is locked out and must not be activated.
Scaffolding	Install scaffolding in a two-story industrial warehouse to service wall-mounted air conditioning units.

Table 9: Controls to Implement During Work	
Control measure	**Job application example**
Use PPE	Wear fall protection while inspecting an overhead crane.
Monitor combustible gases and oxygen	Use combustible gas and oxygen detection equipment to check LEL and oxygen levels while replacing a control valve in a gas line.
Work procedures	Follow step-by-step work procedures when applying toxic two-part adhesives.
Housekeeping	Clean up sawdust, debris, tools, and other material after each stage of a task is completed.
Applying forces in a safe direction	Hold a chainsaw securely; avoid cutting with the upper part of the saw (the upper part of the saw is prone to kickbacks).
Safety watch	Stand watch when a worker enters a vessel to inspect it. Ensure you are properly trained and equipped to perform an emergency rescue if necessary. Maintain communication.
Notify/communicate	Maintenance personnel notify the machine operator when making adjustments to operating equipment. A Control Room Operator notifies a field operator of a pending remote startup of a pump.

Table 10: Controls to Implement After Work is Completed	
Control measure	**Job application example**
Clean up	Work surfaces, coveralls, and footwear used when loading perforating guns with explosives are cleaned and washed thoroughly to prevent explosive residues from being tracked to other areas of the facility.
Collect and mark hazardous or dangerous wastes	Broken glass tubing is placed in a metal container to prevent injuries. Empty pesticide containers are collected for disposal at an approved location.
Quality check	The QA person inspects and measures one in every twenty tools assembled to ensure the work meets specifications. Inspection is documented.
Purge equipment	An empty gasoline tank is purged to remove all vapors before using a cutting torch to cut the tank into scrap.
Post hazard warnings	Place wet floor signs after warehouse floor has been washed.
Remove tags and locks	Remove tags and locks from control valve and electrical breakers after service work on a motor is complete.
Remove blinds	Remove blinds from the lines leading into and out of a vessel after the inside walls of the vessel have been recoated.
Perform cautious startup	Start a repaired pump at minimum throughput.
Inspect equipment after startup	Inspect pump for operation and for leaks after repairs are complete.
Fire watch	Post a fire watch for the night after emergency welding operations in the storage yard are completed late in the evening.
Notify/communicate	Notify Control Room Operator that hot work performed at a refinery is now complete.

Another book by Gordon D. Shand

Interviewing to Gather Relevant Content for Training

Effective training contributes to business success—**improved corporate, job, and employee performance**. But how do you figure out what training is effective? This book provides the strategies you need to identify training that will give you the best return on your investment in training.

Part A:
- provides criteria and strategies you can use to identify:
  - training content that is relevant
  - what content you should address and not address
- describes pitfalls that you can encounter and ways to resolve these pitfalls

Part B describes an interviewing process where you provide leadership to identify and gather content that is relevant, useful, and practical. You will learn how to:
- help the subject matter expert provide quality content
- select content that is relevant and eliminate content that will not improve performance
- keep the subject matter expert engaged
- structure the content to effectively and efficiently develop training and assessment resources

The suggestions in this book are the accumulated experiences of many training and performance consultants who have encountered the challenges of gathering relevant content and developing effective training.

Who can benefit?
- educational, training, and performance consultants
- training program designers
- instructional designers
- technical writers
- trainers and coaches
- internal staff who develop training

www.ingramcontent.com/pod-product-compliance
Lightning Source LLC
Chambersburg PA
CBHW061123070526
44584CB00033B/4206